Strategy and Dynamics in Contests

LSE Perspectives in Economic Analysis

Series editors

Timothy Besley and Frank Cowell

The LSE Perspectives in Economic Analysis series provides concise and original insight into a wide range of topics in economics. Each book is accessibly written but scholarly to appeal to advanced students of economics, and academics and professionals wishing to expand their knowledge outside their own particular field.

Books in the series

A Primer in Social Choice Theory by Wulf Gaertner
Strategy and Dynamics in Contests by Kai A. Konrad

Forthcoming books

Econometric Analysis of Panel Data by Vassilis Hajivassiliou

Strategy and Dynamics in Contests

Kai A. Konrad

OXFORD
UNIVERSITY PRESS

Great Clarendon Street, Oxford OX2 6DP

Oxford University Press is a department of the University of Oxford.
It furthers the University's objective of excellence in research, scholarship,
and education by publishing worldwide in

Oxford New York

Auckland Cape Town Dar es Salaam Hong Kong Karachi
Kuala Lumpur Madrid Melbourne Mexico City Nairobi
New Delhi Shanghai Taipei Toronto

With offices in

Argentina Austria Brazil Chile Czech Republic France Greece
Guatemala Hungary Italy Japan Poland Portugal Singapore
South Korea Switzerland Thailand Turkey Ukraine Vietnam

Oxford is a registered trade mark of Oxford University Press
in the UK and in certain other countries

Published in the United States
by Oxford University Press Inc., New York

First published 2009

British Library Cataloguing in Publication Data

Data available

Library of Congress Cataloging in Publication Data

Data available

Typeset by SPI Publisher Services, Pondicherry, India
Printed in Great Britain
on acid-free paper by
CPI Antony Rowe, Chippenham, Wiltshire

ISBN 978–0–19–954–9597 (Hbk.)
ISBN 978–0–19–954–9603 (Pbk.)

1 3 5 7 9 10 8 6 4 2

For Kathrin

Preface and acknowledgements

This book should be interesting for researchers in public choice, political economy, industrial economics, international politics, the economics of sports, theoretical biology on conflict, and in other fields in which contests govern the process of allocation of resources, or for researchers who study the theory of contests. The book can be used as an introduction, a survey, a reference manual, a textbook for a short course on this topic, or as supplementary reading for courses on political economy or public choice.

The book focuses on two aspects of contests: first, it highlights strategy and commitment in such games. Second, emphasis is placed on describing dynamic contests that consist of series of component contests. In the trade-off between simplicity and generality, I leaned heavily towards simplicity and intuition. Ideas that hold much more widely are often illustrated using parametric versions or even numerical examples, even if more general results are easily available. The reader who would like to find out about maximum generality is referred to the original literature.

The theory of contests, tournaments, or all-pay auctions is a rapidly expanding field. Keeping pace with the speed with which progress is being made has been difficult. This is one of the reasons why the book is partial, subjective, and biased as a survey. Some of the biases have been introduced deliberately. I have not done justice to the large number of empirical studies of particular contest environments and have concentrated instead on contributions that illustrate the theoretical aspects of contests that seem to be generalizable and applicable to a wide set of contest environments. The work is also biased by the specific aspects and topics that I became interested in during my own past research.

There are several important lines of research which show up only marginally in this manuscript, even though whole books could be written about them. For instance, from a variety of starting points, researchers study investment, savings, trade, and other economic activities in a world where property rights are not exogenously defined but where players continuously struggle and expend effort to appropriate and defend resources. These 'economics of conflict' have been most recently surveyed by Garfinkel and Skaperdas (2007), and the existence of this excellent survey is perhaps a good excuse for not treating this aspect more extensively here. In addition, a whole school of researchers has analysed the implications of rent-seeking in many specific contexts based on Tullock (1967) and a number of other seminal papers. Several volumes have been published over the years that collect some of the most important contributions in this field, including Buchanan, Tollison, and Tullock (1980), and more recently, Lockard and Tullock (2001). Nitzan (1994) surveyed the rent-seeking literature some time ago. Since then it has taken numerous new directions that are partially surveyed by Corchón (2007). A recent collection of published papers on rent-seeking has been edited by Congleton, Hillman, and Konrad (2008), who survey and discuss these contributions. The rent-seeking literature has also made substantial contributions to the theory of contests. But rather than providing a balanced survey of the rent-seeking literature, the focus here is on the theoretical insights into contests as games that allocate resources more generally. Some theoretical aspects of this literature are covered in this book, but the empirical studies, for instance, are not surveyed here. Further, a large theoretical and empirical literature on tournaments has been developed, particularly in the context of internal labor markets, and also in the context of patent races in industrial organization. There is also a large literature on contests or conflict in biology which I will not consider. A focus of this literature is on wars of attrition, and on equilibrium in evolutionarily stable strategies. These are important omissions. I hope that the many many authors who have made significant contributions in these fields, and whose work is not appropriately represented here, will be lenient in their judgement.

Many persons have been important and influential and many events have been instrumental in the writing of this book. A joint course on contest theory with Derek J. Clark at the University of Bergen many years back as well as conferences that focused on the advances in contest theory at the Tinbergen Institute at Rotterdam in 1997, and at the Social Science Research Center Berlin (WZB) in Berlin laid the ground for this project. But the ultimate impulse came from Frank Cowell, who told me about the book series on *Perspectives in Economic Analysis*. I would very much like to thank him for his continuing encouragement and his patience with me as an author.

The book has been written over several years, and the communication with many colleagues, collaborators, and friends during this process was an important source of encouragement and inspiration. Many students and a considerable number of colleagues also read preliminary versions of the manuscript most carefully. An early version circulated under a different title (Konrad 2007). They provided most generous advice. Their comments eliminated many flaws, shaped the focus of the analysis, and changed many of my perceptions. The total list of persons is far too long, but I feel that I should thank explicitly Atsu Amegashie, Kyung Hwan Baik, Michael R. Baye, Derek J. Clark, Florian Engelmaier, Gil S. Epstein, Joan M. Esteban, Qiang Fu, Mark Gradstein, Hans Peter Grüner, Refael Hassin, Arye Hillman, Heidrun Hoppe, Aron Kiss, Dan Kovenock, Matthias Kräkel, Johan Lagerlöf, Wolfgang Leininger, Benny Moldovanu, Florian Morath, Johannes Münster, Shmuel Nitzan, Mattias K. Polborn, Mikael Priks, Amnon Rapoport, Brian Roberson, Stergios Skaperdas, Heinrich Ursprung, Karl Wärneryd, and Donald Wittman. I am also most indebted to the group of researchers who have collaborated with me on the theory of contests, particularly Helmut Bester, Derek J. Clark, Roger Congleton, Amihai Glazer, Mark Gradstein, Arye Hillman, Dan Kovenock, Wolfgang Leininger, Wolfgang Peters, Harris Schlesinger, Stergios Skaperdas, and Karl Wärneryd. Several sections in this book draw on the results we have developed and published jointly in previous research.

It is thanks to Nina Bonge, that the figures in this book gained shape and I would very much like to thank her for her competent editing of the text. Several cohorts of work students provided useful research assistance. As a non-native speaker I also owe much to Juli Leßmann, who carefully language-edited the manuscript and also made many suggestions that improved its readability more generally.

Tim Besley and Frank Cowell at the London School of Economics played a crucial role not only in giving the initial impulse for this book, but also in providing advice and accepting the manuscript for this new series. Last but not least, I would like to thank Jennifer Wilkinson, the editor at Oxford University Press, for both her patience and her guidance through the process of turning the manuscript into a book.

Contents

1

An Introduction to Contests

There are many types of interaction in which players expend effort in trying to get ahead of their rivals. Such interactions include marketing and advertising by firms, litigation, relative reward schemes in firms, beauty contests by firms, and rent-seeking for rents allocated by a public regulator, political competition, patent races, and entertainment activities such as sports. Unpleasant events such as military combat, war, and civil war are also some of the examples. These have been studied in the field of contest theory both within these specific contexts and at a higher level of abstraction. The purpose of this book is to survey this work, focusing on the strategic and dynamic aspects of such games, their interaction with each other, and within a more general decision framework. Before outlining the basic structure of the book, I briefly sketch the core object that is studied: a particular type of interaction that is referred to as a contest.

1.1. A definition

A contest can be characterized by the following elements. First, there is a prize to be allocated among the contestants who belong to a set of contestants $N = \{1, \dots n\}$. Each contestant $i \in N$ can make an effort x_i, chosen from a given set X_i of typically non-negative effort levels. The vector of efforts is denoted $\mathbf{x} = (x_1, \dots, x_n)$. These efforts determine which contestant will receive which prize, where, in the most simple case, only one contestant gets a positive prize of some size b and all other contestants get zero. The function that maps the vector of efforts into probabilities for the different contestants winning the prize is

$$p_i = p_i(x_1, \dots, x_n). \tag{1.1}$$

Usually this function is called the *contest success function.* This suggests that, for a given vector $\mathbf{x}$ of efforts, the p_i's are between zero and one, sum up to one, or to something smaller than one, if there is a chance that the prize is not given to one of the contestants.

The contest is about a prize. Contestants may value the prize differently. Contestant i's valuation of winning the prize is denoted $v_i(b)$. Further, contestants may differ in their cost of providing a given level of effort. If contestant i chooses an effort x_i then i's effort cost is $C_i(x_i)$. In most cases, and if not explicitly stated otherwise, we will assume that $C_i(x_i) = x_i$. This yields contestant i's payoff as

$$\pi_i(x_1, \ldots, x_n) = p_i(x_1, \ldots, x_n)v_i(b) - C_i(x_i). \tag{1.2}$$

More formally, simple contests are games that are defined by a set N of players, pure strategy spaces described by the sets X_i of feasible pure strategies, and by the set of payoff functions as in (1.2). In what follows, this framework will sometimes be extended along some dimensions and reduced along others.

Departures from this baseline framework include sequential effort choices, endogenous sequencing of effort choices, decisions on entry and admission, the role of the cost of effort, and of the structure of prizes and the rules that govern their allocation. Contest rules may be chosen by nature, but some elements of contests may also be chosen purposefully by the designer of a contest, according to a multiplicity of possible objectives. Contestants may commit and delegate their decision-making to others; they may use more than one type of effort, including sabotage activities. Contests may take place between groups of players, and the behavior among the players may govern their inter-group contest efforts. Also, contests need not be isolated events, but may repeat or be component contests that are of a more complex, dynamic structure. Also, contests need not take place in an environment of complete information, and a whole set of possible characteristics can be private information.

1.2. Examples

The number of areas in which a contest is an appropriate description of how some allocation outcomes are determined, and the quantitative and qualitative significance of the phenomenon, will be evident when a few examples are considered. Rosen (1988) emphasized the large range of applications of contest or tournament theory and mentioned applications such as examinations, college admission, quality control and medical trials, athletic competitions, elections, litigation, auctions, R&D races, work-points incentive schemes, and relative payment schemes in organizations. One may want to add advertising and other types of promotional competition, rent-seeking, and appropriation conflict in which players use resources to try to define or reallocate property rights between them, and also one of the most violent types of conflict: civil war or war between countries. We discuss a selection of these examples here and illustrate some of the research questions that emerge in this context.

1.2.1. *Promotional competition*

Firms try to increase their market shares by advertising campaigns and other marketing activities. The most obvious cases are newspaper advertisements or TV spots and, similarly, sales agents who try and persuade customers to buy a particular product. Such activities have in common that the major share of these efforts is made up-front, prior to actual sales, and can be understood as efforts in a contest in which the effort choices determine the market shares of all firms. The contest success function may, but need not, have a probabilistic interpretation in this case. For instance, the cigarette producers promote their brands, and their sales efforts determine or influence the share of each brand in the total market. What makes promotional competition a contest activity is the sunk cost nature of promotional effort. The cost of this effort cannot be recovered, whether or not the firm achieves its goals.

The expenditures on marketing and advertising are substantial, and sometimes they are subject to regulation. In the German insurance markets, for instance, the maximum amount of promotional activities by insurance companies was regulated and constrained from above to 30 percent of premiums, and commissions paid to sales agents were limited to no more than 11 percent of premiums (Rees and Kessner, 1999). Figures for pharmaceutical companies are similar. Figures 1.1 and 1.2 depict both the advertising-to-sales ratio and the marketing-to-sales ratios for the industries with the highest ratios in 2003 for the US.

The share of promotional effort in sales revenue is even higher if this is measured not only by advertising campaign costs but also by marketing effort more generally, as is shown in Figure 1.2.

These figures document the fact that advertising and other types of promotional or marketing activities are very commonly used tools in

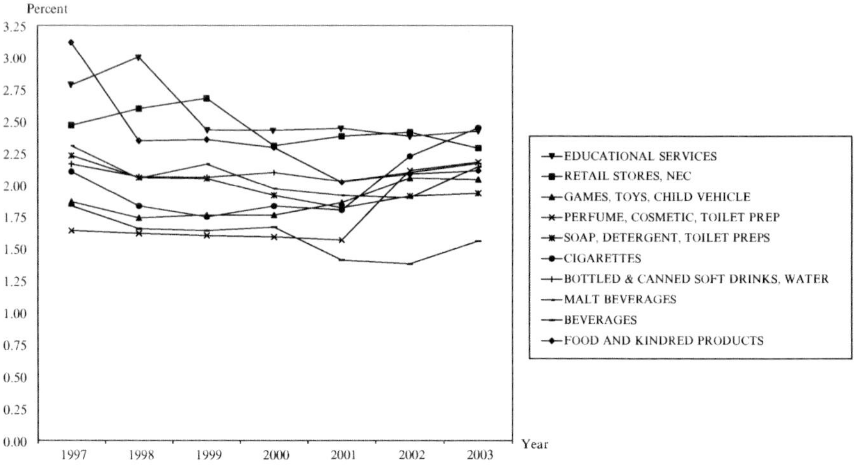

Figure 1.1 Advertising expenditure as a percentage of sales revenues in a number of advertising intensive sectors in the US.

Source: <http://www.AdAge.com>, advertising to sales ratios, various years.

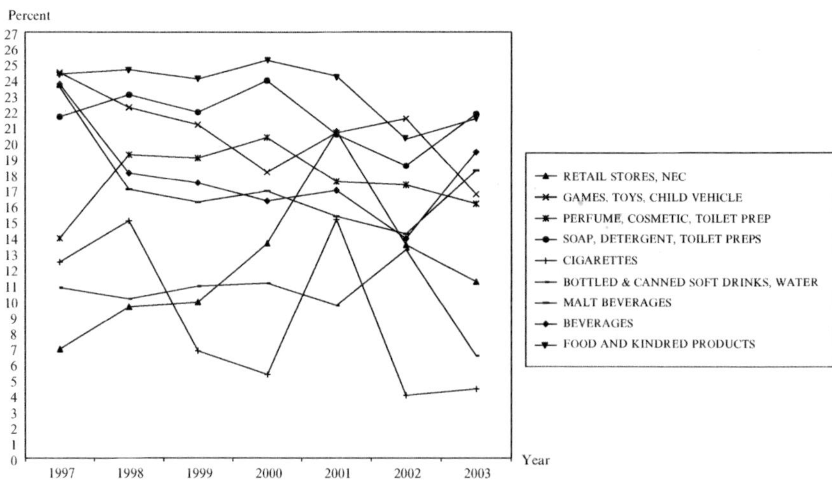

Figure 1.2 Marketing expenditure as a percentage of sales revenues in a number of advertising intensive sectors in the US.

Source: <http://www.AdAge.com>, for various years.

competition between firms. The contest nature of this type of competition was noticed quite early by Friedman (1958), Mills (1961), and Schmalensee (1976).

Firms that spend resources on advertising will generally affect their market share, but advertising may also change the total size of the market.[1] Advertising expenditures therefore have the properties of a contribution to a public good. But they also have a negative externality if such expenditures affect market shares. This specific effect makes promotional competition a contest in which the prize at stake is a function of the contestants' efforts. This aspect will be considered from a theory point of view in section 4.3.[2] Of course, the advertising game is more complex than the simple contest game in section 1.1 because repetition, the dynamics of advertising and the effects on the stock of consumers, possible collusive behavior between the competitors, and the size of firms within the group of largest firms may also affect the results. Advertising expenditures, and marketing activities more generally, also have the property that they may be used to hurt particular competitors, and thereby reduce one particular competitor's market share. This activity could be called sabotage and is different from effort that enhances a firm's own market size, as it will benefit not only this firm but also other firms that are not affected by the sabotage effort. The role of sabotage more generally will be considered in section 5.3.

A variant of promotional competition occurs in industries in which firms expend considerable effort in the composition of an attractive offer. Examples are architecture contests or competition for defence contracts, in which firms expend considerable resources trying to convince the government that they can deliver the superior product.

1.2.2. *Litigation*

Another practical example is litigation. If several parties litigate, typically they expend effort trying to influence the court decision in their own

[1] The two roles of marketing effort, with aggregate effort affecting market size and relative effort affecting market share, has been pointed out by Bell, Keeney, and Little (1975: 136) among others. The empirical assessment of how advertising influences market size and market shares for a particular type of consumer good is still a matter of ongoing research.

[2] See, e.g., Piga (1998) and Gasmi, Laffont, and Vuong (1992). The latter report that the soft drink producer Coca-Cola's advertising expenditure prior to 1977 had adverse effects on the demand for Pepsi, whereas Pepsico Inc.'s advertising expenditure had a weakly stimulating effect on the demand for its rival, the Coca-Cola Company. The differential effects on market share and market size are, however, not the only possible explanations for this, as price competition, for instance, may also have played a role.

favor.[3] The cost expended can be quite extensive. Litigation is potentially a serious cause of welfare loss. International comparative evidence on the cost of litigation is not very extensive. Seemingly, there are inter-country differences with respect to conflict that is resolved in court. The European Union Labour Force Survey 2003 gives the number of legal professionals for European countries. Normalizing these numbers by population size gives the number of legal professionals per 1,000 citizens, and this ranges from 0.93 for France up to 3.41 for the Netherlands. Not all legal professionals work in litigation, and not all litigation effort is expended on hiring legal professionals. However, these numbers may provide a rough measure of the magnitude of these cost. Business law, institutions, and, in particular, the institutional design of the litigation process play major roles in the quality of property rights in a country, and in the amount of resources used in litigation. Shavell (1982) has drawn attention to the importance of fee-shifting rules for plaintiffs and defendants, and Spier (2007) surveys the theoretical literature. Baye, Kovenock, and de Vries (2005) discuss the importance of fee-shifting rules for litigation efforts in a contest model of litigation. They discuss the 'American rule', by which each litigant covers his own cost, the 'English rule', by which the loser pays the costs of both parties, and other cost-shifting arrangements.

Litigation is a complex matter. Plaintiffs have to decide whether to make demands, and what kind of demand these will be; defendants have to decide how to react, how to negotiate in a pre-litigation period, whether to employ lawyers at that stage, and whether to enter into litigation in court, and this, again, becomes a multi-stage game with multiple options. The design of the legal system determines the rules of this game. The game has elements of contests at many stages. The theoretical analysis in the main part of the book will implicitly address strategic aspects as far as they are related to the contest nature of litigation. Among these are the role of fee-shifting rules (section 2.1), the entry decision (section 3.2), delegation (section 3.4), information, and information asymmetries in contests (sections 2.1 and 2.3).

1.2.3. *Internal labor market tournaments*

Tournaments, or relative performance reward schemes, are well established in many working environments. Promotion decisions in organizations are

[3] Formal analyzes of litigation as contest problems are in Farmer and Pecorino (1999), Wärneryd (2000), Baye, Kovenock, and de Vries (2005), Priks (2005), and Robson and Skaperdas (2008).

also often based on relative performance, and sometimes firms explicitly, and repeatedly, award prizes to employees, typically rewarding individuals or a subset of their best-performing employees. These schemes have the structure of a contest, as the employees expend effort in trying to win a prize, and the prize is awarded as a function of these efforts. Kalra and Shi (2001: 171) cite evidence found in various sources regarding the prevalence of sales contests and also describe some specific formats. Some of their examples are Toshiba, which rewarded its top sales representatives with 40,000 USD, and handed out a further 60 smaller prizes of 5,000 USD each, or Merrill Lynch, which gave its 'top 100 brokers' trips to London, and smaller prizes for the follow-up group. Investment bankers also have complex mechanisms and rules to assign bonuses to their employees (for anecdotes, see, e.g., Lewis, 2006). The prizes in sales contests are sometimes symbolic, or award status or prestige to the winner or the group of winners, and sometimes the prize involves both prestige and serious money. The prize structure is not generally uniform, and is often not the winner-takes-all type.

Tournaments inside firms serve many purposes. Motivating employees to deliver high performance or to produce much output is only one aspect. Welch (2001) describes the process of finding his successor as CEO of General Electric (GE). In cooperation with the Board, he first produced a shortlist of 23 candidates in 1994. This list was reduced to eight names later, and finally three persons entered into the final successorship contest: Jim McNerney, Bob Narelli, and Jeff Immelt. These persons were assigned several, carefully chosen tasks and to several divisions of GE sequentially over the years. These challenges were meant to enhance their abilities and human capital, but their performance and progress were also carefully screened during these years. Although all finalists were considered to be extremely valuable assets for the company, the finalists were told that only the winner could stay on with GE; those not promoted to CEO had to leave the company. To make this transition process smooth, replacements for all three persons were assigned early on and these worked together with the respective candidates. This example illustrates the many dimensions that have to be considered when a promotion tournament is designed. The one chosen by Jack Welch had a dynamic structure. It had several rounds with elimination (or attrition) of some candidates in each round. Candidates did not know their competitors in the early stages, but did know their competitors in the later ones. The requirement in the last stage that the unsuccessful competitors had to leave GE potentially increased the size of the prize for the winner: it reduced internal rivalry and established the winner as the uncontested leader, making the leadership position more attractive, and it possibly reduced the reservation utility of losing the contest in the final stage. Hence, the design increased the difference in participants' payoffs between winning and losing. The allocation of replacements for the candidates was also an interesting design aspect, as these replacement persons most likely had strong incentives to support the person they were supposed to replace in the contest, as this person would be the new CEO. Elimination contests and the GE example will be discussed further in section 8.1.

There are many other aspects which played a role and which Jack Welch made transparent when listing the fundamental goals he wanted to achieve regarding leadership succession. First, he wanted to select the strongest leader with an optimal mix of personal characteristics and abilities. He anticipated that the selection process could cause attrition: candidates of high potential could become frustrated and leave GE. He wanted to minimize this loss. He also recognized the possibility of harmful competition. Candidates could devote effort to sabotaging their competitors rather than focusing on own performance. Responsibilities and job design for candidates that minimized the potential for harmful competition had to be chosen. Also, it was desirable to design the tasks of the competitors in a way that made their performance transparent and easily observable. He also recognized the trade-off that exists between some of these goals.

Lazear and Rosen (1981) and Rosen (1986) started the formal study of such structures in the labor market context. Dynamic aspects of multiple stages and elimination tournaments, and issues of incomplete information are already discussed in this work. The empirical importance and the theoretical properties of internal labor market tournaments have been studied carefully in a large literature that had its origin in these two papers.[4] Many issues that have been analyzed, and are highly relevant in these contexts, are surveyed in later sections here. Tournaments in both the labor market and organizations are typically carefully designed, as suggested by Jack Welch's report on the successorship contest he designed. Among the issues to be chosen are the prize structure, the dynamic structure of the contest, in particular regarding the number of rounds, information available to competitors in each round, the design of the narrowing down of the group of competitors, and the initial choice and admission of participants. The designer also may have various objectives in mind. In some firms, the

[4] See, e.g., Lazear (1995) for a brief survey of the early literature.

tournament may simply serve as a reward scheme meant to induce workers to expend effort that translates into output. In other firms, the tournament may also serve as a screening device through which the firm tries to identify employees who are particularly good at pursuing superior tasks, or at assuming more responsibility, and this motivation may even dominate in some firms and in some internal labor market tournaments. Firms may also consider that relative rewards may induce employees to exert destructive effort, effort that does not improve their own performance but reduces the performance of their competitors, and they may consider how to organize the tournament so as to reduce such sabotage incentives. The report given by Welch includes these goals, but adds further goals. These are some of the strategic and dynamic aspects that play a role in labor market tournaments which will be considered further below.

Inside the firm, promotions, bonuses, salary increases, and other allocation decisions on rents may sometimes be the outcomes of designed tournaments. Jack Welch and his board were perhaps able to abstract from personal feelings or empathy and make a completely unbiased decision that relied purely on objectively measurable facts, when they designed a tournament to find a successor for Jack Welch as CEO of General Electric, as is described in more detail in section 8.1. But the judgement of ordinary man is typically susceptible to flattery and may be influenced by other means of persuasion. Milgrom (1988) and Milgrom and Roberts (1988) highlighted the importance of such activities and their potentially detrimental role in production efficiency and in efficient decision-making inside organizations. They coined the term 'influence activities' for the type of unproductive effort that aims to reallocate resources and income or influence promotion decisions inside the firm. They highlighted the role of organizational design in how susceptible organizations are to this problem. The problem of such unproductive activities that aim at redistribution of income, wealth or economic rents more generally has been recognized more generally in the literature on rent-seeking.

1.2.4. *Rent-seeking and beauty contests*

Economic rents are often allocated by bureaucrats, politicians or other decision-makers in organizations. Those who are the possible beneficiaries of their decisions may try to influence these decisions. Firms or consumer groups may attempt to receive favorable treatment from a regulator, firms may lobby for tariffs or other forms of import protection, and these are early examples of rent-seeking that were discussed, for example, in the classical contributions on rent-seeking by Tullock (1967), Krüger (1974), and Posner (1975). The description of rent-seeking as a contest was introduced by Tullock (1980) and taken up by many further contributions dealing with rent-seeking issues. An early survey is that of Nitzan (1994). More recent surveys of the theory of rent-seeking and its applications are by Corchón (2007) and Congleton, Hillman, and Konrad (2008). The latter also reprint and survey a collection of papers that apply the rent-seeking idea far beyond the political economy context. The literature on the various applied aspects of rent-seeking contests is vast. Protectionist trade policy was a prominent example early on.[5] But as discussed in their volumes, industry regulation, privatization, development policy, and foreign aid are only some of the further topics in which rent-seeking can be addressed from a contest theory perspective. Many of the aspects that are dealt with in this literature will be discussed later on, for example, issues of who is willing to participate, and who is admitted to the contest, who defines the rents, who benefits from the rent-seeking expenditure, and who sets the rules of the rent-seeking game.[6]

In many examples of rent-seeking, the relationship between rent-seeking effort and the decision process that leads to favorable legislation or decisions that allocate valuable assets or rights is not very transparent. Sometimes, however, the allocation procedure takes the form of a competition that is openly announced. These types of competition are often called 'beauty contests'. In these contests, the participants are invited to produce proposals that are costly to make, and a committee is supposed to choose the best proposal. Examples of beauty contests that regularly receive public attention are the games that determine the choice of location for the Olympic games by the International Olympic Committee (IOC), or for soccer championships by the Fédération Internationale de Football Association (FIFA). The locations that want to host these events expend considerable resources on trying to influence the decisions favorably. Stewart and Wu (1997) survey some of the literature on decision-making by the IOC. They report the officially stated campaign costs for the cities that applied for the 2000 Olympic games: 25.2 million Australian dollars for Sydney, and 86 million D-Mark for Berlin, and these official numbers may underestimate the actual costs of effort.

[5] See, e.g., Hillman and Ursprung (1988) and Hillman (1989).

[6] For these aspects, see, e.g., Appelbaum and Katz (1986a), Hillman and Katz (1987), Ellingsen (1991), Drook-Gal, Epstein and Nitzan (2004), and Epstein and Nitzan (2004, 2006, 2007).

Beauty contests are also common in other contexts. For instance, the allocation of broadband telecommunication rights have often occurred in beauty contests. Goeree and Holt (1999) discuss the case where the US Federal Communications Commission awarded 643 licenses among 320,000 applications, before switching to auctioning licenses. Hazlett and Michaels (1993) estimate that the application costs added up to about 40 percent of the value of the licenses, for which they give an estimate of 1 billion USD. In recent years, the allocation of spectrum rights by way of a beauty contest has not been unusual. According to Börgers and Dustman (2003), who describe the different processes throughout Europe for awarding broadband (3G) spectrum licenses, beauty contests have been used in Finland, Spain, Sweden, Portugal, France, Ireland, and Luxembourg. Considering the rent-seeking cost of these cases, influence activities could emerge both at the stage where the design of the allocation method had to be chosen, and in the actual contest between rival competitors for the spectrum rights for a given design and a given set of licenses.

1.2.5. *Education filters*

Education is another, perhaps less obvious, example of contest games. Education may serve as an input that enhances individual human capital and translates into higher labor productivity. However, education may also function as a filter which reveals the true characteristics and abilities of a person, thus allowing an improved and more productive use of the person's abilities in the assignment of tasks. The latter purpose of education was highlighted by Arrow (1973), and this aspect is popular among sociologists. Hirsch (1976), for instance, considers the role of the education system in filling a number of attractive positions in a society, and acknowledges the tournament aspect of such systems. The scarcity of attractive tasks in the assignment process on the one hand, and the relative comparisons in the filtering process on the other, make the assignment problem similar to a rent-seeking contest. To the extent that the allocation of jobs and tasks is decided on the basis of relative qualification or performance, some of the effort that is expended in education could be wasteful.[7] To the extent

[7] The tournament structure of education systems has also been recognized by contest theorists. Amegashie and Wu (2004) consider national exams as a contest that is devised to assign students to the different institutions of higher education. They find that students' selection choices about where to apply for higher education prior to preparing for the exams that produce the basis for the admission procedure can be dysfunctional. Konrad (2004d) considers the role of mobility and transition options between different, multi-stage education tracks for efficiency. Fu (2006) considers favoring applicants from minorities in college admission competition.

that education is a costly signal rather than acquisition of useful skills, many of the strategic aspects discussed in later sections therefore apply to this context. Empirically, the effort expended on education is substantial. In 2002, the average overall expenditure in the OECD was 5,273 USD per student at the primary level, 6,992 USD per student at the secondary level, and 13,343 USD per student at the tertiary level (OECD, 2005: 161). These numbers underestimate total effort, as they mainly measure the actual resources spent on teachers and teaching institutions, and do not include the full opportunity cost of time.

1.2.6. *R&D contests*

One of the areas of application in which the tournament character of players' interaction is also very visible, and in which the theory of contests and tournaments made major progress early on, is the area of research and development (Loury, 1979; Nalebuff and Stiglitz, 1983). The firm which introduces a new product or a product improvement first will generally derive some benefit from it. The firm may earn some monopoly rent as long as there are no competitors who can offer a similar product or quality, and patent protection may further increase this rent. Accordingly, firms may spend effort on research and development when chasing these rents.

Many R&D contests emerge naturally from firms' competition, the potential profitability of introducing new products, or the advantage of cost-reducing innovations. However, a large number of technology prizes are also awarded for which several firms may contest. Windham (1999) has collected a considerable list of examples. He mentions the famous contest for a "practical and useful" means of determining longitude at sea (Windham, 1999, p. A-3) for which the British Parliament offered a prize of 20,000 GBP in 1714, the 'Wolfskehl Prize for proving Fermat's Last Theorem', the EU Information Technology prizes, and a long, and non-exhaustive, list of today's recognition prizes.

1.2.7. *Campaigning, committee bribing, and vote buying*

Political competition is another area in which contest theory has major applications. Parties spend resources in trying to influence voters and win elections, whereas party members and politicians expend effort to advance within the party hierarchy or to be nominated for an important office. Such electoral competition and party politics partially resemble the promotional activities of firms who use advertising with the aim of both increasing the market—in electoral markets the aim is an increase in voting turnout—and increasing their own share in this market. Stratmann (2005) surveys and discusses the various motivations for campaign contributors and the possible channels by which campaign contributions may be used to influence electoral outcomes. The empirical significance of the phenomenon is large. One measure, for instance, is the considerable size of campaign budgets of parties or candidates who run for government or office in democratic election campaigns. Some illustrative figures are reported by Alexander (1996). According to this source, Abraham Lincoln's campaign costs were about 100,000 USD, John F. Kennedy and Nixon spent about 9.7 million USD and 10.1 million USD respectively. Bill Clinton could draw on more than 130 million USD. Stratmann (2005: 135) surveys further figures. George W. Bush and Albert Gore accordingly expended 307 million USD and Bush and John Kerry are reported to have expended more than 550 million USD, not including the spending by advocacy groups or political parties. *The New York Times* (December 10, 2007) reported in an editorial that the cost of congressional and presidential elections may reach 5 billion USD in 2008. But, even in parliamentary systems, the cost of campaign spending is significant. In a much smaller country such as Germany, the two largest parties' expenditures were estimated to sum up to about 50 million Euro (Korte, 2006). Campaign money is spent on a variety of categories. The German newspaper *Die Welt* (January 19, 2008, p. 5) reported that Nicolas Sarkozy expended 34,445 Euro for make-up in the campaign for President of France. His female opponent, Ségolène Royal, is reported in the same issue to have expended 52,000 Euro for make-up and hair-styling.

One difference between campaigning prior to elections and firms' ordinary promotional competition using advertising is the payoff function in elections: in markets with promotional competition, all firms typically benefit from a large market, and their payoff can be assumed to be a monotonic and smooth function of the market size and their market share. In electoral markets, the payoffs of parties or candidates are often noncontinuous. Thresholds, such as, for example, the 50 percent majority of all votes, are important. This is particularly true in presidential systems or two-party competition, but thresholds also matter in electoral systems with many parties and coalition formation.[8] Moreover, parties and politicians need to collect campaign contributions in order to use them

[8] These thresholds are also important in another political game that could be called the committee bribing problem. In this problem, two (or more) rival players need to influence a majority of the members of a committee to support their prefered policy alternative. This

for their campaigns, which makes the political game more complex than a simple one-stage contest.[9]

This is not to say that all aspects of political competition can be mapped appropriately by a simple contest for votes with discontinuous payoffs. The political economy theory of political and electoral competition is a large field that cannot be surveyed here. However, it can, and has been, argued convincingly in the literature that the all-pay nature of campaigning and the non-trivial relationship between campaign effort and election outcomes makes contest theory a useful tool for studying this type of competition.

1.2.8. *Military conflict*

Arms races, or even military conflict in the form of war or civil war, are probably among the most important and most obvious examples of contests. The rival players are typically countries, or power groups within countries. As suggested by the textbook example on economic principles, a country's resources can be used to produce 'butter', representing the set of standard consumer goods, or 'guns', representing the set of instruments that improve the country's ability to wage war, or to be the victor if attacked by another military force. Building up military force therefore has opportunity costs in terms of consumption goods sacrificed, whether or not the military goods are used, and whether or not the country is successful in an armed conflict or in negotiations taking place in the shadow of possible military conflict. From a contest theory point of view, the production of weapons constitutes effort in a contest.

Many contest problems of war or combat have been analyzed in a context that is called the 'Colonel Blotto' game. In this game, two (or more) rival army leaders have to make simultaneous choices about where to allocate which share of their troops among different frontiers.[10] War has also been a field of study in international policy. Researchers asked questions

problem has been addressed, e.g., by Young (1978), Congleton (1984), Groseclose and Snyder (1996), Banks (2000), and others.

[9] This is widely acknowledged in the literature. A recent example is Glazer and Gradstein (2005). Examples of contest models of electoral competition with further references are Congleton (1986), and Skaperdas and Grofman (1995), who focus on negative campaigning.

[10] According to Young (1978: 392), 'The first example of a lobbying game seems to have been considered by Borel [(1938)]', and variants of this game have received considerable attention from theorists from time to time. Early contributions are, e.g., Blackett (1954, 1958) and Friedman (1958). Shubik and Weber (1981) and Coughlin (1992) make further contributions and provide further references. Most recent Colonel Blotto games are by Matros (2006) and Robson (2005).

such as why does war take place, given the opportunity to negotiate and settle, and similarly, once war has started, why is it so difficult to terminate it. Much of the literature, and many good answers to these questions, are surveyed in Fearon (1995), who considers asymmetric information and incomplete contracts as the main reasons for a conflict situation turning into a war. Further contributions that explain why war may take place in a context with perfectly rational players in a full information framework are Garfinkel and Skaperdas (2000) and Slantchev (2003), both of whom add explanations based on incomplete contracts.

From an empirical point of view, military conflict could be studied at various levels of aggregation. Even a single battle consists of a whole set of combat events. Sets of battles are sometimes called a campaign. War is an even more complex, dynamic type of interaction in which single battles or campaigns are important components. I will consider some aspects of this complexity in Chapter 8 on the dynamics of contests. Another important aspect of military contests is asymmetry. One type of asymmetry between the attacker and the defending player was already emphasized by Clausewitz (1832/1976): the advantage of defense. However, turning to battles and the nature of contest outcomes, this advantage is not easy to verify from the relationship between numerical superiority and battle success. Dupuy (1977) surveys evidence on ground combat in the time period 1805–1973. He surveys 42 battles. From these battles, 28 attackers and 14 defenders were successful. There were 13 numerically inferior attackers, and 12 of these were successful. In 18 of these battles the victors were numerically superior, in 24 cases the victors were numerically inferior. These data do not show a strong advantage of defense, and the relationship between numerical superiority and battle success is also a loose one. Other qualitative aspects not well described by these numbers seemingly play a role, and these aspects may include morale, leadership, a superior strategy, technological advantage, and luck. Also, the decision to attack is endogenous. Rivals have to decide whether to attack now or later, and whether to attack at all. Moreover, there could be other asymmetries that also play a role. A defending player may be vulnerable at several points, and, to be successful overall, may need to defend all these points successfully in order to win the war, whereas an attacker may be victorious if he can successfully surmount the defense lines of his rival successfully at one point.[11]

[11] Aspects of this type are considered, e.g., in Shubik and Weber (1981), and, more recently, in Clark and Konrad (2007) and in Kovenock and Roberson (2006).

1.2.9. *Sports*

Sport provides the final, and most obvious, application of contest theory. Athletes spend years in training effort, months in preparing for a particular championship or event, and the actual sports event also requires that each participant expends effort that cannot be recovered even if the athlete does not win. Not surprisingly, the contest aspect of sport has received considerable attention in the literature on the economics of sport. In his careful survey, Szymanski (2003) addresses, for instance, issues such as the role of the contest success function, multiple prizes, asymmetry between contestants, the role of contest architecture, and dynamic aspects of actual contests in which the contestants repeatedly expend effort, with a feedback effect via the observed prior efforts by their rivals. He also surveys the empirical literature on individualistic sports, before he turns to team sports.

Consider, for instance, tennis. A tennis match is a complex structure of sequential contests, with points, games or sets being seen as battles in a larger contest. In turn, a match is only one of many battles in a tournament, and a tournament is only a battle in the grand contest for top rankings or annual awards. Sometimes it may be useful to look into this contest architecture more closely, and I will survey some work on this. However, the simple structure of the contest outlined in section 1.1 maps a central aspect of sports competition, and the analysis of single contests, which can be interpreted as a match or a whole tournament, can therefore reveal interesting insights, for instance about the role of barriers to entry or entry fees, rules that make participants in a contest more homogeneous, the number of prizes and their structure, etc. In professional golf, for instance, the 'purse' consists of a number of prizes that decline with the player's rank. Figures 1.3 and 1.4 describe the prize structure for the tournaments on the PGA tour for 42 of 47 tournaments of the European Professional Golf Association (PGA) tour in 2003.[12] Figure 1.3 shows, for the best 20 players in the respective tournament on the European Tour

[12] Data were not available on the internet for all championships. The tournaments included in the figures are: BMW Asian Open, the Diageo Championship at Gleneagles, Omega Hong Kong Open, Open de France, South African Airways Open, Smurfit European Open, Dunhill championship, the Barclays Scottish Open, Caltex Masters presented by Carlsberg, 132nd Open Golf Championship, Heineken Classic, Nissan Irish Open, ANZ Championship, Scandic Carlsberg Scandinavian Masters, Johnnie Walker Classic, Nordic Open, Carlsberg Malaysian Open, US PGA Championship, Dubai Desert Classic, BMW Russian Open, Qatar Masters, WGC-NEC Invitational, Madeira Island Open, BMW International Open, Algarve Open de Portugal, Omega European Masters, Canarias Open de España, Trophée Lancôme, Italian Open Telecom Italia, Linde German Masters, Benson and Hedges International Open, Dunhill Links Championship, Deutsche Bank-SAP Open TPC of Europe, WGC-American Express Championship,

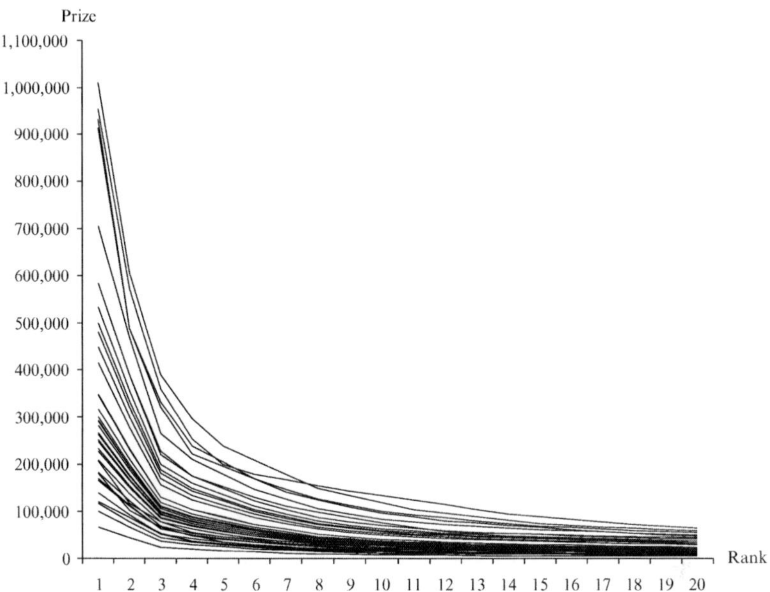

Figure 1.3 European Tour 2003, prize money in Euros.
Source: Various internet homepages.

2003, how the size of the prize money is highest for the player who scores best and declines slowly for players who do less well. Figure 1.4 shows prize money as a percentage of the total purse for the same set of tournaments. The latter reveals that the set of prizes seemingly has an invariant structural pattern. The reasons for awarding multiple prizes and the structure of these prizes will be discussed in detail in section 4.2.

It should be noted that the structure of monetary prizes in Figure 1.3 does not fully describe the full prize structure, as there are implicit, or non-monetary, benefits of performance. Winners of major tournaments have the benefits of qualifying for future tournaments, they get more media attention that can be transformed into monetary payoffs via promotion contracts with producers of brand products, they improve their score with regard to the contest for best performance in a given year, or lifetime, and they probably obtain some ego rent from winning.

Volvo PGA Championship, Dutch Open, the Celtic Manor Resort Wales Open, Turespaña Mallorca Classic, the Daily Telegraph Damovo British Masters, Telefonica Open de Madrid, Aa St Omer Open, Volvo Masters Andalucia.

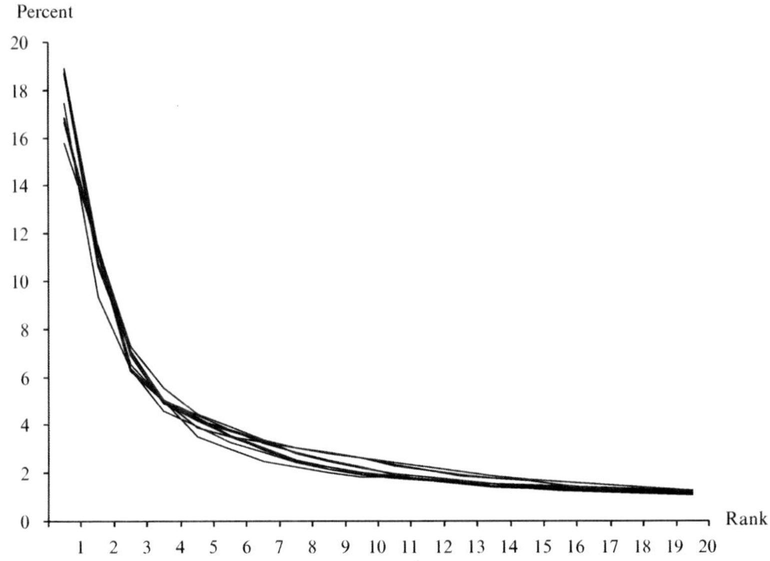

Figure 1.4 European Tour 2003, prize money in percent.
Source: Data from Figure 1.3 and own calculations.

Many types of sport are team sports. This implies that a team player's own effort benefits himself primarily via the improvement in his team's performance, which hints at a free-riding problem in the competition between teams. Moreover, the winning team in a championship is not fully homogenous. Not only do players have different, more or less attractive, appearances, and their own personalities. They also differ visibly in their contribution to their team's success. Accordingly, they do not all get the same prize from winning the championship, and it is probably true that, within teams, there is rivalry concerning who receives higher recognition and can earn higher benefits from media attention, sponsoring and ego rents. Team sports constitute an example of contests that take place both between, and within, the groups, and such structures will also be studied carefully in Chapters 5, 6 and 7.

1.3. Outlook: the structure of the book

The formal definition in Section 1.1 introduced the particular type of interaction that is the focus of the analyzes that follow. Chapter 2 will analyze this structure in more detail. It will focus on three classes of contest success functions and analyze the comparative static properties of the equilibrium. Some common patterns emerge from the analysis of these cases that will also play a role in the modifications and more complex versions of contests that are considered in later chapters. Chapter 2 is also used to present and discuss some of the experimental evidence on where individuals behave according to the equilibrium predictions of contest theory and where they seemingly depart more systematically from these. Also a possible explanation for this behavior is given that potentially reconciles theory with the empirical results.

Chapter 3 is used to study the first set of strategic aspects. Players need not act simultaneously in contests, and the timing of their choices of contest effort may even emerge endogenously. One of the results from studying endogenous timing is that this may benefit all participants in a contest. Other issues in this chapter are the contestants' decisions whether to participate in a contest or not. Also, players may choose to send an agent who participates on behalf of a player, and design the agents' incentives by way of an appropriate contract. On the part of the contest designer, admittance of contestants may be a strategic choice, and a contest designer may like to restrict entry to a contest. Perhaps surprisingly, a contest designer may want to exclude players whose willingness to pay to win the prize is very high.

Chapter 4 focuses on prizes and the prize structure. Particularly if a contest is not generated naturally by the institutional environment but carefully orchestrated by a contest designer, then the structure of the prizes is one of the most important and relevant decision variables in the hands of the designer. Another element that may be influenced by the designer is the participants' cost of effort. As it turns out, it may be worthwhile to make it more costly for some participants in a contest to expend effort, even if the contest designer is interested in maximizing the aggregate amount of effort.

A contest is a game with strong mutual externalities: a contestant who expends more effort increases his likelihood of winning the prize. But at the same time, this increase in winning probability must imply that other contestants have a reduced probability of winning. This is the fundamental externality that is at work in contests. However, there are further externalities that are studied in Chapter 5. For instance, governments often tax the revenues of lotteries, or even own 'state lotteries' and use these revenues to finance public goods. In this case, making an expenditure in a lottery contest has an additional side-effect: the expenditure contributes to a public good. Another aspect may emerge if, in a contest with more than two players, players who lose are not indifferent about the identity of the winner. Suppose, for instance, among three players, player A has a preference for player B to win, rather than player C. In this case, apart from the negative externality of making it less likely for A to win, player B's effort also has a positive externality for A, as it makes it less likely that C wins. Other types of externalities emerge if players can sabotage each other. Here, if one player sabotages another player, then this also benefits competitors other than the sabotaging player. Also, the chapter discusses externalities that emerge in campaign contests, and positive externalities inside groups if groups compete for prizes and all group members can contribute to the aggregate effort expended by their group.

Chapter 6 is used to analyze the dynamics that emerge if groups compete with each other, but if the prize that is awarded to one of the groups needs to be allocated inside the group. The role of the intra-group allocation process in the inter-group contest is carefully studied. The possibility that the members of a victorious group may quarrel about the allocation of the winner prize and dissipate a large share of the prize in the intra-group contest reduces the amount of resources that can be mobilized for the inter-group contest, and this constitutes a strategic disadvantage of groups as organizational units when fighting with other players in a contest. This disadvantage makes it difficult to explain why players may join forces and fight against other competitors as a group. This alliance formation puzzle is the starting point of the analysis in Chapter 7. The chapter also offers some reasoning why alliances may be advantageous for group members, despite the strategic disadvantages of possible internal fighting.

In Chapter 8, a whole set of dynamic contest structures are discussed, including multi-round elimination tournaments, contests that are decided on the basis of multiple component contests that may constitute strictly finite games, and dynamic contests that may potentially continue forever. Another type of dynamics emerges in iterated incumbency fights. In these, an incumbent may be attacked by a challenger in each period, and potentially be replaced by the challenger if the challenger wins the battle between them. Finally, unlike in a strictly static framework, in a dynamic framework, the timing of attack becomes a matter of choice. Problems of timing of attack are also discussed in this chapter. The chapter concludes with a section on a common pattern in dynamic contests which is called the discouragement effect.

Chapter 9 contains some final remarks. In particular, this chapter addresses the difficult issue of welfare in contests. Taking stock of the different structures and the multiplicity of applications, the main conclusion is that the welfare properties of allocation processes that follow the rules of contests very much depend on the nature of contest effort. This ambivalent conclusion on welfare explains why the analysis in chapters 2 to 8 is mainly positive and abstains from a welfare analysis of the structures analyzed.

2

Types of Contest

Many dimensions can be distinguished for a typology of contests. Hirshleifer and Riley (1992, chapter 10), for instance, distinguish dimensions such as whether random elements play a role in the contest success function, whether contestants are informed about their co-players' costs or their co-players' valuations of the prize, whether the contestants' costs of their effort choices are determined by themselves or partially by their co-players, as in wars of attrition, etc. With so many such dimensions, classification is cumbersome. I will follow an alternative strategy and present the three types of contest technology described by the contest success functions that are most prominent in the literature.[1]

I will concentrate on contests in which players have to pay their own bids in full, that is, on what could be called 'first-price contests' or 'first-price all-pay auctions'. Contests in which the player's effort is determined not only by his own choice, but also by the choices of other players will not be considered in detail. In particular, waiting games, wars of attrition, or what could be called second-price all-pay auctions are of considerable empirical importance, with applications ranging from the war of attrition in biology applications to exit games in declining industries in industrial organization. I will also concentrate on contests in which the contestants know each other's valuation of the prize and what their effort cost is and will only touch on the theory of contests with incomplete or asymmetric information.

[1] A further important variant that is not covered here is developed by Anderson, Goeree, and Holt (1998).

2.1. The first-price all-pay auction

Consider the following imagined situation. A person decides to auction a 100-dollar bill among two bidders, 1 and 2. Each bidder chooses a dollar amount x_1 and x_2 and turns this in as a sealed bid, simultaneously with the other bidder.[2] The bidder who bids the higher amount wins the 100-dollar bill, and each receives 50 dollars if they make exactly the same bid. These procedures are known to both of them. If you are one of the two bidders, how much would you like to bid?

As stated, this is an example of a contest in which the contestant who expends the highest effort wins the prize with probability 1. This case is most relevant, for instance, if the contest effort chosen translates deterministically into an observable quality or quantity variable, and if the allocation of the prize is made on the basis of a comparison of the values of this variable for the various contestants. Performance differences are decisive, even if they are small, in many contest applications. In sports, for instance, differences in the size of fractions of seconds, or millimeters can be decisive. But also in many other examples the prize is awarded to the player who has the better performance, even if the difference in performance is rather small. The relationship between a contestant's effort or 'bid' and the revealed performance is frequently less predictable. There will often be noise in the process that maps effort into measured performance. In what follows, we will first consider contests that follow the rules by which the 100-dollar bill is allocated, and then turn to cases with noise. The reader who is impatient to consider cases with noise may jump to the next section. However, as a benchmark case, the deterministic case is interesting and will be used frequently when analyzing strategic or dynamic aspects.

Two contestants

Let us concentrate on the case with two contestants $i = 1, 2$ who attribute positive valuations to the prize that is allocated in the contest. Let these valuations be v_1 and v_2. The players know both their own valuation and the valuation their opponent attributes to winning the contest. By appropriate renumbering of the two contestants, $v_1 \geq v_2 > 0$. Contestants choose their efforts $x_i \in [0, \infty)$ simultaneously, and the cost of effort is simply $C(x_i) = x_i$.

[2] Simultaneity makes this problem different from the Dollar Auction Game as described by Shubik (1971), in which both bidders also pay their own bid and the dollar bill is handed to the bidder with the higher bid, but with ascending bids being made alternatingly by the bidders.

Contestant 1 wins with probability

$$p_1(x_1, x_2) = \begin{cases} 1 & \text{if} \quad x_1 > x_2 \\ \frac{1}{2} & \text{if} \quad x_1 = x_2 \\ 0 & \text{if} \quad x_1 < x_2. \end{cases} \tag{2.1}$$

The probability that contestant 2 wins is $p_2 = 1 - p_1$.[3]

Consider the optimal effort choices of the contestants. Each contestant i maximizes the payoff (2.1) that was specified more generally in section 1.1, subject to $x_i \geq 0$, with win probabilities defined by (2.1), and with $C(x_i) = x_i$. Accordingly, if contestant 1 thinks that contestant 2 will choose some x_2, the optimal effort from the perspective of contestant 1 is either some x_1 slightly above x_2 that makes contestant 1 win the prize with certainty, or $x_1 = 0$. The latter is the case if x_2 is very high so that it does not pay to outcompete contestant 2. The reasoning is similar for contestant 2. Hence, there is no equilibrium in pure strategies in this game. A formal proof of this is by contradiction and starts with the assumption that (x_1, x_2) is such an equilibrium, showing that x_2 can never be contestant 2's optimal reply to x_1 if x_1 is the optimal reply of contestant 1 to this x_2.

The Nash equilibrium is in mixed strategies and these mixed strategies are described by contestants' cumulative distribution functions that describe the distribution of effort choices,

$$F_1(x_1) = \begin{cases} \dfrac{x_1}{v_2} & \text{for} \quad x_1 \in [0, v_2] \\ 1 & \text{for} \quad x_1 > v_2 \end{cases} \tag{2.2}$$

and

$$F_2(x_2) = \begin{cases} \left[1 - \dfrac{v_2}{v_1}\right] + \dfrac{x_2}{v_1} & \text{for} \quad x_2 \in [0, v_2] \\ 1 & \text{for} \quad x_2 > v_2. \end{cases} \tag{2.3}$$

The mixed strategies that are described by (2.2) and (2.3) are mutually optimal replies, meaning that they characterize an equilibrium. This is verified as follows. Contestant 1's payoff equals $v_1 - v_2$ for all choices $x_1 \in (0, v_2]$, and is smaller than this difference for all non-negative x_1 outside this interval if the contestant plays against a contestant 2 who randomizes his effort according to $F_2(x_2)$. Contestant 2's payoff, on the other hand, equals zero for all choices $x_2 \in [0, v_2]$, and is negative for all effort choices that are

[3] Equilibrium of a contest with this contest success function was analyzed by Hillman and Riley (1989).

even higher than v_2 if he plays against a contestant 1 who randomizes according to the cumulative distribution function $F_1(x_1)$.

Baye, Kovenock, and de Vries (1996) show that this equilibrium is also unique. Their proof develops and builds on the insights that equilibrium mixed strategies cannot have mass points other than at $x_i = 0$, that the equilibrium cumulative distribution functions cannot have 'holes'—that is, whole intervals of effort levels that have zero mass—and that there can be, at most, a mass point for one of the contestants at $x_i = 0$. These insights can be verified by contradiction. Some intuition for the result is as follows. Note that 2 is never going to expend more than $x_2 = v_2$. But if contestant 2 never expends more than $x_2 = v_2$, then contestant 1 can be sure of winning with probability 1 if he expends $x_1 = v_2$ (or an arbitrarily small amount more than this). This defines the upper limit of reasonable efforts and reduces the problem to showing how the contestants randomize on the interval $[0, v_2]$. Note also that contestant 1 could guarantee an own payoff equal to $v_1 - v_2$ by simply choosing an effort that infinitesimally exceeds v_2, and, indeed, this is 1's equilibrium payoff, whereas 2's equilibrium payoff is zero. Finally, the slope, and even the whole equilibrium cumulative distribution functions, can be obtained from this equilibrium payoff. The payoff of contestant 1 must be equal to this $v_1 - v_2$ for any strategy that belongs to those used in the mixed strategy. Accordingly, for all these strategies we have

$$\pi_1(x_1) = F_2(x_1)v_1 - x_1 = v_1 - v_2. \tag{2.4}$$

This can be transformed to (2.3). Similarly, if the payoff for all choices x_2 that belong to the mixed strategy for contestant 2 is zero, this means

$$\pi_2(x_2) = F_1(x_2)v_2 - x_2 = 0, \tag{2.5}$$

and this can be transformed to (2.2).

The equilibrium payoffs for contestants 1 and 2 are $v_1 - v_2$ and zero, as discussed. Their expected efforts are

$$Ex_1 = \frac{v_2}{2} \quad \text{and} \quad Ex_2 = \frac{(v_2)^2}{2v_1}. \tag{2.6}$$

This shows that the sum of expected efforts falls short of the effort in a standard second-price auction, as the sum of efforts falls short of v_2 if $v_1 > v_2$. Also, the contest has a peculiar inefficiency property in that the prize is not necessarily allocated to the contestant who has the highest valuation of the prize. This is a peculiarity that is not robust in the sense that it will disappear if the order of moves between the two contestants is changed so that they move sequentially. The prize is also efficiently allocated in some all-pay auctions with incomplete information, particularly in the symmetric independent valuation all-pay auction if the contestants know their own valuations of the prize, but not those of their competitor. Sequential moves for a structure that is equivalent to the all-pay auction without noise have been considered in Deneckere, Kovenock, and Lee (1992), and in the particular all-pay auction context, by Jost and Kräkel (2000). Sequential choices will be re-considered in a separate section, together with endogenous timing. Issues of incomplete or imperfect information will also be discussed later.

Convex cost

Before turning to the case with more than two contestants, consider alternative cost functions. Let $C(x_i)$ be (weakly) convex, that is $C(0) = 0$, $C'(x_i) > 0$ and $C''(x_i) \geq 0$. Consider two contestants with identical valuations, v, of winning the prize, and identical cost of effort. For reasons similar to those just discussed, an equilibrium in pure strategies does not exist. The payoff of player 1 equals

$$\pi_1(x_1) = F_2(x_1)v - C(x_1). \tag{2.7}$$

This equals zero if $F_2(x_1) = C(x_1)/v$. Accordingly, using the symmetry assumption, the equilibrium density becomes $F_1'(x) = F_2'(x) = C'(x)/v$ in the range $[0, \bar{x}]$, with $\bar{x}$ defined by $C(\bar{x}) = v$, and zero elsewhere (see, e.g., Kaplan, Luski, and Wettstein, 2003).

More than two contestants

Let there be $n \geq 2$ contestants. In this case, the nature of the equilibrium and its uniqueness properties depend on the distribution of valuations of winning for the different contestants. In the most simple case with valuations $v_1 \geq v_2 > v_3 \geq \cdots \geq v_n$, the equilibrium is unique and has $x_i = 0$ for all $i > 2$, and contestants 1 and 2 choose the equilibrium cumulative distribution functions as in the $n = 2$ case.[4] Intuitively, the equilibrium play between 1 and 2 must be described by (2.2) and (2.3) if all other contestants do not make bids. But, even if only contestant 1 chooses (2.2) and contestant 2 abstains, this makes the payoff negative for any positive

[4] Baye, Kovenock, and de Vries (1996) give a rigorous analysis of the all-pay auction with more than two players and a full characterization of the equilibria. Some of their results are surveyed here.

effort by any contestant whose valuation of the prize is smaller than v_2, and this explains why all other players find it optimal to abstain from making positive bids.

Uniqueness of equilibrium does not hold once there are more than two players who have the highest valuation of winning the prize. In this case, all these players can take an active role in the equilibrium, and there can be several combinations of active roles that constitute an equilibrium. To illustrate the nature of the equilibrium in these cases, let there be $n \geq 2$ contestants and valuations $v_1 = v_2 = \cdots = v_j > v_{j+1} \geq \cdots \geq v_n$. In any equilibrium, $x_i = 0$ for all $i > j$. Players who have valuations lower than the valuations of two other players with higher valuations will not be active in the equilibrium. In the set of contestants with the highest valuation, any number between 2 and j may actively participate and make positive bids. For instance, one type of equilibrium has only two of these j contestants active. These choose their efforts according to the equilibrium cumulative densities of the two-player game as in (2.2) and all other players stay out. But there are also sets of equilibrium cumulative distribution functions in which more than two contestants make positive bids.

The cases here are not exhaustive, but this example may explain the nature of equilibrium if there are more than two players in the set of players who have the two highest valuations of winning the prize.

Other cost variants

The all-pay auction with complete information and without noise has been well studied, and the equilibria are not only described for the various combinations of relative valuations of the prize. For instance, Baye, Kovenock, and de Vries (1998, 2008) consider the class of symmetric two-player contests along a different, interesting dimension. For this purpose, they assume that the contest success function is as in (2.1) and define the payoff of player 1 as follows:

$$\begin{array}{ll} v - bx_1 - dx_2 & \text{if player 1 wins,} \\ -\gamma - ax_1 - tx_2 & \text{if player 1 loses,} \end{array} \tag{2.8}$$

half of the sum of these payoffs if both players expend the same positive effort. They assume that the payoffs are zero for both players if both players expend zero effort. The payoff of player 2 is obtained by replacing all number 1 subscripts by 2 and vice versa. They give a considerable number of relevant examples for special cases of (2.8). For instance, the case $b = a = 1$ and $d = t = \gamma = 0$ refers to the standard contest case with $v_1 = v_2 = v$ and a loser prize of zero. The case $b = d = 0$, $a = t = 1$ refers to a system in which the contestants have to pay both their own and their opponent's effort if they lose and have a possibly negative loser prize γ. The case $b = t = 0$, $d = a = 1$ refers to a situation in which the winner and the loser both pay the effort made by the loser. An example of this is the war of attrition. Here, both contestants choose the maximum efforts they are willing to expend. They expend this as a constant flow: for instance, as waiting time. Once the stock of effort that one of the players was willing to expend is used up, the other player wins and also stops expending further effort. The nature of the equilibrium depends on the parameters. Baye, Kovenock, and de Vries (2008) provide an extensive characterization of the symmetric equilibria for the general case (2.8) and the conditions for which this characterization applies. In particular, for a large parameter range, a symmetric equilibrium in mixed strategies exists, for which the cumulative distribtion function of equilibrium effort is

$$G(x) = \frac{a}{a-b}\left[1 - \left[\frac{V+\eta m}{V+\eta\omega}\right]^{\frac{a-b}{\eta}}\right] + C\left[\frac{V+\eta m}{V+\eta\omega}\right]^{\frac{a-b}{\eta}} \tag{2.9}$$

for some $m > 0$ and $1 \leq C \leq 0$ being functions of (a, b, d, t), $V \equiv v + \gamma \geq 0$ and $\eta \equiv a + t - b - d$. The reader may consult Baye, Kovenock, and de Vries (2008) for further details and a discussion of the special cases and applications.

Constraints on effort

Contestants are sometimes exogenously constrained regarding the amount of effort they can choose. An important example is discussed and solved by Che and Gale (1998): campaign contribution regulation in the US determines the maximum campaign contribution that a single individual can make to a candidate. Other examples may emerge if the effort expended in the contest is measured by time devoted to it. Candidates may then have only a limited amount of time between the start of the contest and its end, as in many sports games or in some scoring tests in which individuals solve one or many tasks within a given time limit.

If there are n contestants and all have the same spending limit of size m as the maximum effort they can choose, and if this is

$$m < (1/n)\min\{v_1, v_2, \ldots, v_n\}, \tag{2.10}$$

all will simply choose the maximum effort. Intuitively, if (2.10) holds, contestants i have the opportunity to take part in a lottery in which their win probability is $1/n$ if they pay m and their lottery prize is equal to v_i.

However, given that others pay m, in order to hold a ticket that can actually win, they must pay m. This is worth it in a lottery with $n - 1$ other participants even for the participant with the lowest valuation of the prize if $m < 1/n \min\{v_1, \dots v_n\}$.

This intuition structurally determines the equilibrium for a whole range of higher effort limits up to the effort limit that is determined by

$$m < (1/2) \min\{v_1, v_2\}, \tag{2.11}$$

where, by appropriate renumbering, $v_1 \geq v_2 \geq \cdots \geq v_n$, that is, v_1 and v_2 are the two highest valuations among the valuations $v_1, \dots v_n$. For this whole range, only a set of players with the highest valuations will participate, with the contestant with the lowest valuation determined by the condition

$$m < (1/k) \min\{v_1, \dots v_k\}. \tag{2.12}$$

If m becomes even larger than the largest m that fulfills condition (2.11) with equality, only the two contestants with the highest valuation matter, but the solution becomes more cumbersome. If the maximum feasible effort is higher than v_2 with v_2 the second highest valuation, the effort limit is non-binding in the equilibrium and can be ignored. If m is from the interval $[1/2 \min\{v_1, v_2\}, \min\{v_1, v_2\}]$, the solution is less straightforward. As shown in more detail in Che and Gale (1998), the generic equilibrium cumulative distribution functions are as drawn in Figure 2.1 for $v_1 > v_2$.[5] The cumulative distribution functions are identical with the ones in (2.2) and (2.3) in the range from 0 to $2m - v_2$, have zero mass in the range from $(2m - v_2)$ to m and both players have a mass point at m. It can be confirmed that these cumulative distribution functions of effort characterize an equilibrium by showing that contestant 1's payoff equals $v_1 - v_2$ for all effort choices from the set $(0, 2m - v_2] \cup \{m\}$ and is lower for all effort choices from outside this set, and that contestant 2's payoff equals zero for all effort choices from the set $(0, 2m - v_2) \cup \{m\}$, and is lower for other effort choices.

A related problem, treated in Che and Gale (1997), emerges if there are n contestants who face different constraints as regards their maximum effort. For instance, firms may know the profit increase from winning a particular R&D contest with certainty, but they may have a limited amount of equity and there may also be credit market imperfections due to non-contractibility problems that lead to liquidity constraints. To concentrate

[5] Che and Gale (1998) discuss whether additional equilibria are feasible for some non-generic parameters, particularly for $m = v_1/2$ and $m = v_2/2$. They show, for instance, that there is a continuum of equilibria for $m = v_2/2$, with $x_1 = x_2 = m$ being one of these equilibria.

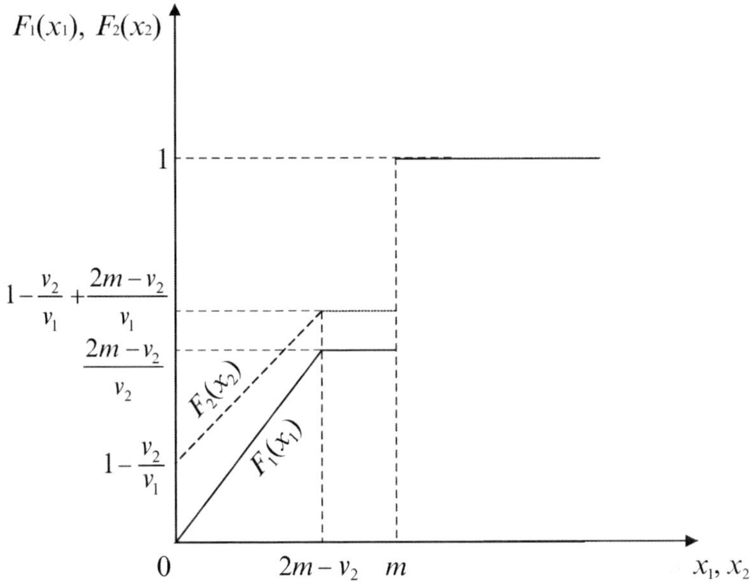

Figure 2.1 The equilibrium cumulative distribution functions for $v_1 = 1, v_2 = 0.8$ and a cap $m = 0.6$.

on the liquidity problem, let all contestants value winning the prize by v, but assume that the wealth that determines their maximum effort limit is sorted such that $w_1 > w_2 > w_3 \geq \cdots \geq w_n$, with $w_2 < v$. The equilibrium in this case is described by cumulative distribution functions

$$F_1(x_1) = \begin{cases} \dfrac{x_1}{v} & \text{for} \quad x_1 \in [0, w_2) \\ 1 & \text{for} \quad x_1 \geq w_2 \end{cases} \tag{2.13}$$

and

$$F_2(x_2) = \begin{cases} 1 - \dfrac{w_2}{v} + \dfrac{x_2}{v} & \text{for} \quad x_2 \in [0, w_2) \\ 1 & \text{for} \quad x_2 \geq w_2, \end{cases} \tag{2.14}$$

and zero effort by all other contestants (see Figure 2.2). The equilibrium properties of these functions can be confirmed by calculating the payoffs of the contestants. Given F_2 and zero effort by all contestants $3, \ldots n$, the payoff of contestant 1 equals $(v - w_2)$ for all $x_1 \in (0, w_2]$, and is smaller for all other effort levels $x_1 > w_2$. This makes contestant 1 indifferent with respect to all effort levels $x_1 \in (0, w_2]$. He may therefore randomize according to F_1. Similarly, F_2 turns out to be an optimal reply to F_1 and

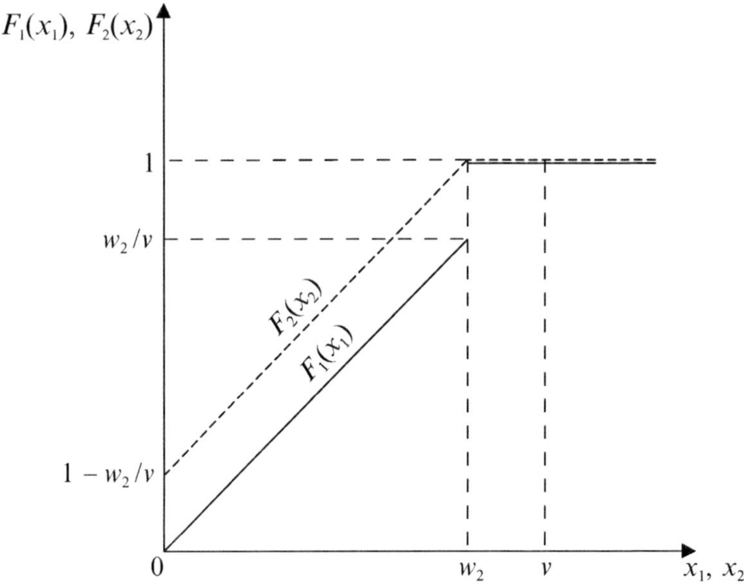

Figure 2.2 The equilibrium with budget constraints.

to the non-participation of other contestants, and yields a payoff equal to zero to contestant 2. All other contestants $3, \ldots, n$ would make losses from any feasible positive effort level given F_1 and F_2 and have zero payoff from choosing an effort level of zero.

Incumbency advantages

In many real-world contests for a prize, the contestants are not fully homogeneous. Differences with respect to contestants' valuations of the prize translate equivalently into differences in contestants' cost of providing a given level of effort. More precisely, a situation in which $C_1(x_1) = x_1$ and $C_2(x_2) = x_2$, but $v_1 > v_2$ can be mapped into an equivalent situation in which $v_1 = v_2$, but $C_1(x_1) = x_1(v_2/v_1)$ and $C_2(x_2) = x_2$. This becomes clear from writing down the two contestants' objective functions for the two types of problem, noticing that one problem is obtained from the other by dividing the objective function of contestant 1 by v_1/v_2 (see Baye, Kovenock, and de Vries (1996) for a discussion).

A different type of asymmetry comes into play if one of the contestants has some kind of a headstart advantage; suppose, for example, that the contestants are symmetric with respect to provision cost ($C_i(x) = x$) and their valuation of the prize $v_1 = v_2 = v$, but let the contest success function be given as

$$p_1(x_1, x_2) = \begin{cases} 1 & \text{if} \quad x_1 > x_2 - \delta \\ \frac{1}{2} & \text{if} \quad x_1 = x_2 - \delta \\ 0 & \text{if} \quad x_1 < x_2 - \delta. \end{cases} \tag{2.15}$$

In this case, contestant 1 has a 'headstart advantage'. His opponent needs to expend an effort that exceeds contestant 1's effort by more than δ units of effort for winning the contest. There are many environments in which such a headstart becomes relevant. For instance, Konrad (2002) considers a situation in which an incumbent leader of a country fights with an opposition. A similar problem shows up in an R&D problem considered by Kaplan, Luski, and Wettstein (2003), and in Konrad (2004c) in the context of parties' campaign contributions.

The equilibrium outcome in the problem with a headstart advantage is given by the cumulative distribution functions

$$F_1(x_1) = \begin{cases} \frac{\delta}{v} + \frac{x_1}{v} & \text{for} \quad x_1 \in [0, v - \delta) \\ 1 & \text{for} \quad x_1 \geq v - \delta \end{cases} \tag{2.16}$$

and

$$F_2(x_2) = \begin{cases} \frac{\delta}{v} & \text{for} \quad x_2 \in [0, \delta) \\ \frac{\delta}{v} + \frac{x_2 - \delta}{v} & \text{for} \quad x_2 \in [\delta, v) \\ 1 & \text{for} \quad x_2 \geq v. \end{cases} \tag{2.17}$$

Again, by considering the resulting payoffs, it can be verified that these effort distributions are optimal replies to each other and establish an equilibrium.

Incomplete information

Possible asymmetries between contestants may often go along with incomplete information, and private information may pertain to a whole set of possible characteristics. Singh and Wittman (1998), for instance, allow for productivity differences in contestants' ability to transform their contest resources into effective contest effort. Essentially this suggests differences in the cost of effort, and the cost of effort may be information that is private to each contestant. Similarly, contestants often know their own valuation of winning the prize, but have only an opinion based on experience or a guess about their opponent's valuation of the prize. The all-pay auction is then one with incomplete information. This case has attracted considerable interest in the literature for various assumptions about the distributions of types, cost functions, and bidding constraints.

To see how the equilibrium differs from the full information case, consider the symmetric case with two contestants 1 and 2. Each values the prize of winning according to some $v_i \in [0, 1]$. The valuations v_i are drawn independently from a distribution $F(v)$ on the unit interval $[0, 1]$. The following is an equilibrium candidate. Let each contestant choose effort that is a function of the contestant's valuation of the prize, say, $x = \xi(v)$ such that the valuation that belongs to a given bid x is $\xi^{-1}(\xi(v))$, provided that this inverse exists. Consider now contestant 1's optimal choice if contestant 2 follows this pattern. The objective function of contestant 1 with a valuation equal to v_1 becomes

$$\pi_1(x_1) = F(\xi^{-1}(x_1))v_1 - x_1. \tag{2.18}$$

Maximization of this objective function yields the first-order condition

$$\pi_1'(x_1) = F'(\xi^{-1}(x_1))\frac{d\xi^{-1}}{dx_1}v_1 - 1 = 0. \tag{2.19}$$

Using symmetry according to which the two contestants will follow the same bid function $\xi(v)$ in the equilibrium, this can be transformed into

$$\frac{dx}{dv} = F'(v)v. \tag{2.20}$$

This is a differential equation. Taking into account the starting condition $\xi(0) = 0$, it can be solved for a given distribution function $F(v)$ as

$$\xi(v) = \int_0^v F'(v)vdv. \tag{2.21}$$

Hence, a general property of this solution is $\xi(1) = E(v)$. The specific bidding function can be obtained explicitly by solving (2.21). This can, but need not, be a difficult task. For instance, if $F(v)$ is uniform on the unit interval, then (2.20) becomes

$$dx = vdv \tag{2.22}$$

and has a simple solution:

$$\xi(v) = \frac{v^2}{2}. \tag{2.23}$$

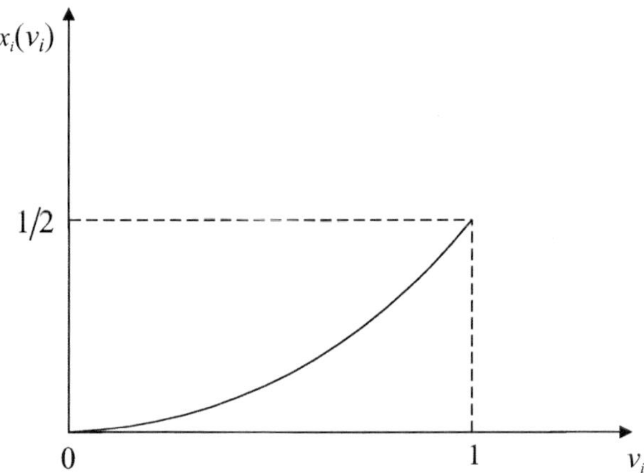

Figure 2.3 The equilibrium bidding function.

The solution in this simple case is illustrated in Figure 2.3. It has nice properties that are robust for other distribution functions of valuations for a priori symmetric contestants. The inefficiency, according to which the prize can go to the bidder with the lower valuation that emerged in the full information case, disappears in this example. In the equilibrium, the contestant with the highest valuation of the prize wins the good. This is a nice property and also holds if the distribution of types has mass points. The efficiency property of the allocation outcome in the all-pay auction with incomplete information is not fully robust. It will, for instance, not hold in general if the players are drawn from non-identical distributions of types.

The equilibria in the cases with complete and with incomplete information have something in common. The equilibrium effort choices of a contestant's opponent is a distribution of effort levels. In the complete information case, to overcome the non-existence problem of mutually optimal replies, players need to randomize. In the incomplete information case, the randomness of types imposes randomness of one's opponent's bids, and this randomness is sufficient to make the decision problem of a contestant of a given type smooth. The duality of these two types of randomization is discussed in Amann and Leininger (1996).[6]

[6] A selection of contributions focusing on different problems in such a framework are Glazer and Hassin (1988), Amann and Leininger (1996), Krishna and Morgan (1997), Baye, Kovenock, and de Vries (1998), Clark and Riis (2000), Moldovanu and Sela (2001), Feess, Muehlheusser, and Walzl (2002), Gavious, Moldovanu, and Sela (2002), Kura (1999), Lizzeri and Persico (2000), and Singh and Wittman (2001).

One-sided asymmetric information

Consider again two contestants. Suppose both contestants' valuations are drawn from the same distribution, but contestant 1's valuation v_1 is publicly observed, whereas contestant 2's valuation v_2 is this contestant's private information. For the class of 'smooth' contests with contest success functions that make the objective function sufficiently concave, Wärneryd (2003) has addressed a common value problem.[7]

For an illustration of the nature of asymmetric information, let us consider the bivariate case with independent values for the all-pay auction without noise. Let v_i be drawn randomly and independently from the set $\{a, b\}$ with $a < b$, and with probabilities $q_a = 1 - q_b$ for both contestants. Let v_1 be publicly observed and let v_2 be contestant 2's private information. In this case the equilibrium has cumulative distribution functions

$$F_1^a(x_1) = \begin{cases} q_b \dfrac{b-a}{b} + \dfrac{x_1}{a} & \text{for} \quad x_1 \in [0, aq_a) \\ \dfrac{b-a}{b} + \dfrac{x_1}{b} & \text{for} \quad x_1 \in [aq_a, a] \end{cases} \tag{2.24}$$

for contestant 1 if $v_1 = a$ and

$$F_1^b(x_1) = \begin{cases} \dfrac{x_1}{a} & \text{for} \quad x_1 \in [0, aq_a) \\ q_a\left(1 - \dfrac{a}{b}\right) + \dfrac{x_1}{b} & \text{for} \quad x_1 \in [q_a a, q_a a + q_b b] \end{cases} \tag{2.25}$$

if $v_1 = b$, and cumulative distribution functions for contestant 2 that depend on both contestants' types,

$$F_2^{aa}(x_2) = \frac{x_2/q_a}{a} \quad \text{for} \quad x_2 \in [0, aq_a] \tag{2.26}$$

$$F_2^{ab}(x_2) = \frac{(x_2 - aq_a)/q_b}{a} \quad \text{for} \quad x_2 \in (aq_a, a] \tag{2.27}$$

$$F_2^{ba}(x_2) = \frac{b-a}{b} + \frac{x_2/q_a}{b} \quad \text{for} \quad x_2 \in [0, aq_a] \tag{2.28}$$

$$F_2^{bb}(x_2) = \frac{(x_2 - q_a a)/q_b}{b} \quad \text{for} \quad x_2 \in (aq_a, q_a a + q_b b] \tag{2.29}$$

and zero and one respectively for x_2 to the left and to the right of these intervals with F_2^{rs} being the function for the case where contestant 1 has

[7] For an independent value problem with incomplete information see Hurley and Shogren (1998).

a publicly observed valuation of r and contestant 2 has a valuation equal to s.

The expected equilibrium payoff of the informed contestant is

$$(b-a)\,q_a q_b\left(2-q_a\frac{b-a}{b}\right) \tag{2.30}$$

and the expected equilibrium payoff of the uninformed contestant is

$$q_a q_b(b-a). \tag{2.31}$$

The better informed contestant receives an information rent.

In the case with two-sided full information, a rent is obtained only in the cases in which the contestants' valuations differ, and the rent in this case equals $(b-a)$. Each contestant has an ex ante chance of winning this rent of $q_a q_b$. Accordingly, the total expected rent is $2q_a q_b(b-a)$ and, in expectation, it is equally distributed between the two contestants. In the case of asymmetry, the increase in the payoff is earned by the contestant who is better informed.

One may also compare this outcome with the expected equilibrium payoffs in the two-sided incomplete information case considered by Konrad (2004a). There, the contestants who have the high valuation receive an expected payoff equal to $q_a(b-a)$, and, given their probability of having a high valuation, each contestant has an ex ante expected payoff equal to $q_a q_b(b-a)$, just as in the full information case. Of the three cases, the asymmetric one has the highest expected payoff in the binary distribution case. Whether this is a general pattern is unclear, but it is intuitively plausible that the better informed contestant will earn an information rent.

2.2. Additive noise

For various reasons, noise or randomness plays an important role in contests. Consider, for example, two architects who compete to receive the contract to build a museum. Let them both be equally talented and productive. Typically, if the prize is high, they will expend considerable manpower and come up with good project proposals. A committee or the builder-owner then decides. The number of office hours expended on thinking about a project proposal will generally improve it, but there is no need for the architect who expends the largest number of hours to win the architecture contest for sure. The decision will generally depend on many random factors. For instance, the decision-maker's preferences are not perfectly known to the architects, and they may like, or dislike, one or the other proposal for reasons not related to the effort put into the project. The decision may also depend on the architects' look, haircut, mood, or performance when presenting their proposals, thus adding further elements of noise.

A simple way of mapping this kind of noise was chosen by Lazear and Rosen (1981) and also in much of the labor market tournament literature partially surveyed in Lazear (1995).[8] The underlying assumption of this contest success function is that the contest success probabilities of the set of contestants are not affected if all contestants increase their contest efforts by the same, arbitrary, absolute number, as long as the contest efforts are positive both prior to and after this shift in effort. This is a strong assumption, of course. However, it does help to generate a simple framework that has been popular, particularly for studying problems in the labor market.

The two-player case

Consider two contestants. They choose contest efforts x_1 and x_2. But their efforts do not translate in a deterministic way into the observable characteristics that are the basis of decision-making as in the section on the first-price all-pay auction. An easy way to describe this is to allow for some additive noise: the observed characteristic for contestant i is $x_i + \epsilon_i$, where ϵ_i is a realization of a random variable, and the prize is awarded to the contestant for whom $x_i + \epsilon_i$ is largest. Written differently, and lumping the two noise parameters ϵ_1 and ϵ_2 into a single parameter $\epsilon = \epsilon_2 - \epsilon_1$, the contest success function can be written as

$$p_1(x_1, x_2) = \begin{cases} 1 & \text{if} \quad x_1 - x_2 > \epsilon \\ \dfrac{1}{2} & \text{if} \quad x_1 - x_2 = \epsilon \, . \\ 0 & \text{if} \quad x_1 - x_2 < \epsilon \end{cases} \tag{2.32}$$

Much now depends on the distribution of the noise variable ϵ. We denote the cumulative distribution function of ϵ by G and the support of this distribution by the interval $[-e, e]$, with $e > 0$.

The tournament is often designed by an organizer. The organizer may be able to determine the prize b_W obtained by the winner of the tournament, the prize b_L received by the loser of the tournament, which may also be positive. Let the contestants' valuations of winning or losing be $v_i(b_W)$

[8] Related structures have also been analyzed in the literature on contests under the 'difference-form contest success function' (see, e.g., Hirshleifer, 1989; Baik, 1998; and Che and Gale, 2000. See also Skaperdas, 1996, for axiomatic reasoning).

and let the valuation of losing be $v_i(b_L)$ for $i = 1, 2$. Each single contestant then maximizes

$$p_i(x_1, x_2)(v_i(b_W) - v_i(b_L)) - C(x_i) + v_i(b_L). \tag{2.33}$$

Unlike in the previous section, the cost $C(x_i)$ of effort is not assumed to be linear, but instead it is a convex function of effort with $C(0) = 0$, $C'(x_i) > 0$ and $C''(x_i) > 0$. This convexity assumption brings about a situation in which the marginal effort cost for an increase in the probability of winning the prize is increasing in this probability.[9] If this cost function is sufficiently convex, the contest equilibrium can simply be described by the first-order condition for contestant 1,

$$\frac{\partial G(x_1 - x_2)}{\partial x_1}[v_i(b_W) - v_i(b_L)] = C'(x_1), \tag{2.34}$$

and analogously for contestant 2, provided that the contestants' expected payoffs in the resulting equilibrium are larger than their payoffs from not participating in the contest. When setting up a contest, this participation constraint can be accounted for by making the loser prize b_L sufficiently large.

The problem can be simplified if one of the following assumptions are made. First, if $v_i(b) = b$, and if both contestants have the same cost function, then $x_1 = x_2$ in the equilibrium. This reduces both contestants' first-order conditions in the equilibrium to

$$G'(0)(b_W - b_L) = C'(x_i). \tag{2.35}$$

Second, if ϵ is distributed uniformly on an interval $[-e, +e]$ this causes the first-order conditions of the two contestants to be independent of each other, as this makes $\partial G(x_1 - x_2)/\partial x_1$ independent of x_2 and equal to $1/(2e)$. Accordingly, the strategic interdependence of effort choices disappears. In what follows, I will concentrate on this particularly simple and illustrative case.

The first-order condition suggests in this case that an increase in the dispersion of ϵ, or a reduction in the value of the winner prize, will generally reduce the optimal effort of a contestant. The contestant who values

[9] A suitable combination of convexity of the cost function and the distribution of ϵ is required for the first-order condition to describe the equilibrium. Otherwise corner solutions become important and the equilibrium may be in mixed strategies. For $C(x) = x$ and a uniform distribution of ϵ, for instance, the problem converges towards the standard all-pay auction if the support of ϵ becomes small.

winning $v_i(b_W) - v_i(b_L)$ more highly will expend more effort than his competitor, given that they face the same function describing their cost of effort.

When the tournament is designed by an organizer, the optimal design question emerges. If the distribution of noise is exogenously given, and, for simplicity, uniform, the contest designer can still choose along several dimensions, for instance, the choice of the winner and loser prizes. Let us concentrate again on the simple case in which $v_i(b) = b$. Two benchmark cases need to be distinguished for the contest design problem. The contest designer could be at the shorter side of the market and, much like a monopolist, may design the contest in a way that maximizes his own payoff from organizing it, or the participants in the contest could be on the short side of the market, that is there could be many contest designers (like firms) which compete for hiring contestants.

Consider first a firm that has monopoly power when hiring two contestants. In this case, the problem of choosing b_W and b_L is the problem of maximizing

$$\varphi(x_1^* + x_2^*) - b_W - b_L \tag{2.36}$$

subject to the participation constraints of the contestants, that is $p_i(x_1^*, x_2^*)(b_W - b_L) + b_L \geq C(x_i^*)$, where the contestant's payoff from not participating is normalized to zero. Here, (x_1^*, x_2^*) denote the equilibrium efforts. The contest designer's benefit from the contestants' efforts x_1 and x_2 is denoted φ and is assumed to be a function of the sum of these efforts. Of course, (2.36) is only one of many reasonable objective functions which the tournament organizer may have, some modifications of which have been considered in the literature.

The firm can always set b_L sufficiently high to fulfill the participation constraint. If the optimization problem has an interior solution, using symmetry, the contest designer chooses $b_W - b_L$ in a way such that $x^* = x_1^* = x_2^*$ for which

$$G'(0)(b_W - b_L) = C'(x^*) \tag{2.37}$$

also fulfills

$$C'(x^*) = \varphi'(2x^*). \tag{2.38}$$

This condition is the efficiency condition for the equilibrium effort. The contest designer can induce each of the two contestants to expend an additional unit of effort, and $\varphi'(2x^*)$ is the additional benefit this brings to the contest organizer. However, the organizer will have to motivate the contestants to do this by increasing the contest prize. The optimal structure is reached if the additional marginal benefit generated by additional effort equals the actual marginal cost of the contestant in providing this additional effort.

Alternatively, the contestants may have all the market power. In this case, the optimal contest is characterized by the same condition (2.38), but the contestants will receive the maximum feasible compensation for participation that reduces the contest organizer's expected payoff from organizing the contest down to his reservation utility.

Note that the first-best optimal contest is not necessarily implemented for a number of reasons such as asymmetry between the contestants, risk aversion on the side of the contestants or the contest designer, and issues of incomplete information (see, e.g., O'Keefe, Viscusi, and Zeckhauser (1984) for some considerations). For many of these issues, the first-best outcome will become unattainable as an equilibrium outcome.

Some considerations about the optimality of a tournament as a designed incentive mechanism when the designer cares about total output net of compensation are given in Nalebuff and Stiglitz (1983). An important insight in this paper is that tournaments have useful properties as incentive contracts even if the contestants are risk averse, if the relationship between individual effort and individual output is 'disturbed' by considerable systematic noise, that is, if the ϵ_i's that add to actual efforts x_i to determine i's observed output have a large common component. In this case, the tournament works similarly to a compensation scheme that is used to set up yardstick competition. A few other positive aspects of tournaments have been highlighted in the literature. Tournaments make it feasible for the organizer to commit to paying out a prize to at least one contestant, which may be useful if the actual output is observable, but not verifiable in court[10] or if the moral hazard problem is double-sided in the sense that the principal can also affect the agent's output (see Malcomson, 1984; Carmichael, 1983 and a discussion in Tsoulouhas, 1999). Other aspects that may improve the theoretical properties of tournaments as incentive mechanisms have been discussed. See, for instance, Levin (2002), Quintero (2004), and Fernández and Galí (1999). The latter consider the role of credit market constraints for the optimality of a tournament. Gibbons and Waldman (1999) and, in particular, Lazear (1995) also survey further negative aspects of tournaments, highlighting in particular the problem of sabotage, or the disincentives for providing help to co-workers if they

[10] The importance of this argument has also been questioned in the literature, as, once the tournament designer and the participants observe the actual output, the participants may try to bribe the designer to award the prize not in accordance with true output.

are rivals in a tournament, and also how such problems could in theory be reduced by an appropriate design of the tournament. They also consider some empirical applications.

Note that the tournament turns into the all-pay auction without noise if the distribution of ϵ becomes degenerate. Hence, the all-pay auction without noise in the previous section can be seen as the limiting case of the tournament. This convergence, however, is not a smooth process. If the dispersion of ϵ becomes smaller and smaller, at some point a pure strategy equilibrium typically disappears. Mixed strategy equilibria that can emerge in this case are described for some cases in Che and Gale (2000).

2.3. The Tullock contest

Perhaps the most popular contest success function that has been suggested and used in several areas of economics assumes that a contestant i's probability of winning the contest equals the ratio between this contestant's own effort and the sum of all efforts, or a variant of this. Some examples and early references in the context of promotional competition and in military applications have been discussed in Chapter 1.

The standard Tullock contest

While Tullock (1980) was not the first to analyze contests with this particular structure in economic applications, the following contest success function is typically attributed to him as he was the first to use it to study the problem of rival rent-seekers who expend resources to influence the decision outcome in their favor:

$$p_i(x_1, \dots x_n) = \begin{cases} \dfrac{x_i^r}{\sum_{j=1}^n x_j^r} & \text{if} \quad \max\{x_1, \dots x_n\} > 0 \\ \dfrac{1}{N} & \text{otherwise.} \end{cases} \tag{2.39}$$

For $r = 1$, this function has also been called the 'lottery contest': the win probability equals the share of expenditure of a contestant in the total expenditure, as in a lottery in which one monetary unit buys one lottery ticket, and in which the winner is drawn from the set of all tickets, with each ticket winning with the same probability. However, the parameter $r > 0$ in the function (2.39) allows for slightly more general types of contests. This parameter will be important for the marginal impact of an increase in a contestant's effort.[11] Together with functions

$$C_i(x_i) = x_i \tag{2.40}$$

describing individuals' cost of providing efforts x_i, this describes the 'Tullock contest'.[12]

The function (2.39) converges towards the contest success function (2.1) with no noise as $r \to \infty$. Note that p_i is a probability for all feasible combinations of effort, and that the probability for i to win the contest is increasing in i's own effort and decreasing in other contestants' effort.

The Tullock contest and its variants have been studied extremely carefully. The contest success function (2.39) has been used in the literature describing rent-seeking (see Nitzan, 1994, for an early survey and Lockard and Tullock, 2001, for a more recent collection of papers). Rent-seeking has not been the first area in which its formal structure has been used. Friedman (1958) used the function (2.39) to describe the relationship between the persuasive advertising of different firms and their respective shares in the markets. He considered the advertising game between two firms which compete in several products or product categories. Firms have given global advertising budgets and must decide how to allocate their budget to advertising expenditure for these different products. This game with exogenously given sums of effort, but different parallel contests has been called the 'Colonel Blotto game' and different variants of this game have been studied in the literature (see section 1.2.8). Bell, Keeney, and Little (1975) axiomatized (2.39); also in the context of advertising, Schmalensee (1976) considered more general functions describing the relationship between advertising expenditure and market shares and introduced and discussed a number of plausible properties of such functions. He considered (2.39) with $r = 1$ as a special case (p. 495). A more recent application in the context of promotional competition is Barros and Sørgard (2000). In sports, the outcome of sports tournaments has been described by (2.39) by Hoehn and Szymanski (1999) and Szymanski (2003). The function has also been used for describing R&D contests (Fullerton and McAfee, 1999) and has emerged in the literature on status-seeking (Congleton, 1989; Konrad, 1990, 1992) in a structurally related context to describe preferences for relative-standing comparisons. An important

[11] A whole set of modifications of this function is discussed in Corchón and Dahm (2007).

[12] As discussed in Michaels (1988), the effective effort x_i by contestant i can also be a function of a number of inputs which generate this effective effort. In this case, the contestant will typically choose a cost-efficient mix of the different effort inputs.

implicit assumption that is made in (1.2) and throughout this book is risk neutrality. Because contests most naturally involve uncertain outcomes, risk aversion may play an important role.[13]

The function (2.39) with $r = 1$ has been particularly popular, perhaps because of its analytical tractability. By adding some constants in the numerator or the denominator, or by allowing for a different cost of making contributions x_j, the contestants can be made asymmetric, and handicaps for one or the other contestant can be analyzed.

Existence, uniqueness, and comparative statics

The existence and uniqueness of the Nash equilibrium in the Tullock contest follow from the analysis in Szidarovszky and Okuguchi (1997) if x_i^r is concave in r, that is, if $r \leq 1$. They prove this property for an arbitrary finite number of contestants and for a more general class of contest success functions.[14]

For the Tullock contest, the scope for existence and uniqueness of a Nash equilibrium can be extended. In the symmetric contest with n contestants, $r \leq n/(n-1)$ is the condition that ensures that the second-order condition is fulfilled. If this condition is violated, a pure strategy Nash equilibrium will typically not exist. This fact has caused considerable confusion for quite some time and has raised the question of whether contestants may, on aggregate, expend more effort than the value of the prize they can win (Tullock, 1980). As can be seen from inspecting the first-order conditions for a player's contest effort, r enters as a factor that determines the impact of a marginal increase in a player's own effort. If r becomes larger, then, at any symmetric level of contest effort, an increase in own effort has a higher marginal impact on the player's win probability. Hence, a large r tends to make additional effort profitable at the margin. But the locally optimal effort levels that are then determined by the first-order conditions could be so high that participation at this level is unprofitable.

Baye, Kovenock, and de Vries (1994, 1999) have shown that the equilibrium solutions that emerge if the contestants' objective functions are not concave cannot have higher expected aggregate contest efforts in an equilibrium than the value of the prize and have shown the existence of an equilibrium. They have also characterized the equilibrium which is

[13] Early seminal contributions are Hillman and Katz (1984); Long and Vousden (1987). See also Skaperdas and Gan (1995) and Konrad and Schlesinger (1997). A most elegant and powerful approach to the analysis of risk aversion in a class of contests that includes the Tullock contest has been developed by Cornes and Hartley (2003), who also provide a short survey of the literature on this subject.

[14] For a discussion of stablity properties of the equilibrium see Xu and Szidarovszky (1999).

in mixed strategies if there is a finite set of possible effort choices. Even though the equilibrium mixed strategies are different, the results regarding dissipation resemble qualitatively the all-pay auction with complete information. Given that the contestants choose mixed strategies, the total effort can, in some instances, exceed the valuation of the prize, but the expected total effort in the equilibrium cannot exceed the value of the prize. As long as contestants cannot be forced to expend positive effort, or to participate in the contest, they can always abstain from expending effort. Some contestants would prefer to abstain from expending effort if participation implied an expected effort that would exceed their expected reward if they were to take part in the contest.

A characterization of the contest equilibrium and its comparative static properties can be obtained from the first-order conditions, where these characterize the equilibrium (see, e.g., Nti, 1999).[15] For the simple case with only two contestants, the first-order conditions for the maximization problem with an objective function (1.2) of a contestant with contest success function (2.39) and a cost-of-effort function (2.40) are

$$\frac{rx_1^{r-1}x_2^r}{(x_1^r + x_2^r)^2}v_1 = 1 \quad \text{and} \quad \frac{rx_2^{r-1}x_1^r}{(x_1^r + x_2^r)^2}v_2 = 1. \tag{2.41}$$

The reaction functions that result from solving these first-order conditions are depicted for the case $v_1 = 2$, $v_2 = 1$ and $r = 1$ in Figure 2.4.[16]

The intersection determines the Nash equilibrium if the first-order conditions determine the equilibrium. The equilibrium values are

$$x_1^* = r\frac{v_2^r v_1^{1+r}}{(v_1^r + v_2^r)^2} \quad \text{and} \quad x_2^* = r\frac{v_2^{1+r} v_1^r}{(v_1^r + v_2^r)^2} \tag{2.42}$$

$$p_1^* = \frac{v_1^r}{v_1^r + v_2^r} \quad \text{and} \quad p_2^* = \frac{v_2^r}{v_1^r + v_2^r} \tag{2.43}$$

$$\pi_1^* = \frac{v_1^{r+1}(v_1^r + v_2^r(1-r))}{(v_1^r + v_2^r)^2} \quad \text{and} \quad \pi_2^* = \frac{v_2^{r+1}(v_2^r + v_1^r(1-r))}{(v_1^r + v_2^r)^2}. \tag{2.44}$$

Note that the contestant with the higher valuation of the prize expends more effort and wins with a higher probability, but not with probability 1. The Tullock contest equilibrium does not always award the prize

15 For an early solution of a structurally equivalent problem in the context of promotional competition see Mills (1961: 293). Mills solves a slightly more general problem which, by imposing symmetry restrictions on some parameters, reduces to the Tullock problem. For comparative statics on more general contest success functions that are based on a ratio $f(x_i)/\sum f(x_j)$ see Nti (1997).

16 See Pérez-Castrillo and Verdier (1992) for more general cases.

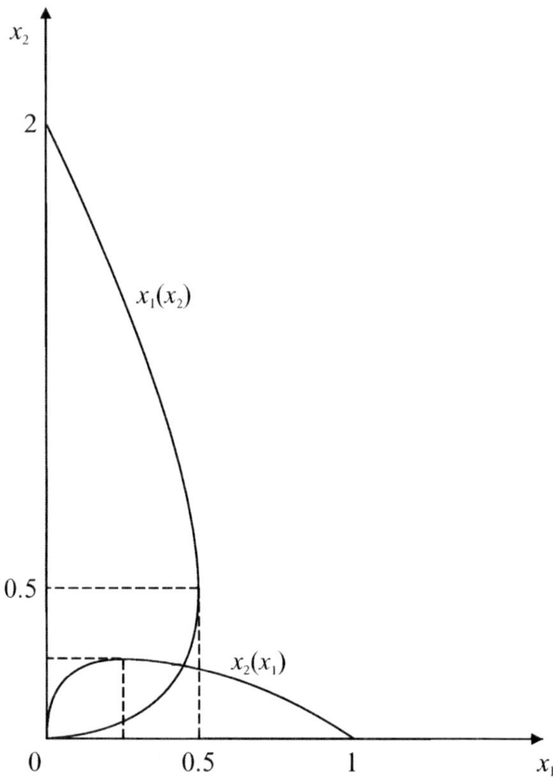

Figure 2.4 Reaction functions for $v_1 = 2$, $v_2 = 1$ and $r = 1$.

to the contestant who values it most, but the equilibrium win probabilities are biased favorably for the contestant with the higher valuation. Also, total rent-seeking effort is generally reduced if the contestants differ more in their valuation of the prize. This can be seen as follows. Consider valuations $v_1 = v + D$ and $v_2 = v - D$. The sum of efforts can be written as

$$x_1^* + x_2^* = (v_1 + v_2)\frac{rv_1^r v_2^r}{(v_1^r + v_2^r)^2} \tag{2.45}$$

$$= (v + D + v - D)\frac{r(v + D)^r (v - D)^r}{((v + D)^r + (v - D)^r)^2} \tag{2.46}$$

$$= 2v\frac{r(v + D)^r (v - D)^r}{((v + D)^r + (v - D)^r)^2}. \tag{2.47}$$

Differentiating $(x_1^* + x_2^*)$ with respect to D reveals after some transformations that this sum decreases in D.

Many participants

The symmetric Tullock contest with an arbitrary, but sufficiently small, r or the asymmetric Tullock contest with $r = 1$ can be generalized to the case with any finite number $n > 2$. See, for example, Stein (2002) and Meland and Straume (2007). For an elegant and very powerful approach to the comparative statics on more general contest success functions that are based on a ratio $f(x_i)/\sum f(x_j)$ but cover also the case in (2.39) and asymmetric valuations, see Cornes and Hartley (2005), who also address existence, uniqueness, and limit results.[17]

The symmetric case shows that the ratio between the aggregate effort that is expended in the equilibrium and the value of the prize is increasing in the number of contestants, and converges towards r for all $r \leq 1$ for very large numbers of identical contestants. In particular, the prize is fully 'dissipated' by aggregate effort, if $r = 1$.[18] The fact that the prize is not fully dissipated even with free entry and a large number of identical contestants for $r < 1$ has received some attention, as it seems to contradict the intuition that rents cannot survive with perfect competition among an infinite number of identical contestants. Some discussion of this can be found in the collected papers volume by Lockard and Tullock (2001). Ellingsen (1991) carefully explains why an expected effort that exceeds the valuation of the prize or 'overdissipation' cannot occur.[19]

Gradstein and Konrad (1999) also address this issue. They show that full dissipation also results for $r < 1$ if the contest takes place, not as a simultaneous Tullock contest among all n contestants, but in a multi-stage contest in which a number of parallel contests take place at each stage, where two contestants always compete with each other in a two-player Tullock contest, and only the winner in each of the parallel-stage contests is promoted to the next stage of contests, as in a pairwise elimination tournament.

The insight used in Cornes and Hartley (2005) to solve for the case with asymmetric valuations of the prize results from the observation that the

[17] Cornes and Hartley (2002) consider entry fees for contests with this structure. Earlier comparative static results on this structure are by Nti (1997) and Wärneryd (2001).

[18] This result is intuitive, but should not simply be extrapolated, as is shown in Wärneryd (2001).

[19] Fabella (1995) and Keem (2001) make further additions to the framework and the result in Ellingsen (1991).

payoff of player i depends only on player i's own effort and the sum of all other players' effort. For this purpose, define $X = \Sigma_{i=1}^{i=n} x_i$ and note that $p_i(x) = x_i/X$. Inserting this in the payoff function (1.2) and calculating first-order conditions yields

$$x_i = \max\left\{0, X(1 - \frac{X}{v_i})\right\}. \tag{2.48}$$

If all contestants expend non-zero effort in the equilibrium, this can be re-arranged to characterize

$$\sum_{i=1}^{n} x_i^* = X^* = \frac{n-1}{n} \frac{n}{\Sigma_{i=1}^{i=n} \frac{1}{v_i}}. \tag{2.49}$$

Note that, from the first-order condition (2.48), corner solutions in which some contestants prefer to choose zero effort are likely to emerge if contestants are sufficiently heterogeneous. In this case, X^* is found by an equation similar to (2.49), for which n is replaced by the number of players who make non-zero bids in the equilibrium.

Why is this contest so popular?

Why has the function in (2.39) been invented and used independently in so many different areas of applied theory? The contest success function is a mapping that associates win probabilities with players' effort choices. Whether a contest success function appropriately maps the allocation rule that applies in a given empirical context is ultimately an empirical matter. However, in most instances in which contest efforts are chosen to influence the win probabilities, the whole process that translates individual actions into win probabilities is very complicated. Moreover, actual contest effort and ex ante asymmetries between the contestants are often difficult to measure. This makes it difficult to assess or measure what is the 'true' contest success function in a given institutional context. Researchers have therefore resorted to other instruments when trying to identify the 'true' contest success function, or its properties. I will briefly discuss two such instruments.

Axiomatic reasoning

One possible means used in the search for the 'true' contest success function or its properties is borrowed from other contexts in economics: some plausible properties of such probabilistic allocation rules are introduced. These properties impose constraints on what the contest success function can look like, and jointly they may narrow down the set of alternatives to a reasonably small class. This 'axiomatic' approach has been taken by Bell, Keeney, and Little (1975), Skaperdas (1996), Clark and Riis (1998a), and Kooreman and Shoonbeek (1997). They give systems of axioms about how conflict is decided as a function of the contestants' efforts, so that these sets of axioms imply that the contest success function that conforms with these axioms must belong to a certain class of contest success functions. The different approaches offer different sets of axioms for different classes of contest success functions. Some sets of axioms yield the Tullock contest success function.

The early analysis of Bell, Keeney, and Little (1975) was conducted in the context of promotional competition for market shares, and they aim at an axiomatic foundation for how marketing effort translates into market shares. Their work is pioneering in this field.[20] They highlight the potential importance of an axiom that leads to what is called 'aggregative games' in other areas of economics,[21] where individual payoffs depend only on own choices and the aggregated values of all other players' efforts.

In the context of contest theory and the theory of conflict, Skaperdas (1996) offers sets of axioms for different types of contest success functions. Among these, he derives the Tullock function from several axioms. Some of these axioms are extremely intuitive: $p_i(\mathbf{x})$ should be a probability, strictly positive if i expends positive effort, increasing in own effort everywhere, and decreasing in other players' effort, and exhibit an anonymity or symmetry property. Two further axioms relate to how the contest success function that applies in a contest that is among a set of contestants that is a subset $M \subseteq N$ with $\#M \geq 2$ inherits properties of $p_i(\mathbf{x})$: it can be stated as a ratio function of these $p_i(\mathbf{x})$ and is invariant as regards the components x_j for which $j \notin M$. Once the structure of the contest success function is narrowed down for a contest between the members of any subset M to

$$p_i^M(\mathbf{x}) = \frac{f(x_i)}{\sum_{i \in M} f(x_i)}, \tag{2.50}$$

where $f(.)$ is a positive and increasing function of its argument, the Tullock contest success function is obtained if p_i is required to be homogenous of

[20] Kotler and Bliemel (2001: 277) call a function that is structurally identical to the Tullock contest success function with $r = 1$ the *fundamental theorem* for the determination of market shares.

[21] See, e.g., Cornes and Hartley (2007).

degree zero in all players' contest efforts, that is, if

$$p_i^M(\lambda\mathbf{x}) = p_i^M(\mathbf{x}) \tag{2.51}$$

for all $M \subseteq N$.[22]

Clark and Riis (1998a) extend Skaperdas' work. An alternative set of axioms is stated by Kooreman and Shoonbeek (1997) and leads to a modified version of the Tullock contest success function that allows for asymmetry between players. One of their axioms makes an assumption about the functional form of the derivative of the contest success function with respect to effort choices, yielding the contest success function essentially by integrating this derivative.

Microeconomic underpinnings

An alternative approach that is used to find out about the structure of contest success functions, given that a direct measurement approach is not feasible, is the search for microeconomic underpinnings. A careful study of particular institutional set-ups in which players' efforts are converted into win probabilities can sometimes reveal a probability model that is describing this process. This suggests that the win probabilities may result from some stochastic process that can be identified more closely. It is then possible to state some formal results on the relationship between the stochastic properties of the underlying selection processes and effort choices and this may lead to the contest success function (2.39). Such approaches can be found in Hirshleifer and Riley (1992), Fullerton and McAfee (1999), and Baye and Hoppe (2003), and they make a strong case for the Tullock contest success function with $r = 1$.

A Tullock contest structure emerges from a simple search problem. The result can be obtained along intuitive lines of reasoning. Suppose there are two players 1 and 2. For concreteness, let us consider them as two competing interest groups who lobby by making design proposals for two mutually exclusive projects 1 and 2. The choice between the projects is made by a benevolent, but uninformed, decision-maker who, for the sake of the argument, will decide favorably either for interest group 1 or for interest group 2, depending on who proposes the project that is superior from a welfare point of view. Assume that the projects can be carried out with various designs, and the designs may benefit or harm a greater public

[22] Skaperdas (1996) also identifies further axioms that, given the axioms essentially yielding (2.50), yield a contest success function that is a special case of the contest success functions with additive noise as discussed in section 2.2.

by more or less, and may also (but need not) change the interest group's benefits from having their project implemented. Let x_i be the number of design proposals produced by interest group i, for all interest groups $i = 1, 2$, and suppose that the policy-maker chooses the proposal of the group which produced the design that benefits a greater public most. Then, if the design proposals are independent draws from identical distributions, the probability that interest group i produces the most preferred design equals its share in the total number of proposals, that is, (2.39) with $r = 1$.

Moreover, let v_1 and v_2 be the interest groups' benefits from a favorable decision on one of their proposals. These benefits may, but need not, depend on the interest groups' efforts. For instance, if the various designs do not change the interest group's benefit or cost from being granted the right to carry out their project, but do change the benefits that the project has to a greater public, v_1 and v_2 are exogenous with respect to the choices of x_1 and x_2. More generally, the valuations of winning will be functions of x_1 and x_2 that depend on the particular framework. For instance, in the context of R&D races in which the design draws can be understood as experiments in innovating a particular product, and where the firm that succeeds in doing this first wins the patent, the number of experiments will be related to the overall speed of innovation, and the rent from successfully innovating is likely to have a different present value if the innovation takes place earlier. Also, if the innovations are seen as improvements in product quality, with the firm that has the best product winning a contest, the number of trials may affect the expected quality of the product that finally wins the race, and this, in turn, may change the firm's valuation of winning.

Baye and Hoppe (2003) provide a formal analysis of this aspect in the context of R&D contests. Their analysis can be framed in the context above.[23] For concreteness, return to the lobbying example with two groups who can expend resources. Suppose they can expend resources trying to increase the public benefits of their own project if adopted. They simultaneously and independently choose amounts x_i of resources, for $i = 1, 2$. Each unit of resource is invested in research and generates a new project design with a different public benefit value z_i for contestant i, where these valuations are independent random draws from a given distribution of values z with a distribution function $F(z)$ that is continuous on $[0, 1]$

[23] Related ideas have been put forward by Lagerlöf (1997, 2007) and Austen-Smith (1995, 1998). In Lagerlöf (1997) the interest groups produce competing information about their own proposals that makes their own proposal look better.

and differentiable on $(0, 1)$, where the choice of the maximum valuation equal to unity is for simplicity only. Each contestant then presents to the decision-maker the project that has the highest public benefit. The decision-maker chooses the project with the higher valuation.

Consider the payoff function for contestant 1 that results from this setup. Let x_1 and x_2 be the numbers of draws chosen by the two contestants and let v_1 and v_2 be the highest project valuations. Then the probability that a given maximum valuation v_1 is higher than the highest z_2 that emerges from the other firm's draws is equal to $[F(v_1)]^{x_2}$. If contestant 1 makes only one draw that costs one unit, the expected payoff is

$$\int_0^1 F(v)^{x_2} v f(v) dv - 1. \tag{2.52}$$

Each additional draw costs an additional unit and yields a positive expected benefit if it is more successful than all other draws. Summing up all these benefits and costs yields group 1's payoff as

$$\pi_1(x_1, x_2) = x_1 \int_0^1 vF(v)^{x_2} F(v)^{(x_1-1)} f(v) dv - x_1. \tag{2.53}$$

Note that this makes use of the fact that the event for which two or more draws generate the same project quality is a zero probability event. Making use of symmetry and defining $u(v) = F(v)^{x_2+x_1}$ and, hence, $du(v) = (x_1 + x_2)F(v)^{x_2+x_1-1} f(v)dv$ yields

$$\pi_1(x_1, x_2) = x_1 \int_0^1 \frac{1}{x_1 + x_2} v du(v) - x_1. \tag{2.54}$$

Integrating by parts yields

$$\pi_1(x_1, x_2) = \frac{x_1}{x_1 + x_2} v_1(x_1, x_2) - x_1 \tag{2.55}$$

with

$$v_1(x_1, x_2) = \left[1 - \int_0^1 F(v)^{x_2+x_1} dv\right]. \tag{2.56}$$

Accordingly, the groups' efforts translate into a payoff function that resembles their payoff function in a Tullock contest with the minor difference that the contest prize may depend on x_1 and x_2 as well.

Hirshleifer and Riley (1992) suggest a different microeconomic underpinning in one of the exercises in their chapter about contests. Assume, for instance, the prize in an R&D race is given and equal to v for both contestants. Let contestant 1 win if $q_1 x_1 > q_2 x_2$, where x_1 and x_2 are effort levels chosen by the two contestants, and q_1 and q_2 are independent draws from an exponential distribution $F(q) = 1 - e^{-aq}$. The noise that is introduced by the exponential distribution translates this all-pay auction problem into the Tullock problem as follows: for a given $\hat{q}_1$, contestant 2 wins for given (x_1, x_2) if $\hat{q}_1 x_1 < q_2 x_2$ which happens with probability

$$\begin{aligned} prob(\hat{q}_1 x_1 &< q_2 x_2) \\ &= prob(q_2 > \hat{q}_1 x_1 / x_2) \\ &= 1 - prob(q_2 \leq \hat{q}_1 x_1 / x_2) \\ &= 1 - (1 - e^{-a\hat{q}_1 x_1 / x_2}) \\ &= e^{-a\hat{q}_1 x_1 / x_2} \end{aligned} \tag{2.57}$$

In a next step, consider the unconditional probability for contestant 2 to win for (x_1, x_2). It can be written as

$$\begin{aligned} prob(q_1 x_1 &< q_2 x_2) \\ &= \int_0^\infty e^{-aq_1 x_1 / x_2} f(q_1) dq_1 \\ &= \int_0^\infty e^{-aq_1 x_1 / x_2} [a e^{-aq_1}] dq_1 \\ &= a \int_0^\infty e^{-aq_1 \frac{x_1 + x_2}{x_2}} dq_1 \\ &= a \left[-\frac{1}{a} \frac{x_2}{x_1 + x_2} e^{-aq_1 \frac{x_1 + x_2}{x_2}} \right]_0^\infty \\ &= -\frac{x_2}{x_1 + x_2} [0 - 1] \\ &= \frac{x_2}{x_1 + x_2} \end{aligned} \tag{2.58}$$

This is a straightforward foundation for using the ratio of efforts as a probability for winning the contest. It is based on the all-pay auction contest success function, but with some multiplicative noise that follows a particular type of distribution.

Information aspects

Tullock (1980) assumed complete information; the players who enter into the contest know everything about each other. The microeconomic foundation reveals that this structure is basically a short cut to more explicit competitive search problems in which a substantial amount of uncertainty is involved. One may consider elements of incomplete and imperfect information in the Tullock contest too. Contestants may have some uncertainty about their own abilities or their valuations of the prize, and/or the abilities and valuations of their opponents.

For instance, each contestant may know his own valuation of the prize, but may know only the distribution from which the opponent's valuation of the prize is drawn. Malueg and Yates (2004) provide an analysis of the case in which two contestants' valuations are drawn from the same bivariate distribution but need not be the same. In their framework each player knows his own valuation of the prize.

Some players could also have superior information compared to others, and there are several problems of asymmetric information that could be distinguished. For instance, the prize valuation could be the same for all players, but one player may know the true valuation of the prize, while his competitor does not. The valuation of the prize could be different for two players, where only one player knows his true valuation. Similar aspects could be analyzed regarding the cost of effort or the mechanism that maps effort choices into win probabilities. Wärneryd (2003) addresses this problem: two contestants' valuations are from the same distribution. Contestant 1 knows the true value of the prize. Contestant 2 knows the distribution from which this value is drawn, but does not know the true value of the prize. Wärneryd shows that, for a contest success function somewhat more general than (2.39), the uninformed contestant is more likely than the fully informed contestant to win the contest in the equilibrium. He also considers the special case of (2.39), and several specific distributions of the prize.

Hurley and Shogren (1998) address a problem of asymmetric information in which the contestants' valuations of the prize are independent. The valuation of the prize of one of the contestants is publicly observed. They consider the impact on the contest outcome of the distribution from which the informed contestant's valuation is drawn.

2.4. Experimental evidence

Contests have also attracted experimental game theorists. In an influential contribution, Davis and Reilly (1998) consider Tullock's lottery contest and the all-pay auction without noise with both symmetric and asymmetric players in an experimental setting. They confirm some of the qualitative predictions for the participation of an additional player with a higher valuation of the prize in an otherwise symmetric environment. Their most important result is that effort levels exceed the predictions resulting from the Nash equilibrium, taking effort cost and the value of the prize at face value for both the lottery contest and the all-pay auction. This 'overdissipation' is reduced if players participate more often, but it does not fully disappear. In Potters, de Vries, and van Winden (1998), the overspending results in Davis and Reilly (1998) are critically reviewed. They find overdissipation for the lottery contest, but dissipation that is close to the predicted values for the all-pay auction without noise.

Further experiments look at whether agents who play modifications of the Tullock lottery game or the all-pay auction without noise choose the predicted equilibrium efforts. Currently the literature is expanding rapidly, as many different structures can be studied experimentally.[24] Small changes in the set-up may have consequences. Rapoport and Amaldoss (2004) consider modifications of the all-pay auction, taking into consideration that the space of possible effort choices from which players choose has a finite grid, that players are resource constrained, and that there is a particular tie-breaking rule if the highest effort is made by more than one player. Dechenaux, Kovenock, and Lugovskyy (2003, 2006) draw attention to the importance of these assumptions for the possibility of multiplicity of equilibria, and draw conclusions about how the results in Rapoport and Amaldoss (2004) could be reconciled with the theory results for players who maximize their monetary payoffs.

By and large, the perceptions in the literature are that the experimental results can often be reconciled with the theory predictions for players who maximize their monetary payoffs. If they do not do this, players are frequently biased towards overdissipation. These results on overdissipation, which occur more frequently in the context of the Tullock contest than for the all-pay auction without noise, need to be explained. Potters, de Vries, and van Winden (1998) suggest that players may randomize uniformly across the whole range of possibly reasonable or feasible bids, and this may explain the overdissipation they found for the lottery contest case. Another explanation that can be considered suggests that contestants gain additional psychological benefits from their choices and from the outcomes. Lugovskyy, Puzzello, and Tucker (2006) mention the 'desire to win', and the 'desire to punish'. A desire to win that adds to the monetary reward

[24] See, e.g., Millner and Pratt (1989, 1991), Shogren and Baik (1991), Schmitt et al. (2004), Öncüler and Croson (2005), Anderson and Stafford (2003), Parco, Rapoport and Amaldoss (2005), Amaldoss and Rapoport (2008), Barut, Kovenock, and Noussair (2002), and Gneezy and Smorodinsky (2006).

that is gained from winning in a laboratory experiment need not be ad hoc; instead it can be founded in the evolutionary game theory on contests.

2.5. Evolutionary success

Evolutionary biologists and evolutionary game theorists found an important reason why individuals sometimes behave in a way that is different from the straightforward maximization of their monetary payoffs. Biologists like Maynard Smith and Price (1973) and Maynard Smith (1982) explored a simple but powerful idea: suppose that individuals do not consciously solve the problem of maximizing their monetary payoffs when interacting with other individuals. Instead, their choice of action is predetermined by some rules that are hard-wired in their genes. Then what would the forces be that determine these hard-wired actions? For instance, if individuals who behave in a way that makes them more successful than other individuals in a given group reproduce faster, and eventually outgrow the less successful individuals, this would eventually breed types of individuals whose hard-wired actions make them successful in the interaction with others. Unaware of whether they were behaving rationally or cleverly, they would simply follow their genetic code. In doing so, they would be behaving as if they were rational and clever. Their cleverness would, however, have one element that is different from the cleverness of individuals who simply maximize their monetary payoffs: for an individual behavioral type to outperform another type, it is not sufficient just to perform well. Performing better than the other type is more important. Accordingly, what matters for the evolutionary success of a given type of behavior is whether this behavior is relatively more successful than other behavior. This led Maynard Smith to a concept of equilibrium behavior in an evolutionary context called equilibrium in evolutionarily stable strategies (ESS).[25] More formally, applied to a symmetric two-player game, a strategy x would be called an evolutionarily stable strategy if the following condition holds for all $\hat{x} \neq x$:

$$\pi(x; x) \geq \pi(\hat{x}; x) \tag{2.59}$$

$$\text{if} \quad \pi(x; x) = \pi(\hat{x}; x), \quad \text{then} \quad \pi(x; \hat{x}) > \pi(\hat{x}; \hat{x}).$$

In words, the first condition states the requirement for a Nash equilibrium: if x is an evolutionarily stable strategy, then it should be a best reply if

[25] For an intuitive introduction and a careful formal treatment of evolutionary game theory see Samuelson (1997).

the other player chooses this strategy. The second condition is a stability requirement that makes sense if one adds a dynamic story: Suppose there is a sequence of periods. In each period there is a set of players. Each player has a type and the type invariantly determines the choice of action (for instance, 'x', or '$\hat{x}$'). This invariant choice of action is the player's strategy. Suppose players are teamed up pairwise. Each player behaves according to his type. Players receive payoffs depending on their own choice and the choice of their matched player. Then, the composition of the set of players in the next period is determined. It is suggestive to assume that the shares of player types who had high payoffs grow, whereas shares of player types who had low payoffs in comparison to other types shrink. Coming back now to the stability requirement: Suppose that, at some point, the whole set of players consists of players of type x. Now, for some exogenous reason, let some tiny share of the population change its type to '$\hat{x}$'. Then, players of this type have a probability of 1 of being matched with players of type 'x'. If $\pi(x; x) = \pi(\hat{x}; x)$, they are not doing worse than players of type 'x'. However, the second part of the second condition puts a limit on the growth of this subset: if the type who plays x interacts with a type playing this mutant strategy $\hat{x}$, then he is doing better than if he also played the mutant strategy $\hat{x}$. The strategy 'x' is a superior reply to '$\hat{x}$' than '$\hat{x}$' itself. Hence, once the share of the '$\hat{x}$'-type had grown, the type that is the candidate for an evolutionarily stable strategy has an advantage against this type and will outgrow it.

Applied to the Tullock contest, let there be a set N of infinitely many individuals i, and assume that these individuals $i \in N$ participate all together in a pairwise Tullock contest for a prize of size 1, each of them choosing his own effort level x_i. Assume further that the contest has the standard lottery contest success function and is symmetric. Then, as derived, maximization of their individual monetary payoffs, and anticipation of this equilibrium play, will induce all players to choose efforts equal to $1/4$. This yields a monetary payoff to each individual equal to $1/4$. Also, $x = 1/4$ is a unique best reply to $x = 1/4$ by a player's adversary. Hence, $x = 1/4$ fulfills the condition (2.59). As discussed, the stability condition (2.59) is stated for a static game in which players choose one action or strategy once and then payoffs materialize, but should be interpreted in a dynamic context, in which a changing population of players plays this static game repeatedly, and where the material payoffs of different types of players in each static round of the game affect their reproductive success and induce a change in the composition of player types in the set of players from one round to another. The important aspect in this dynamic process is that what matters for the success of a particular type in a population of a given size is not this type's absolute payoff. His share in the population will grow or shrink, depending on whether he does better or worse *relative* to the other types. Now, this comparative aspect is one-sided in a very large population: for instance, if a person in the US wants to move up into a higher income percentile, the only realistic option he or she has is to earn more income, rather than trying to reduce the average income of all others.

In a small group with a finite number of players, there is another option for increasing one's own income position: instead of becoming rich, a person can do something to make other group members worse off. This important consideration was introduced by Schaffer (1988), who argued that the condition used by Maynard Smith and Price is appropriate for large populations, but does not take into consideration the option that a mutant may follow a strategy that makes him slightly worse off, but makes others even more worse off. Schaffer introduced an alternative, generalized, ESS equilibrium condition which applies particularly for small populations.

The implications of Schaffer's observation can be made transparent in a simple contest environment.[26] Consider a population N consisting of $n < \infty$ members. In each period all members fight in a grand contest about a given amount of resources that is normalized to $v = 1$, for a series of periods $t = 0, 1, \ldots$ This set-up also differs from the pairwise matching that was used for an illustration of evolutionary stability, and is called 'playing the field'. However, this difference is not crucial for insights to be obtained. Suppose that players fight about shares in this prize, and that each player is awarded a share equal to his share in the total effort. If players choose efforts $x_1, \ldots x_n$, then i's share is determined by (2.39) with $r = 1$. Accordingly, the payoff of each player i is simply $\pi_i = x_i/\Sigma_{j=1}^{n} x_j - x_i$. This 'state game' repeats in every period among the set of players that constitute this group in the respective period. The idea of evolution enters into this picture by using two assumptions. There are potentially heterogeneous types of players; a player's type is essentially given by the amount of effort this player chooses. The space of possible types in this case is $[0, \infty)$. Second, the composition of the set of n players as regards their types changes from one period to the next, and this change follows a process that could be described as a random process

[26] Leininger (2003) and Hehenkamp, Leininger, and Possajennikov (2001) adopt Schaffer's (1988) concept for finite populations of contestants to consider evolutionarily stable strategies in contests with finite numbers of players.

with some drift: loosely speaking, a type that has a higher monetary payoff than another type in period t will be likely to be better represented in the period $t+1$ population than the other type. Without specifying these dynamics more precisely, intuitively, the types that have higher monetary payoffs than their competitors will outgrow their competitors in the long run. Given the constant and finite population size, this growth will be at the expense of the number of competitors of this other type. This already suggests that population composition will be governed by types' payoffs relative to other types' payoffs, and not by their absolute payoffs.

Leininger (2003) defines Schaffer's notion of evolutionary stability formally as: a strategy (or type) $\hat{x}$ can invade a population of type x if the player who expends $\hat{x}$ earns a higher monetary payoff than all the other players in the group who expend x. Moreover, a homogenous population of players consisting of type x^{ESS} cannot be invaded by players of a different type $\hat{x} \neq x^{ESS}$, if, given the effort choices $\hat{x}$ by the invader and x^{ESS} by all others, the payoff of such a player expending $\hat{x}$ is not larger than the payoffs of all other group members who expend x^{ESS}, for all possible levels of effort $\hat{x} \geq 0$. This defines evolutionary stability, once the meaning of 'invading' has been made clear. Let us do this in the context of the lottery contest. Here, the n players simultaneously choose their efforts, and this yields a vector of efforts $(x_1, \ldots, x_n)$. A population of types who play x can be invaded by a type who plays $\hat{x}$, if $\pi_1(\hat{x}, x, x, .., x) - \pi_i(\hat{x}, x, .., x) > 0$ for $i \in \{2, 3, \ldots, n\}$.

We can now consider whether a population of types who choose the Nash equilibrium efforts x can be invaded. The Nash equilibrium in the lottery contest, given the assumed symmetry, is characterized by $x = (n-1)/n^2$. The equilibrium payoff of each player is equal to $1/n^2$. This effort choice does not constitute an evolutionarily stable strategy. To confirm this, suppose all players $i = 2, \ldots n$ are of type $x = (n-1)/n^2$. Consider the question of whether a population of players who expend this effort can be invaded. The question can be rephrased as whether a player 1 of type $\hat{x}$ could attain a higher payoff than the players $i = 2, \ldots n$ who all choose x, for some choice $\hat{x} \neq x$. Formally, the question is whether an $\hat{x}$ exists such that the difference between the mutant's payoff and the average payoff of all other players can become positive for this $\hat{x}$. Defining this payoff difference as $\Phi(\hat{x}; x)$, this condition is

$$\Phi(\hat{x}; x) \equiv \left[\frac{\hat{x}}{\hat{x} + (n-1)^2/n^2} - \hat{x}\right] - \left[\frac{(n-1)/n^2}{\hat{x} + (n-1)^2/n^2} - \frac{n-1}{n^2}\right] > 0.$$

By symmetry, $\Phi(x;x) = 0$. Moreover, note that

$$\frac{d\Phi((n-1)/n^2;(n-1)/n^2)}{d\hat{x}} = 0 + \frac{1}{n-1} > 0.$$

This shows that a type with effort slightly higher than the effort $x = (n-1)/n^2$ could successfully invade this group.

If the strategies in the Nash equilibrium are not evolutionarily stable, what constitutes an equilibrium in evolutionarily stable strategies in this case? Leininger finds: a population in which all players choose $x^{ESS} = 1/n$ cannot be invaded. This effort level constitutes an equilibrium in evolutionarily stable strategies. Note also that this equilibrium outcome is a sad outcome from the point of view of the group as a whole. It suggests that the efforts chosen in the evolutionarily stable outcome fully dissipate the value of the prize.

Hehenkamp, Leininger, and Possajennikov (2001) consider also a Tullock contest with $N = \{1, 2, \ldots n\}$ and a contest success function with $r \in (1, n/(n-1))$, that is a situation in which the marginal impact of contestants' efforts is higher than in the lottery contest. As is known from the literature on the Tullock contest, the symmetric Nash equilibrium exists and is characterized by $x = r(n-1)/n^2$. Turning to the equilibrium in a finite population in evolutionarily stable strategies, such a strategy can be found by searching for the own effort x that maximizes the difference between own payoff and the average payoff of all other players,

$$\left[\frac{x^r}{x^r + (n-1)\hat{x}^r} - x\right] - \left[\frac{\hat{x}^r}{x^r + (n-1)\hat{x}^r} - \hat{x}\right]$$

and solving the first-order condition at $x = \hat{x}$. This yields $x^{ESS} = r/n$, where Hehencamp, Leininger, and Possajennikov show that this solution also fulfills the second-order conditions for a local maximum if $r < n/(n-2)$. This effort x^{ESS} implies that, if $r \in (1, n/(n-1))$, the evolutionarily stable equilibrium has a sum of contest expenditure $nx^{ESS} = r > 1$. Accordingly, the contestants expend more effort in the aggregate than the value of the monetary prize. This is feasible, as the contestants do not compete for the monetary prize, but instead for a higher chance of surviving. Intuitively, fitness in an evolutionary context is a relative concept, and the strategy that is relatively more successful than competing strategies makes the type of player who chooses this strategy outperform other types. If all other players choose the effort that characterizes the Nash equilibrium level in the single-period game, a single player's increase in effort compared to this level yields no increase in the player's payoff. By the nature of the problem, such a marginal change only has a second-order effect as regards his own payoff. However, for this player this higher effort can still pay off in terms of fitness because it also reduces other players' expected reward.[27]

One may go one step further, taking into consideration the complexity of the environment in which human beings interact and their cognitive abilities. The standard concept of evolutionary game theory considers the evolutionary stability of types, with types typically being defined as players whose actions are hard-wired. However, evolution need not shape or determine particular actions or efforts. Evolutionary forces may shape more complex decision rules that take into consideration the particular structure and characteristics of the problem. A type's effort may not simply be a scalar number, but a function of the type of contest success function, the prize structure, the number and composition of other players etc. Such types may behave as if they choose their efforts by trying to maximize a given objective function, taking into consideration a set of constraints. Evolutionary forces may shape the objective functions which then make humans choose different efforts in different environments. Konrad (1990) argued that, during the process of evolution, a disposition for enjoying relative rewards, that is status preferences, could have developed that is hard-wired in the biology of mankind. This is an example of what is called the 'indirect approach' in the more formal part of evolutionary economics. The point has been made formally by Eaton and Eswaran (2003).[28] They show that a contest environment can induce status preferences in the process of evolutionary selection of preferences.

[27] A large literature in economics postulates the existence of preferences for relative income, relative performance, or status. Such preferences have far-reaching consequences. They change the equilibrium wage profile in organizations (Frank, 1984a, 1984b), lead to excessive spending on observable goods (Frank, 1985a), affect growth, may lead to overaccumulation of wealth and separation into a class society (see, e.g., Cole et al., 1992, 1998; Konrad, 1992) and have other interesting effects (Weiss and Fershtman, 1998). Hirsch (1976) justifies the assumption of such preferences by arguing that some absolutely scarce goods may be allocated according to relative standing. Frank (1985b: 23–6) also surveys empirical findings on sociophysiological experiments in biology and psychology that reveal connections between status and social interaction and physiological measures. For a formal analysis of contests for status, see Moldovanu, Sela and Shi (2007).

[28] Early formal analyzes of the indirect approach are Güth and Yaari (1992) and Huck and Oechssler (1999), in areas other than contest theory. Güth and Yaari (1992) consider the evolution of preferences assuming that players observe the preference characteristics of their co-players. In such a framework, a certain type of preference has strategic effects as it may influence the co-players' actions. Huck and Oechssler (1999) show that the evolutionary stability of preferences that deviate from maximizing own monetary payoff can also emerge in the absence of such observability. An application of this mechanism in contest theory is Konrad (2004a).

This point can be illustrated as follows. Consider a situation with a sequence of periods. In each period there is a set of n players, called the population. They take part in a symmetric Tullock contest with a contest success function (2.39) for a prize of size 1. The expected prize, net of contest effort by player i, is called the *absolute material payoff* of player i and is equal to

$$\pi_i = p_i - x_i. \tag{2.60}$$

The objective functions that govern players' behavior in the respective period may deviate from their material payoff (2.60). Let us allow for the class of objective functions

$$u_i(\alpha) = \alpha\pi_i + (1-\alpha)\left[\pi_i - \frac{1}{n-1}\sum_{j\neq i}\pi_j\right]. \tag{2.61}$$

The case $\alpha = 1$ describes the case in which only absolute performance matters. The case $\alpha = 0$ describes the case of pure status preferences in which only relative performance matters, defined as the difference between own absolute payoff and the average payoff of all other players. The utility function (2.61) is a parametric version of a more general function in which agents' utility depends on their own and their co-player's level of income, wealth or consumption, which is typically assumed in the analyzes of economic consequences of status briefly discussed in the introduction. This particular parametric version is also frequently used. See Reiter (2000), also for further references. Let p_i be defined by the Tullock contest success function with $r = 1$. In this case, the extreme case of preferences for relative standing with $\alpha = 0$ may evolve evolutionarily in a finite population with size n of players.[29]

The result in Eaton and Eswaran (2003) needs to be compared with the outcome of the direct approach that considers the effort choices that develop evolutionarily. The evolutionarily stable actions that are determined by their 'direct' approach differ for games with different numbers of participants. Individuals who simply choose a predetermined effort cannot optimally adjust their choices to temporary or cyclical changes in the

[29] For this problem, the perceptions of players with regard to the other players' objective functions are important. The player may need to form expectations about the co-players' preference type. If, instead, types are observable, this leads to a strategic commitment advantage of some not narrowly selfish types of preferences in the sense that a player's preference type induces behavior by their co-players that depends on the player's actual type. Status preference can then emerge even in infinitely large populations along arguments made by Frank (1987, 1988, 1989) or Bester and Güth (1998).

number n of players. It needs mutations and evolutionary pressure for a population to account for a long-lasting jump in n, or a rather complete programme that makes the genetically determined effort choices a non-trivial function of all the factors that matter in a contest. This problem can be overcome if the genetically determined actions are sufficiently complex; for instance, in a more volatile environment, the choice of effort of a type could be contingent on the number of contestants, their valuations of the prize and their costs of effort, and on the specific nature of the contest success function. Behavior that follows such detailed rules may become behaviorally equivalent to the behavior that follows from maximization of a predetermined objective function.

Unless such a complex rule has developed, a population with predetermined effort choices does even worse with short-run stochastic fluctuation or with deterministic cycles in the number of players. Also, such a rule is not suitable for coping with unforeseen events. Hence, agents whose efforts are predetermined by the evolutionary process behave suboptimally for environments with very reasonable temporary fluctuations, compared to agents who optimize according to a cleverly chosen objective function. Agents who derive their actions from genetically determined preferences characterized by status preferences as in (2.61) behave optimally for contests with different numbers of contestants. They spontaneously respond optimally to such fluctuations in the contest environment. Agents who choose their effort levels on the basis of preferences that are shaped by evolutionary pressure may therefore outperform agent types whose effort choices are shaped by evolutionary pressure directly.

2.6. Summary

This chapter presented results for three main types of static contest. The first-price all-pay auction, as the contest without noise is often called, has been analyzed first. While there will be few real-world situations in which the actual effort choices of contestants translate into such a precise outcome with regard to who wins the contest, this interaction makes it very clear that the outcome in a contest strongly depends on one's own effort relative to the efforts of other contestants, and that this may cause considerable expenditure, particularly for the contestants who value the contest prize most highly, or who are most productive in generating the type of output that is the unit of comparison with respect to determining contest success. It has also been shown that asymmetry between the contestants who participate actively in the contest reduces total expenditure. Incomplete information may, but need not, change total contest expenditure. In particular, the binary example at the end reveals this most clearly. The first-price all-pay contest and its equilibrium under various constraints will be an important building block in the analysis of more complex situations.

The all-pay auction without noise is also interesting as a benchmark case, and both the Tullock contest success function and the contest success function in the all-pay auction with additive noise are obtained from this benchmark case. They have been justified by axiomatic approaches, but also by way of probability models that match reasonably closely the real world situations which they are meant to describe.

Empirical experimental work is often in line with the theory predictions of the underlying contest model in the experiments. Sometimes the subjects exhibit higher effort than would be optimal from the point of view of maximization of their individual payoffs. Evolutionary game theory can provide an explanation for this overly aggressive behavior in contests, if this competition takes place within small groups, such that an individual can benefit not only by an improvement of own performance, but also by reducing the performance of others.

The analysis of equilibrium and of its comparative statics across the three types of contests reveals some common patterns that are potentially important for considering further strategic aspects. Summarizing, three major common patterns can be identified:

First, contests are activities in which one player's increased effort is a negative externality for the other player. As the total win probability is given, if the probability of winning can be increased for one contestant, this necessarily decreases the win probability for someone else. With a given prize, contestants can typically increase their aggregate rents if they succeed in reducing the aggregate equilibrium effort.

Second, for the aggregate effort, not only the size of the prize but also the heterogeneity of contestants is important. If the contestants are more heterogeneous, this typically reduces the aggregate equilibrium contest efforts and increases the contestants' aggregate net payoffs. For the all-pay auction with additive noise, heterogeneity interacts with the specific distribution of this noise, and results are not straightforward.[30] It is a pattern,

[30] Esteban and Ray (1999) provide, apart from other insights, some evidence for the limits of a possible generalization of this result in the context of contests between groups.

however, that is true for many types of contests, including the all-pay auction without noise and the Tullock contest.

Third, the contestant with the higher valuation of the prize is typically more likely to win the prize, and also expends higher effort. This was also true for all three major types of contests. A similar relationship holds for productivity advantages in providing effort. As discussed, for example, by Baye, Kovenock, and de Vries (1996), there is a close one-to-one relationship between differences in the valuation of a contest prize and differences in individual cost of producing given effort levels. Accordingly, the contestants with productivity advantages will generally make more effort and win the prize with higher equilibrium probabilities.

3

Timing and Participation

3.1. Endogenous timing

The importance of commitment, and the advantage or disadvantage from irreversibly choosing one's actions prior to the actions of another player in an interactive situation, can be traced back at least to Stackelberg's (1934) analysis of sequential choice of prices or quantities in a duopoly. In the contest framework, the choice is about effort, and several researchers have considered contests with exogenously given sequential timing.[1] Dixit (1987) asked whether there is an advantage or a disadvantage in being able to commit to an effort choice before other contestants who can observe this choice and react to it. For most strategic games, there is typically an advantage or a disadvantage either for the leader or for the follower and vice versa. The surprising answer to this question in the context of contests is that there may be an advantage for both the leader and the follower, and that contestants may non-cooperatively agree on a sequential choice of moves. Baik and Shogren (1992) and Leininger (1993) independently asked whether contestants would be willing to commit at an early or late point in time to make their own choice of effort, and whether this could lead endogenously to a sequential order of moves in a contest.[2]

[1] Sequential moves are analyzed by Pèrez-Castrillo and Verdier (1992) and Linster (1993a) and are compared with simultaneous moves by Linster (1993a). Morgan (2003) also provides a discussion of the welfare effects of sequential choices, and Glazer and Hassin (2000) consider more than two players. Leininger (1991) considered sequential moves in an all-pay auction if there is an exogenously given finite maximum bid.

[2] From a structural point of view, their analysis is similar to analyzes of endogenous sequential choices in oligopoly games by Deneckere and Kovenock (1992), Hamilton and Slutsky (1990), Matsumura (1999), and Mailath (1993), who show that sequential choices of quantities in Cournot competition can be the outcome of non-cooperative play. Deneckere, Kovenock, and Lee (1992) addressed this question in a pricing game that is structurally very similar to an all-pay auction.

Suppose there are two dates for an irreversible effort choice: early or late. The contestants first make a choice of timing, and this choice is irreversible and publicly observed. Will this lead to both contestants moving early, to both contestants moving late, or will some sequencing of choices emerge endogenously?

The issue can be illustrated using the functional form (2.39) with an exponent r equal to 1 for the case of two contestants 1 and 2 and valuations of the prize equal to v_1 and v_2 that was used by Leininger (1993). Let $v_1 > v_2$ be an appropriate numbering of the contestants. Consider the graphic representation of the problem by Baik and Shogren (1992), which applies also for a more general contest success function.[3] The reaction functions that result from solving the first-order conditions are

$$x_1(x_2) = \sqrt{x_2 v_1} - x_2 \tag{3.1}$$

and

$$x_2(x_1) = \sqrt{x_1 v_2} - x_1, \tag{3.2}$$

provided that these values are positive, and effort x_i is zero otherwise. These functions are shown in Figure 3.1. Reaction function $x_1(x_2)$ reaches $x_1 = 0$ for $x_2 = 0$ and for $x_2 = v_1$. It reaches its maximum at $x_2 = v_1/4$ and this maximum is equal to $x_1(v_1/4) = v_1/4$. The reaction function x_2 is described similarly. The two functions intersect at the point (x_1^*, x_2^*) for strictly positive values of effort and this intersection characterizes the Nash equilibrium that is denoted by N in Figure 3.1.

The set of indifference curves for each player is not shown in the diagram, except for an indifference curve for player 1 that passes through the point S_1. All indifference curves for player 1 have the property that they are concave and have their peak along the reaction function $x_1(x_2)$. The indifference curve slope for player 1 can be made plausible by observing that the player will generally benefit from a reduction in x_2. Moreover, for a given x_2, the player will increase his payoff by moving towards $x_1(x_2)$. Accordingly, for a given x_2, if player 1 chooses an x_1 that differs from $x_1(x_2)$, this will reduce his payoff unless something pleasant happens that compensates him for the suboptimal choice in x_1. For instance, let $(x_1(S_1), x_2(S_1))$ be the coordinates of S_1. For a given level of $x_2 = x_2(S_1)$, if player 1 chooses a higher x_1 than $x_1(S_1)$, this will lower player 1's payoff, compared to a choice of $x_1(S_1)$. The payoff may stay constant, however, if the increase

[3] The case $v_1 = v_2$ is not particularly interesting as locally it does not yield strategic incentives to move early or late, and the Stackelberg and Nash equilibria coincide. This was observed by Dixit (1987).

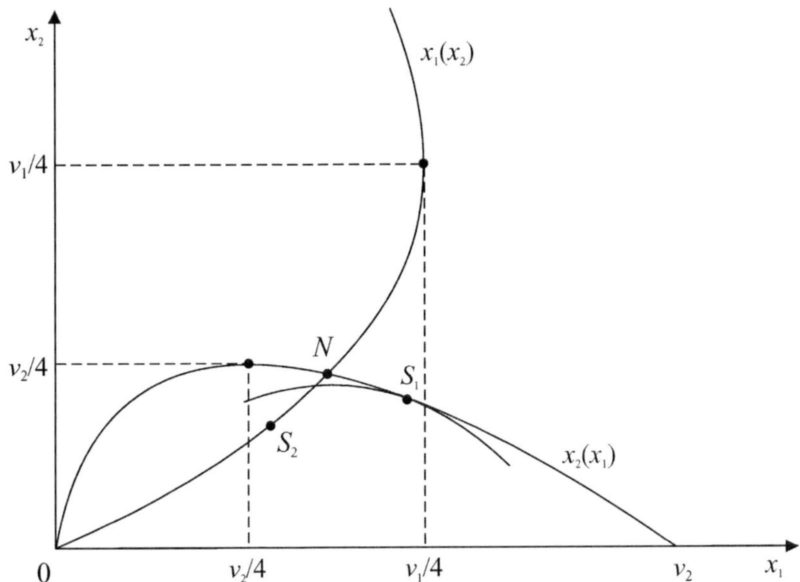

Figure 3.1 Reaction functions.

in x_1 occurs together with a reduction in x_2, as this reduction in x_2 may compensate player 1 for the reduction in utility from moving even further away from his own reaction curve. This explains why the indifference curves bend downwards on both sides of the reaction curve, starting from a point on the reaction curve.

Consider now the choice of timing. Let there be two points in time at which contestants could irreversibly choose their contest effort. These dates are denoted as e(arly) and l(late). Let contestants first decide simultaneously whether to choose their own contest effort early or late. Once this choice is made, what follows depends on the contestants' decisions, which are characterized by the pairs of timing decisions (e, e), (e, l), (l, e) and (l, l). If both contestants have decided to choose their effort early, they enter into a contest in which their contest efforts are chosen simultaneously, and the unique Nash equilibrium at N emerges. Similarly, if both decide to choose their effort late. Hence, for choices (e, e) and (l, l), the Nash equilibrium N and the associated payoffs emerge. These are denoted as π_1^N and π_2^N in this section.

If the contestants have chosen (e, l), then contestant 1 makes his effort choice first. Contestant 2 observes the given choice x_1 and then chooses the optimal reply to this effort choice, which can be found on contestant 2's reaction function $x_2(x_1)$. Given this logic, when contestant 1 makes his choice, he anticipates that contestant 2 will choose $x_2(x_1)$. Contestant 1 effectively chooses the equilibrium outcome among all points on the reaction curve of contestant 2. For contestant 1's indifference curves as in Figure 3.1, this equilibrium is reached at S_1, which characterizes the Stackelberg equilibrium if contestant 1 is the Stackelberg leader and contestant 2 is the Stackelberg follower. All that was needed to construct this point was that $x_1(x_2)$ intersects $x_2(x_1)$ to the right of its maximum (which is at $x_2 = v_2/4$), which follows from $v_1 > v_2$. An 'interior solution' with S_1 to the left of $(v_2, 0)$ is not required for the argument to follow. Denote the equilibrium payoffs as $\pi_1^{S_1}$ and $\pi_2^{S_1}$. As S_1 is to the right of N on contestant 2's reaction curve, $\pi_2^N > \pi_2^{S_1}$ must hold. This in turn implies that (e, l) can be ruled out as an equilibrium, as, given that contestant 1 chooses e, contestant 2 could also choose e and induce the Nash equilibrium N.

If the timing is (l, e), contestant 2 chooses the Stackelberg equilibrium S_2 along the reaction function of contestant 1. This point S_2 must be to the lower left of N. Denoting the equilibrium payoffs in S_2 as $\pi_1^{S_2}$ and $\pi_2^{S_2}$, note that $\pi_1^{S_2} > \pi_1^N$ and that $\pi_2^{S_2} > \pi_2^N$.

Turning to the stage where the contestants decide about the timing of moves, it is revealed that it is a dominant strategy for contestant 2 to move early. Given this choice, the contestant 1 has a choice between S_2 and N only, but prefers the Stackelberg equilibrium S_2.

Summarizing, the asymmetry of the two players with respect to their valuations of the prize leads to an endogenous asymmetry in their timing of moves. The player with the low valuation of the prize moves first, whereas the player with the higher valuation waits and observes this contestant's effort and then chooses the effort that maximizes his own payoff. The player with the lower valuation becomes the Stackelberg leader in this game, not by assumption, but by endogenous choice of the timing of moves.

Recall that having the lower valuation of the prize is equivalent to competing for the same given prize, but with a higher cost of making the effort. Accordingly, player 2 is the 'weaker' player, or the 'underdog', whereas player 1 is the 'stronger' player, or the favourite. In this interpretation, the equilibrium outcome suggests that the underdog may find it in his interest to commit first to an effort that is lower than the Nash equilibrium effort, and the favourite may want to wait and observe this lower effort and then reduce his own effort in turn.

This result is interesting, because it does not conform with what is true in many commitment games. This is that it is either an advantage to commit early, in which case both players choose to commit early, or a disadvantage, in which case both players choose to commit late. Here the asymmetry between contestants translates into an asymmetry as regards their preferences for early or late commitment, which in turn reduces aggregate contest effort.

The result does not necessarily hold for all contest types. However, the result does hold for the all-pay auction without noise. Consider, for instance, two contestants with $v_1 > v_2$. If contestant 1 chooses his effort first, the equilibrium has $x_1 = v_2$ and $x_2 = 0$, and the payoffs are $\pi_1 = v_1 - v_2$ and $\pi_2 = 0$, the same payoffs as with simultaneous moves. If contestant 2 chooses his effort first, the equilibrium has $x_2 = 0$ and $x_1 = 0$ and the payoffs are $\pi_1 = v_1$ and $\pi_2 = 0$. When a choice of timing precedes the choices of effort, there are several equilibria. One of these is the payoff-dominant equilibrium in which player 2 commits to choosing early, and player 1 commits to choosing late. As a result, $x_2 = 0$ and $x_1 = 0$ with $\pi_1 = v_1$ and $\pi_2 = 0$ emerges.[4]

For these results, the assumption that the contestants can commit to their timing and that this commitment choice is observable is quintessential. The weaker contestant who decided to make his effort choice early would certainly like to deviate from this choice and would typically like to add some effort at the point in time when his opponent chooses effort. As the weaker contestant expends less than his Nash effort at the early point in time, then, if a later increase in effort is feasible, this would essentially bring back the simultaneous Nash equilibrium. Romano and Yildirim (2005) consider more formally a game in which there is a stage following stage l in which the contestants make a simultaneous choice about whether they would like to add to their previously expended effort. They show that, starting from S_2 in Figure 3.1, or from $x_1 = x_2 = 0$ in the all-pay auction without noise, they would add to their previous efforts and revert to total efforts characterized by the Cournot-Nash equilibrium N. The same argument also applies if, once the players have chosen $x_1 = x_2 = 0$ in previous stages, they were also to revert to the Nash equilibrium in a stage that follows e and l.

[4] Sequential effort choices in the all-pay auction without noise have been considered, e.g., in Deneckere, Kovenock, and Lee (1992) and in Jost und Kräkel (2000). Konrad and Leininger (2007a) generalize these results for the case of many players and general cost functions.

3.2. Voluntary participation

In many contests, the choice of whether or not to participate is very limited. If one player decides to impose a conflict on another player, the decision not to fight may have severe and rather unattractive consequences. For instance, a country leader who is attacked from inside or outside will typically sacrifice his job or more if he decides to ignore the attack.

The participation question is perhaps more interesting if participation is voluntary. If the winner in a contest is awarded a prize that is valued by a player but all losers receive nothing, intuition suggests that a player may want to expend at least some effort trying to win the prize. However, whether this is a useful strategy will generally depend on how much other players are willing to expend. For instance, if other players value the prize more highly, and, therefore, expend considerable effort, it need not be worthwhile for a player who values the prize less to expend effort. It may be preferable to not compete at all. In the context of the all-pay auction without noise, all players who value the prize less than the valuation of the player who values the prize second most highly were in such a position and did not expend any effort in the equilibrium. Similarly, in the Tullock contest, condition (2.49), together with (2.48), suggests that, if the group of contestants is large and heterogeneous regarding their unit cost of effort, or regarding their valuations of the prize, players whose unit cost is high or whose valuation of the prize is low may prefer not to make a positive effort.[5] Also, asymmetries in how players' efforts translate into win probabilities in the contest success function may induce some players to decide not to enter into the contest (Gradstein 1995).[6]

Participation in a contest often has an entry fee. This fee may be explicit, or, in many cases, may consist of the opportunity cost of what a player might have otherwise done. A tennis player who decides to participate in a particular tournament may have to pay some fee, may have some fixed cost of travel and accommodation, and may sacrifice the option of participating

[5] An early contribution considering entry into Tullock contests is Appelbaum and Katz (1986b). Entry and participation with asymmetric players in the Tullock contest is addressed, e.g., by Stein (2002).

[6] Gradstein (1995) also studies entry deterrence by an incumbent player. This player may have the option to invest in the effectiveness of his own future contest effort. A higher own contest effort has two implications in this context. It gives this contestant a potential advantage in the later contest for a given number of contestants, and it may also deter some players from entering the contest. Marginal calculus can then determine the incumbent's optimal amount of investment.

in another tournament taking place simultaneously elsewhere, or simply spending the weekend with his or her family. Such entry fees are important, as, in some contests, the expected contest effort that is expended in the equilibrium is close to, or even fully dissipates, the rents of contestants.

Entry fees may then induce some contestants to abstain, or may lead to an entry game in mixed strategies. Hillman and Samet (1987) solve the all-pay auction without noise for the case of minimum outlays where even perfectly symmetric players have mass points on zero effort levels. Related to this, consider the following two-stage game with n players who all value winning the prize in an all-pay auction by $v_i = v$ and have cost functions of actual contest effort of $C(x_i) = x_i$. Let them decide whether to enter into this contest in stage 1, in which case they have to pay some fixed positive entry fee $D \in (0, v)$. In stage 2, if none of them has entered, the prize is not awarded. If one of them has entered, the prize is awarded to this player, even if he expends no further effort in stage 2, and if more than one player has paid the entry fee, the standard all-pay auction takes place and in the equilibrium yields zero rents to each participating player. In this case, there are asymmetric equilibria in pure strategies in which one of the players enters and the others do not. Moreover, there is a symmetric mixed strategy equilibrium in which each player enters with a given probability. If all players enter with this probability, this makes each player just indifferent about whether to enter or not; if a player does not enter, his payoff is zero. If he does enter, his expected payoff is $(1 - q^*)^{n-1}v - D$. Accordingly, the entry probability in a symmetric mixed strategy equilibrium is

$$q^* = 1 - \left(\frac{D}{v}\right)^{\frac{1}{n-1}}. \tag{3.3}$$

This equilibrium leads to a situation in which the number of potentially active players in stage 2 becomes a random variable.[7]

The equilibrium with randomized entry describes a possible solution to the participation problem in the symmetric all-pay auction. Note that a more extreme solution with possible non-entry applies if players are heterogeneous, as the most advantaged player can expect to receive a rent from participating in any case, and, hence, will always enter, whereas for other participants, entry becomes unattractive. However, both the case in which players randomly enter, and the solution in which only the most

[7] Unlike in this two-stage game with endogenous uncertainty, Myerson and Wärneryd (2006) and Münster (2006b) analyze situations in which there is an exogenous uncertainty about the number of active contestants that is not resolved prior to players making their choice of contest effort.

advantaged player enters, imply that prizes should be observed where no active players compete for them. Alternatively, there may be cases in which there is only one contestant, particularly in the all-pay auction without noise, or in contest situations with entry fees more generally, in which the equilibrium effort may sum up to a large share of the total prize, making entry of several players unprofitable. The fact that typically we do not observe this type of mixed strategy entry behavior constitutes an entry puzzle.

One reason we typically do not observe sports tournaments in which no players, or only one player, show up is the players' incomplete dissipation and equilibria in which all active players expect to receive some positive rent. A second reason is incomplete information. As has been shown, players have a positive expected payoff in the contest equilibrium with incomplete information. However, there is a third explanation: stochastic ability. This has been discussed by Konrad and Kovenock (2008a). A tennis player's performance on a given day and in a given match may differ considerably from his average performance, and this random element can help in overcoming the entry puzzle. To study this, consider two players, 1, and 2, who, if they both enter, compete in an all-pay auction without noise. Let the valuation of the prize be $v_1 = v_2 = 1$ for both, but let players differ in their cost of effort: $C_1(x_1) = k_1 x_1$ and $C_2(x_2) = k_2 x_2$. For given and known k_1 and k_2, if $0 < k_1 \leq k_2$, the unique equilibrium of the all-pay auction is described by

$$F_1(x) = \begin{cases} k_2 x & \text{for} \quad x \in \left[0, \dfrac{1}{k_2}\right) \\ 1 & \text{for} \quad x \geq \dfrac{1}{k_2} \end{cases} \tag{3.4}$$

$$F_2(x) = \begin{cases} 1 - \dfrac{k_1}{k_2} + x k_1 & \text{for} \quad x \in \left[0, \dfrac{1}{k_2}\right) \\ 1 & \text{for} \quad x \geq \dfrac{1}{k_2} \end{cases} \tag{3.5}$$

in line with Baye, Kovenock, and de Vries (1996), and has payoffs $1 - k_1/k_2$ for player 1 and 0 for player 2. For $0 < k_2 \leq k_1$ the subscripts 1 and 2 in (3.4) and (3.5) need to be interchanged.

Let us now turn to the stage at which the players have not yet learned their actual productivity in expending effort in the all-pay auction. Let k_i be random variables with finite support $[0, \bar{k}]$. For the nature of the equilibrium, it is not the absolute values of k_1 and k_2, but rather their ratio that is important. Let $\alpha \equiv k_1/k_2$. Then the joint distribution of k_1 and k_2

induces a cumulative distribution function $Z(\alpha)$ of α. Let this cumulative distribution function be continuously differentiable with density function $z(\alpha)$. In this case, player 1's payoff can be stated as

$$\pi_1(Z(\alpha)) = \int_0^1 (1-\alpha)z(\alpha)d\alpha. \tag{3.6}$$

The upper limit of the integral is equal to 1, as, for all $\alpha > 1$, the expected payoff of player 1 is zero. Note, first, that this expected payoff (3.6) is non-negative and is strictly positive if the probability by which player 1 has a cost advantage is positive. Accordingly, even if player 1 is disadvantaged in expectation, that is if $E(k_1/k_2) > 1$, his expected payoff is positive, and analogously for player 2.

Intuitively, only the player who has an actual cost advantage in the all-pay auction receives a positive rent. Player 1 may be the weaker player on average. However, as abilities follow a stochastic process, player 1 may have stronger positive productivity on the day of the encounter and be the stronger player in that particular event. For instance, tennis players who are listed at quite different ranks in the ATP list may play against each other in the final of a tournament, and the player who is ranked lower may even be the stronger on this particular day. This need not be the result of luck or of chance, as is assumed in a contest success function with exogenous noise, but can be the outcome of random variations in the physical or mental constitutions of the players. When play starts, the players may quickly find out about their own and their adversary's constitution on a particular day and then, with these current abilities, they may play the all-pay auction with complete information.

Consider two distributions Z and $\tilde{Z}$ of α, such that $\tilde{Z}$ dominates Z by second-order stochastic dominance (with or without a change in the mean). Then $\pi_1(Z) \geq \pi_1(\tilde{Z})$.

For a proof,

$$\begin{aligned}\pi_1(Z) - \pi_1(\tilde{Z}) &= \int_0^1 (1-\alpha)(z(\alpha) - \tilde{z}(\alpha))d\alpha \\ &= \Big[(1-\alpha)(Z(\alpha) - \tilde{Z}(\alpha))\Big]_0^1 + \int_0^1 (Z(\alpha) - \tilde{Z}(\alpha))d\alpha \\ &= \int_0^1 (Z(\alpha) - \tilde{Z}(\alpha))d\alpha \geq 0. \end{aligned} \tag{3.7}$$

The second line follows from the first by integration by parts, and the last inequality holds by the definition of second-order stochastic dominance.

The result, and its implications for tournaments or contests with multiple rounds with or without elimination of some contestants in early rounds, was derived in Konrad and Kovenock (2008a). If $\tilde{Z}$ dominates Z by second-order stochastic dominance, then the two distributions may (but need not) have the same mean, but, intuitively speaking, Z has greater probability weight in small outcomes of k_1/k_2, that is in states in which the advantage of player 1 is large. For instance, if Z is obtained from $\tilde{Z}$ by a mean-preserving spread as defined by Rothschild and Stiglitz (1970), player 1 will prefer Z, that is the player has a preference for randomness in his own relative performance. For instance, if k_1 and k_2 are drawn from stochastically independent distributions, then, if there is a mean preserving spread in own cost k_1, this will cause a mean-preserving spread in α as well, and will generally increase player 1's payoff, and a mean preserving spread in own cost k_2 will of course increase player 2's profit for the same reason.

Where players cannot perfectly predict their own strength in the actual contest, even the weaker of two players, who has a lower expected ability than the stronger player, can anticipate that he has some strictly positive expected rent from participating in the all-pay auction. When players make their entry choices, they are willing to pay an entry fee up to the amount of this expected rent.

3.3. Exclusion

An issue closely related to the decision to participate is the problem of admission of contestants. Contest designers selectively admit contestants or design rules that govern admittance. Indeed, this is a relevant issue in many designed contests. Fullerton and McAfee (1999), for instance, analyze admittance rules for an R&D tournament. On the basis of their analysis, they advocate an auction in which two contestants gain access to the actual research tournament. More obvious examples of rules for admission or elimination of contestants can be found in the literature on the economics of sports. Szymanski (2003) discusses the composition of leagues, and rules and mechanisms that have been generated to increase the homogeneity of the contestants within a league with a given, unchanged set of teams. An example is the 'rookie draft' system that is used in American Football, which allocates the rights to draft new players from the pool of newly entering players in each season as a function of the teams' comparative performance. He also discusses governance structures such as hierarchies among leagues, where teams which over- or underperform compared to the competing teams within a given league are relegated or promoted to the next lower or higher one, respectively.

The contest designer's objective function will generally be essential for the optimal design of admittance rules in contests. Let us assume, as has frequently been done in this context, that the contest organizer cares about aggregate effort. The admittance rules can be used to influence key determinants of the contest, such as the players' valuations of the prize, the number of contestants, and the asymmetry of contestants. Some of the results in this context are straightforward and follow from the comparative static results in Chapter 2. In general, an increase in the contestants' valuations, or a decrease in their cost of effort, will increase their observed effort, and there is a tendency for homogeneity among the contestants to increase their efforts, and the rules, for instance in sports tournaments that improve the competitive balance between teams in open or closed leagues, are in line with these results.

An important, counterintuitive result in this context is found by Baye, Kovenock, and de Vries (1993). They show that there can be a trade-off between participation by contestants with high valuations and contest homogeneity, such that admitting the contestant who values the contest prize most highly need not be optimal. Their result can be illustrated in the context of the all-pay auction without noise. For this purpose, suppose there are three contestants with valuations $v_1 > v_2 = v_3$, and cost-of-effort functions $C_i(x_i) = x_i$.

If all three contestants are admitted to the contest, there are several equilibria. In one of the two equilibria with the highest expected aggregate effort, contestant 3 expends zero effort and contestants 1 and 2 choose the equilibrium strategies outlined in (2.2) and (2.3). It can be verified that expected effort made in this equilibrium equals

$$\frac{v_2}{2}\left(1 + \frac{v_2}{v_1}\right) < v_2. \tag{3.8}$$

Suppose now that a contest designer who cares about aggregate effort excludes contestant 1 from taking part in the contest. As a result, only contestants 2 and 3 will expend positive effort, and the equilibrium is unique and is described again by (2.2) and (2.3) with, however, v_1 replaced by v_2 and v_2 by v_3. Expected aggregate effort becomes equal to

$$\frac{v_2}{2} + \frac{v_2}{2} = v_2. \tag{3.9}$$

In this example, the expected aggregate effort in the equilibrium increases if the contestant who values the prize most highly is eliminated from the contest. The increase in expected effort is higher, the higher the valuation of this player with the highest valuation. Intuitively, asymmetry between players results in some discouragement effect for the weak contestant, making him choose zero effort with a considerable probability. At the same time, the weak contestant determines the effort chosen by the strong contestant. As a result, total effort is reduced by moving from a situation with $v_1 = v_2 = v$ to one with $v_2 = v$ and $v_1 = v + D$ for $D > 0$.

Of course, it is not always optimal to eliminate the strongest contestant from the set of contestants. If this were true, repeated elimination would eventually reduce the set of contestants to zero. The example is based on a trade-off. Effort in an all-pay auction is high if the active bidders have a high valuation of the prize, and if the bidders are symmetric. More precisely, the bidder with the second highest valuation determines the range of possible bids, and the difference in the valuations of the prize between the two bidders with the highest valuations determines the size of the mass point of probability for which the bidder with the lower valuation bids zero. In the example, the elimination of the contestant who values the prize most does not change the range of bids as it does not reduce the second highest valuation of the prize, but it does reduce the heterogeneity between the two contestants with the highest valuation.

More generally, if the contest designer can choose among a set of contestants, who can be sorted according to their valuations of the prize as $v_1 \geq v_2 \geq \cdots \geq v_n$, from Baye, Kovenock, and de Vries (1993), the maximum expected aggregate contest effort that can be obtained from a subset $\{i, i+1\}$ of these contestants with $v_i \geq v_{i+1}$ is

$$\frac{v_{i+1}}{2}\left(1 + \frac{v_{i+1}}{v_i}\right). \tag{3.10}$$

The expected aggregate contest effort is maximized, for instance, for the set of two contestants for which this expression is largest. An optimal set of contestants can be found by computing this value for the sets $\{1, 2\}$, $\{2, 3\}, \ldots \{n-1, n\}$, and choosing the pair that maximizes this number.

The deeper insight provided by this example is that homogeneity of the contestants can be important for generating high expected effort and can be more important than the high valuation of the prize. The intuition holds more generally. Recall the equilibrium solution (2.47) in the asymmetric Tullock contest for valuations $v_1 = v + D$ and $v_2 = v - D$, where it was argued that total effort is decreasing in D.

Heterogeneity is also an important aspect when a contest organizer has some choice with respect to the contest success function. The example above illustrates that the all-pay auction is particularly sensitive to heterogeneity among the contestants who value the contest prize most highly. The Tullock contest success function, or the all-pay auction with noise, is less sensitive to heterogeneity. This suggests that a contest designer who cannot influence the homogeneity of the contestants may want to choose the contest success function accordingly. Che and Gale (1997) illustrate this in an instructive example. This shows that the Tullock contest can induce higher aggregate effort than the all-pay auction without noise if the contestants are sufficiently heterogeneous. Suppose, for instance, that $v_1 = v+D$ and $v_2 = v-D$ with $v > D \geq 0$. The aggregate contest effort in the Tullock contest for $r = 1$ is

$$x_1^* + x_2^* = 2v\frac{(v+D)(v-D)}{4v^2}. \tag{3.11}$$

The expected aggregate effort in the all-pay auction without noise is

$$E(x_1^* + x_2^*) = \frac{v-D}{2}\left(1 + \frac{v-D}{v+D}\right). \tag{3.12}$$

Accordingly, the Tullock contest induces higher expected aggregate effort if

$$\frac{D}{v} > \sqrt{2} - 1. \tag{3.13}$$

Further issues are relevant for the problem of admission. Amegashie (1999, 2000) considers procedures called 'shortlisting' in two-stage Tullock contests in which the semi-finals determine the participants in the final. These aspects are also relevant in the analysis by Gradstein and Konrad (1999) who ask how many rounds should be chosen for an elimination tournament with Tullock contests at each elimination stage if a homogeneous group of contestants is to be induced to generate maximum aggregate effort. The trade-off between homogeneity and the valuation of the prize, which is the basis of the results in Baye, Kovenock, and de Vries (1993), does not show up in this work, given that all players are assumed to be homogeneous. Nevertheless, shortlisting, or the organization of the elimination tournament in several rounds, becomes attractive there because the win probability in the Tullock contest with the Tullock contest success function with $r < 1$ exhibits decreasing returns to scale in contest effort, and this makes it attractive to have a sequence of parallel contests with small numbers of participants rather than one big contest.

Note that the organizers' preferences on the contest design may, but need not, be in line with the contestants' design preferences. Generally, where tournaments are used to elicit effort, the organizers' and the contestants' preferences can indeed be aligned. Recall the contest with additive noise in the context of labor market tournaments with perfect competition between contest organizing firms. In this framework, all rents end up in the hands of workers, and the equilibrium design is also the one that would be chosen by the workers themselves. A deviation from this design may reduce contest efforts, but this would also reduce the contest prizes that can be allocated among contestants, and reduce overall rents. Hence, a trade-off between organizers and contestants mainly emerges if the prizes that are to be allocated are not carefully chosen, but exogenously given.

3.4. Delegation

Delegation is known to be an important strategic option, and this is also true in the context of tournaments or contests. As discussed by Schelling (1960), delegation opens up the option to commit to future actions that are not time consistent from the perspective of the decision-maker, and this may yield him a strategic advantage: as other players anticipate this future behavior, they may accommodate and change their behavior in a way that is in line with the true objectives of the player who chooses this commitment. If two players A and B bargain about sharing a cake and negotiate about their shares, typically the more patient player receives a larger share. Accordingly, if a player A feels he is impatient, he may commit himself and delegate the whole negotiation to a middleman M who is, and is known to be, extremely patient. When M and B meet, under standard assumptions about complete information, the non-cooperative bargaining will lead to an outcome that has a higher share for A than if A has negotiated directly with B. Typically this commitment advantage is symmetric. This often leads to escalation: player B may feel the same concerns as A about the disadvantage of being impatient. So B may also subcontract and send another middleman who is also more patient.

The role of delegation in contests has been explored by a number of authors and in various contexts.[8] In a contest between two players A

[8] Baik and Kim (1997), Baik (2007), Wärneryd (2000), and Kräkel and Sliwka (2006) consider delegation in the context of a Tullock contest. Schoonbeek (2007) considers endogenous delegation in a variant of the Tullock (1980) contest that was developed by Epstein and Hefeker

and B, player A may consider delegating the decision about the amount of fighting effort to a delegate. If the delegate cares more strongly about winning, or discounts the cost of fighting compared to A, then A could expect to win the contest with higher probability. Instead of fighting himself, sending a strong warrior may seem to player A to be a good idea. However, if both players choose such a strategy, this may considerably escalate the conflict, leading to a symmetric outcome that is much less desirable than the equilibrium in absence of delegation. A closer look at the delegation incentives in contest shows that delegation in contests has a particular aspect which makes it different from the standard, symmetric escalation that occurs in many contexts with delegation: asymmetry opens up for an advantage for both the weaker and the stronger contestant in a conflict. This is illustrated in what follows.

Delegation contracts

Suppose there are two individuals who care about winning a prize that is allocated in a contest. The individuals will be called principals 1 and 2. The principal i who eventually receives the prize values it by v_i with $i = 1, 2$. Principals 1 and 2 may delegate the actual bidding to two agents, A_1 and A_2. For this purpose they write a contract with their agent. The contract can be denoted as (φ_i, b_i) and is described by the following arrangements. First, the contract transfers the right to make bids x_i from principal i to his agent A_i. This agent incurs a cost in making this bid, and, for simplicity, let $C_i(x_i) = x_i$. According to the contract, only the agent is allowed to make bids. Principal i abstains from bidding. Second, if agent A_i wins the prize, the agent delivers the prize to his principal and receives a pre-specified payment b_i that cannot be re-negotiated. This price is the agent's valuation of the prize, and will therefore be called 'delegated valuation'. Third, for the contract to be valid, the agent pays an amount φ_i to the principal. This amount is transferred up front, before the actual bidding takes place and will be called 'down payment'.

Two further assumptions are made. For simplicity, the agent's reservation utility of whether to sign this contract or not is zero, implying that agent A_i is willing to sign the contract if (φ_i, b_i) yields it an equilibrium payoff that is equal to or larger than zero. Generally, φ_i and b_i can

(2003). Schoonbeek (2004) considers whether groups may want to delegate the choice of effort in order to overcome their free-rider problem when contesting with another player or group. Brandauer and Englmaier (2005) consider median voter decision-making on the choice of the delegated agent. Wärneryd (2000) adds a hidden action problem in the relationship between the principal and her delegate. Konrad, Peters, and Wärneryd (2004) consider delegation for the first-price all-pay auction without noise.

be chosen from the non-negative real numbers, but we will require that there is a maximum delegated valuation that can be agreed on between a principal and his agent, that is $b_i \leq \bar{b}$ for some arbitrarily large but finite number $\bar{b}$.

Denoting $E(x_i^*)$ as the expected effort expended by agent i and p_i^* the agent's win probability in the contest equilibrium with delegation, the participation constraint requires

$$\varphi_i \leq b_i p_i^* - E(x_i^*). \tag{3.14}$$

As the choice of φ_i does not affect the actual all-pay auction once the delegation contracts are signed, the principals will offer contracts with the highest feasible up-front payments. The participation constraints (3.14) will therefore be binding. Accordingly, principal i's payoff can be written as

$$\pi_i = v_i p_i^* - E(x_i^*), \tag{3.15}$$

where the equilibrium values p_i^* and x_i^* will generally depend on b_1 and b_2.[9]

Delegation in all-pay auctions

Considering standard auctions with complete information, it is typically not in the bidders' interest to send someone else to the auction to make bids if this other person attributes a different valuation to the object that is auctioned. However, this is not true for the all-pay auction, as is shown in Konrad, Peters, and Wärneryd (2004). Instead, principals will choose to sign contracts with delegates and send them to the auction with delegated valuations that differ from the principals' valuation. The result relies on an asymmetry between the valuations of the delegated bidders that emerges endogenously. To study this endogenous asymmetry, it makes sense to start with a framework that is fully symmetric ex ante: two individuals 1 and 2 who have identical valuations of winning the prize, equal to $v_1 = v_2 \equiv v$.

If these individuals make bids in a first-price all-pay auction, they will make bids according to (2.2) and (2.3) as in the standard all-pay auction.

[9] The delegation contract is typically not renegotiation-proof at the stage between the publicly observed writing of the delegation contract and the stage at which the delegated agent and other players choose their actual contest effort. This is a problem with delegation more generally, and is not specific to delegation in contests. Delegation contracts typically have the property that, once they are written and observed by the other players, the principal and the agent in this contract have an incentive to secretly re-negotiate this contract, and the results on delegation are based on the implicit assumption that such secret re-negotiations are not feasible.

As they value the prize equally, their expected efforts and their expected benefits from winning just equalize. Their payoffs from participating in this contest if they choose effort according to their own objective functions are equal to zero.

Turn now to the case with delegation. Let $\bar{b} > v/2$, which is seemingly not very restrictive and leads to the more interesting outcomes.[10] In this case both players like to delegate. Exactly two equilibria with pure strategy choices of contract offers exist in this case, if both players are allowed to delegate and choose the delegated valuations simultaneously. The delegated valuations in these contracts are

$$(b_1^*, b_2^*) = (v/2, \bar{b}) \text{ and } (b_1^*, b_2^*) = (\bar{b}, v/2). \tag{3.16}$$

One of the principals chooses a delegated valuation that is lower than his true valuation of the good and the other principal chooses the maximum feasible delegated valuation. These equilibria do not confirm the intuition that both players may have an incentive to induce their delegate to bid more aggressively than they would bid themselves. Instead, the delegation contracts make the delegates who are the actual bidders highly asymmetric, by inflating the valuation of one agent to the maximum, and by reducing the valuation for the other agent to half the true valuation of his principal. The payoffs of the principals in these equilibria are

$$\left(\frac{3}{4} - \frac{v}{4\bar{b}}\right) v \tag{3.17}$$

for the player i who writes a contract with $b_i^* = \bar{b}$, and

$$\frac{1}{8}\frac{v^2}{\bar{b}}$$

for the player j who writes a contract with $b_j^* = v/2$.

A proof is in Konrad, Peters, and Wärneryd (2004). Only a heuristic argument will be given here to make the outcome intuitive, showing that $v/2$ and $\bar{b}$ are optimal replies to each other. For this, suppose that principal 2 and his agent choose a delegated valuation $b_2^* = v/2$ and that this is anticipated by principal 1 and his agent. What would be the optimal contract from the perspective of principal 1 in this case? His agent A_1 will bid

[10] If $\bar{b} \leq v/2$, both principals choose $b_1^* = b_2^* = \bar{b}$ in the equilibrium. Hence, if the maximum delegated valuation is very small, the solution is a corner solution in which both principals choose the highest feasible delegated valuation. Each principal would prefer not to delegate the choice of effort to an agent; he would prefer to choose the effort directly and not be subject to the agent's effort constraint, given that the other principal delegates.

against agent A_2. Using the fact that (3.14) is binding, principal 1's payoff is given as $p_1^* v - E(x_1^*)$. The equilibrium values p_1^* and Ex_1^* depend on the delegated valuations b_1 and b_2, which take the role of the contestants' valuations as in a standard all-pay auction. If $b_1 < b_2 = v/2$, this leads to $p_1^* b_1 = E(x_1^*) = (b_1)^2/v$. Accordingly, principal 1's payoff for this range of delegated valuations equals $p_1^*(v - b_1)$. Using $p_1^* = b_1/(2b_2) = b_1/v$ in this range, the payoff of principal 1 is strictly increasing in b_1 for $b_1 \leq b_2 = v/2$. For $b_1 > b_2 = v/2$, as p_1^* is strictly increasing in b_1 and $E(x_1^*) = v/4$ for $b_1 > b_2 = v/2$, the optimal reply of player 1 to $b_2 = v/2$ is to choose b_1 as large as possible. The payoff in (3.17) is obtained by replacing the equilibrium values $p_1^* = 1 - v/(4\bar{b})$ and $E(x_1^*) = v/4$ in $p_1^* v - E(x_1^*)$. Given that principal 2 chooses a delegated valuation that is lower than principal 1's true valuation, principal 1 makes his own delegate very aggressive by giving him a delegated valuation that is as high as possible. Principal 1 does not have to worry about the high b_1 that he will have to pay to his agent, because this is compensated for in the high up-front fee φ_1 that A_1 will pay to his principal.

Turn now to principal 2. It seems intuitively plausible that he as a principal also makes his agent more aggressive in the bidding by giving him a high valuation, as this increases his agent's win probability. However, this strategy works only if the other principal does not choose a high delegation value as well. If both agents have high delegated valuations, for example, if $b_1 = b_2 = \bar{b} > v$, then $p_i^* b_i = E(x_i^*)$ and $\varphi_i^* = 0$. Accordingly, $\pi_i = -(\bar{b} - v)/2$ in this case and both principals incur losses. This shows that both principals would be better off not delegating their bidding than they would be in a situation with symmetric delegation in which both choose high delegated valuations. However, this still does not explain why $b_2 = v/2$ is indeed an optimal reply to $b_1 = \bar{b}$. To see why, suppose $b_1 = \bar{b}$ and consider principal 2's optimal delegated valuation. His agent will choose $E(x_2^*) = b_2 p_2^*$; hence $\varphi_2^* = 0$ and $\pi_2 = (v - b_2) b_2/(2\bar{b})$. This payoff is negative for $b_2 > v$ and positive for $b_2 < v$, and reaches its maximum for $b_2 = v/2$. Given that principal 1 has chosen a very high delegated valuation, the optimal strategy of principal 2 is to choose a fairly low delegated valuation. His agent will expend few resources on bidding in expectation, but will still win the prize with some positive probability.

The two principals earn a positive payoff, but they earn these with different margins. Principal 1 makes his agent very aggressive by giving him a high valuation of bidding. This is not very costly, as the expected bid of this agent is not determined by his own delegated valuation but instead by the opponent agent's delegated valuation. An increase in principal 1's valuation does not increase his agent's equilibrium bids, but it will deter principal 2's agent from bidding, and this benefits principal 1. In this situation, it is hopeless for principal 2 to make his agent an aggressive bidder as well, as this would lead to losses. Instead, principal 2 makes his agent a very reluctant bidder—a bidder who expends very little and still wins with some positive probability.

The outcome generalizes if the two bidders face different constraints on the maximum delegated valuation, as long as both maxima are sufficiently large. Moderate differences in the principals' true valuations of the prize also do not change the outcome qualitatively. The symmetry of the true valuations and the constraints was chosen for simplicity and because asymmetric pure strategy equilibria are more surprising as outcomes if all players are symmetric ex ante.

The mechanism that is responsible for the asymmetric delegation equilibrium also underlies a result in strategic trade policy that was shown in Konrad (2000b). He considers two firms that are located in two different countries and compete for business in a third country export market, much as in the standard framework of strategic trade policy by Brander and Spencer (1985). The main difference is that export competition is not via prices or quantities. Sales competition is organized as an all-pay auction where the two firms make simultaneous money payments (bribes) to the consumer or to the person who makes the buying decision and the decision-maker awards one major contract to the firm that pays the higher bribe. The two governments in which these firms are located may change their firms' bribing incentives by trade taxes and trade subsidies. In the equilibrium, one government, say government 1, will subsidize its firm to the maximum amount feasible and endow its firm with a high valuation of winning the bribing contest. The other government 2 will optimally moderate firm 2's incentives to bid by imposing a trade tax on this firm that has to be paid if the firm is awarded the contract. This reduces the firm's benefit from winning the export contract. As a result, the contest will become highly asymmetric, and the total expected equilibrium bribing effort will be much lower than the valuation of being awarded the contract. Moreover, both countries gain from this type of strategic trade policy. The strategic trade policy alters the firms' bribing incentives in a way that is very similar to the effects of a delegation contract and puts the firms in the roles of delegated agents who bribe on behalf of their benevolent country governments.

Delegation in Tullock contests

The equilibrium asymmetries that emerge in the delegation equilibria are not specific only to the all-pay auction without noise and can also emerge in asymmetric Tullock contests. But delegation may lead to less drastic effects in Tullock contests, particularly if the players are fairly homogeneous. The strategic aspects of delegation in the Tullock contest can be studied using reaction curve diagrams. Figure 3.2 depicts the 'true' or undelegated reaction curves $x_1(x_2)$ and $x_2(x_1)$ in a fully symmetric two-player Tullock lottery contest that are formally derived as function (2.41), for values $r = 1$ and $v_1 = v_2 = v$. They intersect in the symmetric Nash equilibrium N. A representative of the indifference curves

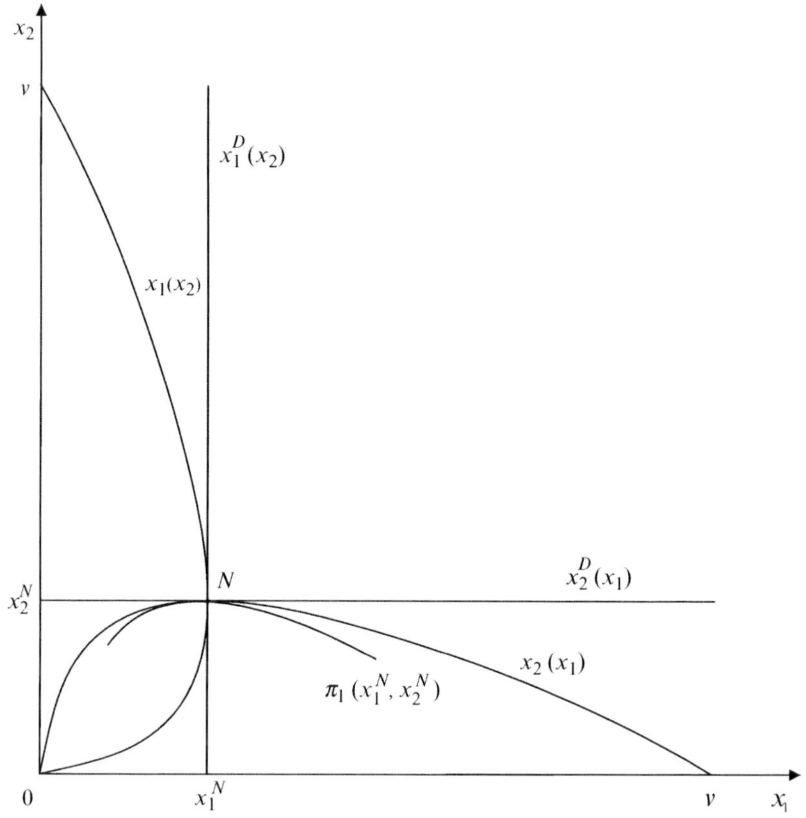

Figure 3.2 The curves show the undelegated reaction curves $x_1(x_2)$ and $x_2(x_1)$ for the symmetric Tullock lottery contest with a prize of size 1 and an equilibrium in the chosen reaction curves for delegates.

of contestant 1 is shown in this diagram. There, $\pi_1(x_1^N, x_2^N)$ is the set of pairs of efforts (x_1, x_2) that yield the payoff level of contestant 1 in the Nash equilibrium (x_1^N, x_2^N). The indifference curves for contestant 2 are obtained analogously. The shape of these indifference curves has already been explained more carefully in section 3.1.

Suppose that contestant 1 chooses to delegate the choice of x_1 to an agent who is motivated by objectives that can be completely specified in a contract and perfectly monitored as in the above framework. If the set of feasible delegation contracts is sufficiently rich, and if the agent's opportunity cost of acting as a delegate is zero, the agent will receive a net payment just equal to his equilibrium choice of effort in the contest, and the choice of the delegation contract can be understood as changing the own reaction curve to some function $x_1^D(x_2)$, without, however, changing the payoff levels associated with given pairs (x_1, x_2) of effort.

As long as contestant 2 does not delegate the effort decision to an agent, this problem resembles the Stackelberg problem discussed previously. Contestant 1's problem reduces to choosing his most favored point along contestant 2's reaction function $x_2(x_1)$. In general, this point is obtained by finding the iso-payoff curve with the highest payoff which 1 can reach along contestant 2's reaction function. Note that, due to the shapes of the reaction functions in the symmetric case, this point is identical with the point N in Figure 3.2. Contestant 1 then may design a contract that will cause N as the equilibrium outcome and the principal will have a payoff equal to this highest payoff.

If contestant 2 can also delegate his effort choice, the problem increases in complexity, particularly if the delegated reaction functions can be chosen as arbitrary functions. If the two players are perfectly symmetric, the undelegated Nash equilibrium N leads to effort choices and win probabilities that also emerge as equilibrium values in a subgame perfect equilibrium in the contest with delegation.[11] To confirm this in the framework discussed here with an arbitrary choice of delegated reaction functions, suppose that contestant 2 chooses a reaction function for his agent

$$x_2^D(x_1) \equiv x_2^N. \tag{3.18}$$

In this case contestant 1 can choose the equilibrium along this reaction function and prefers (x_1^N, x_2^N) among all these points. Contestant 1 can

[11] See Wärneryd (2000).

establish this outcome by a delegation contract that yields a reaction function for his agent

$$x_1^D(x_2) \equiv x_1^N. \tag{3.19}$$

No other delegated reaction function could yield a higher payoff to contestant 1. Of course, the same argument applies to contestant 2, given that contestant 1 chooses the delegated reaction function (3.19). Hence, delegation contracts leading to delegated reaction functions (3.19) and (3.18) constitute optimal replies to each other in the delegation stage.

Delegation and agency problems

Commitment and the strategic effect of commitment may make delegation individually desirable from the point of view of the principal. A possible disadvantage of delegation contracts is that delegation may have an additional agency cost.

Wärneryd (2000) considers one type of such agency cost more formally. He discusses what happens if principals cannot observe the effort that is chosen by their delegated agents. The example he has in mind is litigation, where the conflicting parties usually have to delegate to lawyers the task of providing favorable evidence and of presenting it to the court. The delegation contracts between the principal and his lawyer that are used, or admitted, differ between the legal systems in different countries, but they all have in common the fact that the actual effort of a respective lawyer can hardly be fully observed by the principal. This moral hazard problem typically leads to an equilibrium effort choice of the lawyer that is too small compared to what would maximize their joint surplus. Hence, nobody would hire a lawyer if he felt equally capable (or at least reasonably capable) of collecting evidence himself and presenting it appropriately to the court. However, in many court systems, delegation of court representation to lawyers is mandatory, and, moreover, lawyers do have comparative advantages in what they do, making two-sided delegation inevitable. The effort reduction that is achieved if both conflicting parties have to delegate the effort choice to their lawyers may enhance efficiency of litigation by reducing the aggregate effort that is used in litigation.[12]

A more global picture takes into consideration that the nature of the litigation process has implications for business conduct that may

[12] A further aspect comes into play if the internal organization of the law firm is taken into consideration, as in Priks (2005). He suggests that law firms consist of groups of lawyers, and the specific payment schedules and sharing rules among partners may generate further disincentives inside law firms. The issue of contests between groups and the free-riding incentives for group members will be discussed more carefully in Chapter 6.

potentially lead to future litigation. In such a framework, other aspects gain importance. For instance, litigation effort need not simply be wasteful, but higher effort on both sides may improve the quality or precision of the signal to the court about what is the right or wrong decision. Delegation then also affects the 'truth revealing' quality of the litigation process and changes the precision by which the litigation system enforces contracts or property rights. This, in turn, will change the performance of business life. Despite its limitations with regard to such aspects, viewing litigation as a contest is a very useful simplification: it can reveal some of the implications of the institutional framework for litigation effort.

3.5. Summary

Several strategic dimensions of contest have been considered in this chapter. If the participants in a contest have the ability to make a commitment about the timing by which they make their effort choices, a sequential choice of effort may emerge endogenously as an equilibrium. The weaker player (the 'underdog') becomes the Stackelberg leader. He chooses lower effort than in the Nash equilibrium. The stronger player (the 'favorite') becomes a Stackelberg follower. He observes this lower effort and accommodates to it, typically by choosing effort that is lower than the Nash equilibrium effort. Both players benefit from the mutual reductions in effort in this equilibrium.

If contestants can delegate the effort decision to an agent and endow their agents with incentives different from the players' own incentives, this may also have beneficial effects for all contestants. The contestants may use the opportunity to delegate the effort choice, thereby generating a large asymmetry between the two agents. Given this asymmetry, the agents may dissipate a smaller share in the prize than in a perfectly symmetric contest, and this can benefit both players.

Endogenous sequential effort choices and delegation are instruments which can be used by the contestants who aim at reducing their total contest effort in the equilibrium. The organizer of a contest may also use instruments, but he may try to induce higher effort. It may be optimal from the organizer's perspective to exclude players from participating in the contest, even though they have a very high value of winning the prize. In particular, the aggregate effort in a contest may be higher if the player who values the prize most highly is excluded from the contest. This outcome emerges if the players with the second and third highest valuation have valuations that are similar to each other and considerably lower than the highest valuation. The exclusion of the player with the highest valuation makes the remaining top competitors more similar and the contestants more homogeneous. The effect from an increase in homogeneity may be more important than the effect from the contestants' valuations of winning.

In all these cases, the driving force is a change in the homogeneity of the contestants that is caused by the strategic actions. Contestants may like heterogeneity, as it may reduce their equilibrium efforts. They may act strategically, trying to increase their heterogeneity. Contest organizers who like high effort, on the other hand, may like to take actions that increase the homogeneity of their contestants.

4

Cost and Prize Structure

4.1. Choice of cost

A natural way to influence the outcome of a contest is to influence the cost of the contestants' effort. This is easy if a contest organizer controls this aspect by setting the rules, or by using instruments such as taxes and subsidies that change the cost-of-effort functions for some, or all, contestants.[1] The change in the cost structure that is desirable will generally depend on the point of view. Contestants who want to reduce their overall equilibrium efforts might be interested in the creation of asymmetry. The contest organizer may find a high level of effort desirable, and, as has been discussed in the context of labor market tournaments, to some extent, this may ultimately also be in the interest of contestants if there is a positive relationship between the equilibrium effort and the contest prize.

The contest designer who is interested in maximizing aggregate effort may consider handicapping one or several contestants. This problem has already been addressed by Lazear and Rosen (1981), who suggested that handicapping can be a means of reducing heterogeneity. Clark and Riis (2000) consider a bureaucrat or politician who allocates a prize in an all-pay auction between two contestants whose valuations of the prize may differ. The contestants' efforts are given as bribes to the bureaucrat, who considers these as income. They also assume that the bureaucrat allocates the prize as a function of the contestants' efforts. Each contestant knows only his own valuation, but the distributions from which these valuations are drawn are common knowledge. They show that (in order to make the

[1] Sometimes the change in the cost-of-effort functions in a specific contest is unintended, and is brought about by a policy change that was not motivated by the contest situation. An important example of this is profit taxation, which changes the opportunity cost of spending resources on lobbying. See, e.g., Glazer and Konrad (1999).

contest more symmetric) the bureaucrat may favor the contestant who is more likely to have a lower valuation of the prize, and that, at the same time, this favoritism may decrease the efficiency of the allocation of the prize.

The contest designer's incentive for favouring the contestant who attributes a lower valuation to winning, and the possible decrease in efficiency that may result from equilibrium handicapping, can also be illustrated for the all-pay auction with complete information. Consider the two contestants 1 and 2 with $v_1 > v_2$. The equilibrium outcome of an all-pay auction between these two is given in section 2.1. The total expected effort is $(v_2/2)(1+v_2/v_1)$. Suppose the bureaucrat has no option other than to let the contestants make bids in an all-pay auction, but can handicap one or other player. For instance, the bureaucrat can allocate the prize to contestant 2 unless $x_1 > (1+h)x_2$. As long as $v_2 < v_1/(1+h)$, using this tool will change the total expected effort to $\frac{v_2(1+h)}{2} + \frac{v_2}{2}\frac{v_2(1+h)}{v_1}$. Contestant 2 is less likely to expend zero effort. Hence, the handicap will cause an increase in the probability that the prize is allocated to the contestant who values it less, but may increase the bureaucrat's returns.

4.2. The structure of prizes

Contests with n contestants often have a more complex structure of prizes than just one winner prize and $n-1$ identical loser prizes. Most evidently, sports tournaments explicitly award more than one winner prize: there are gold, silver and bronze medals at the Olympics. In tennis tournaments, there is a scale of prize money for a number of players at the top. In motor sports, the best three drivers are honored and are allowed to pour champagne on each other, but even the lower ranking drivers can earn credits for the world championship. In professional golf tournaments, the 'purse' consists of a number of prizes that decline with the rank a player achieves in the tournament. Recall the prize structure for the tournaments on the PGA tour in Chapter 1. Note, also, that these awards do not fully describe the set of prizes and the prize structure, as there are implicit, or non-monetary, benefits of a player's absolute and relative performances. Winners of major tournaments have the benefit of qualifying for future tournaments, they get media attention that can be transformed into monetary payoffs via promotion contracts with sponsors who want to advertize their brand products, they improve their score with regard to the contest for best performance in a given year, or lifetime, and they probably obtain some ego rents and enhance their self-confidence.

In Chapter 1, other contest examples with multiple prizes were also discussed. In education tournaments, in some entry examinations for the system of higher education, or for admission to some professions, there are explicit or implicit quotas that award winner prizes to all who pass the examination. Hence, such tournaments allocate more than one winner prize. As there are typically multiple grades, there is a whole set of different winner prizes. Also, as discussed in Fernández and Gali (1999), if a heterogeneous population of students may be assigned to different qualities of schools, this may follow the rules of a rank-order tournament with multiple, heterogeneous prizes.[2] In sales contests, the firms often award multiple prizes to the top group of salespersons. Political competition, too, often has a complex prize structure. When two presidential candidates campaign and run against each other, they can be seen as competing for one winner prize and one loser prize. But in party competition with a representative system and coalitions, many outcomes other than victory and defeat are feasible. Moreover, once a party is selected to form the government, the party members can compete for quite a number of positions with different office rents attached to them, making this process a competition with many prizes. Moldovanu and Sela (2001) report a number of R&D contests in which there is more than one prize. But even the numerous annual contests in which a recognition prize is awarded (see, e.g., Windham, 1999 for a list of such prizes) can, to some extent, be seen as contests with many prizes. Such prizes are often awarded in sequential order. Contestants may, for instance, choose how they allocate their efforts in different periods, with prizes awarded period by period. Former winners of a prize may, but need not, be excluded in the a next round. Contestants may also expend their efforts simultaneously, and their relative performance ranking may be used to allocate the different prizes among them. Sports contests and political contests can be examined as illustrations.

Whether or not there are multiple prizes, and also the choice of the allocation function that assigns several prizes to the contestants can sometimes be a matter of design. Are multiple prizes awarded on the basis of the vector of actual efforts or are prizes allocated in sequential contests? Can a contestant win several prizes, or only one? Can contestants take part in all

[2] Fernández and Gali (1999) consider a framework in which the students' abilities are private information. They show that such tournaments, although they dissipate tournament effort, may be more efficient than markets if the markets suffer from borrowing constraints.

contests or do they have to select themselves into groups? Can contestants choose, or are they allocated to, different contests for different prizes, as is the case in league systems in sports? The choice of the prize structure will generally also interact with the type of contest success function, and information aspects play a role, too.

These examples motivate questions about how the prize structure influences contest efforts and the contestants' performance, and the nature of the process that turns efforts into observable performance. Some elements in a contest can be chosen by its organizer, whereas many other elements cannot. What can be chosen, and what cannot be chosen, depend on the particular type of competition and the nature of the application. The nature of the contest success function is often predetermined by the nature of the game, and the discretion the organizer of a contest has may be quite limited in many applications. The structure of prizes as a function of what are the observable outcomes of a contest can often be chosen.

In studying the optimal design of contests, a further complication emerges—which derives from the question of what the objective function of the contest organizer is. In analyzing contests from an optimal design perspective, care is needed when the objective functions of a contest organizer and the contestants are specified. Many analyzes consider this question from the point of view of an organizer who would like to maximize expected aggregate contest effort. Indeed, contestants' efforts and their performance is probably of interest for most contest designers, making this an interesting research task. Contest organizers may, however, care about many other aspects as well. The organizer of a sports competition may be interested in attracting spectators, eliciting high fees from media companies for broadcasting rights, or may pursue other goals, or a combination of these. The organizer will not necessarily maximize the sum of all players' efforts. Aspects such as suspense, competitive balance, and even long-term considerations about the endogeneity of players' or teams' quality and their distribution may become important. Different matches in a tournament are typically differently attractive to spectators. If the designers are interested in media coverage or fees for broadcasting rights, the fundamental laws of media economics further amplify the importance of such differences for tournament organizers. Singh and Wittman (1998) and Hoehn and Szymanski (1999) discuss some of these issues in more detail. In other contest applications, further aspects may come into play.

As discussed, most of the existing papers in the literature have addressed some, but not all, of these aspects and have focused on players' contest effort.[3] Moldovanu and Sela (2001) provide a brief literature survey and give conditions for when one or more prizes are optimal, focusing on the maximization of aggregate effort, or of highest individual effort by some of the contestants. They consider contest design in a framework with n contestants as follows. A contest designer allocates a prize of size 1 that can be awarded as one single prize, or as several prizes. For instance, the total prize money may sum up to 1 and may be split into a large prize of size b_1 and a small positive prize of size $b_2 = 1 - b_1$. Each contestant i chooses his contest effort x_i. The contestant who provides the highest effort wins the highest prize. The contestant with the second highest effort wins the second highest prize etc. Moreover, contestants may differ with regard to their cost of effort. Each contestant i knows his own cost type, described by his cost parameter $c_i \in [m, 1]$, which is private information. All contestants' cost types are independent draws from the same distribution, with a continuous cumulative distribution function denoted $F(c)$. Contestants are risk neutral; their payoffs are simply the expected prize money that they win, minus their actual cost of contest effort $c_i x_i$. One of the main results concerns the optimal prize structure when a contest designer wants to maximize the expected sum of contest efforts. They find that one single big prize is optimal from the contest designer's perspective if the cost of contest effort is linear in effort for all contestants.

Their formal approach can be sketched using a specific example with $n = 3$. The optimal effort x_i for player i who has a cost of effort equal to $c_i x_i$ can be derived from the following intuitive approach: assume that there is a monotonically decreasing bidding function $x(c)$ that is obeyed by all players other than i, with an inverse $c(x)$. If there are two prizes, b_1

[3] For instance, Clark and Riis (1998b) consider the case with several identical prizes and heterogeneous contestants who value these prizes differently, and know each other's valuations. They analyze the case in which the prizes are allocated as a function of simultaneously chosen efforts, with the contestants with the highest efforts winning the prizes, and the case in which there are several rounds of this type, where contestants who win a prize at some stage are not allowed to participate in further contest rounds. Barut and Kovenock (1998) characterize the equilibria in a related all-pay auction framework with multiple prizes of different size. Each player chooses one effort, the highest prize is awarded to the player with the highest bid, the second highest prize goes to the second highest bidder, etc. Clark and Riis (1996) consider multi-prize contests with a Tullock contest success function. Kalra and Shi (2001) consider the optimality of multiple prizes in sales constests that follow the logic of an all-pay auction with additive noise. They focus on risk aversion and convex effort costs. These approaches differ from contests in which the different contests are independent by design, but may be linked through participation decisions (see, e.g., Gradstein and Nitzan, 1989) or overall budget constraints as in Colonel Blotto games and in promotional competition games with fixed overall budgets. Glazer and Hassin (1988) address the optimality of the prize structure very generally. They find that, under some conditions, handing out the same positive winner prizes to all but the worst performing participant can maximize aggregate effort.

and $b_2 = 1 - b_1$, with $1 \geq b_1 \geq 1 - b_1$, then i's optimization problem is to solve for

$$\arg\max_{x_i}\{b_1(1 - F(c(x_i))^2) + b_2\, 2F(c(x_i))(1 - F(c(x_i))) - c_i x_i\}. \tag{4.1}$$

In this objective function, the first term describes the expected prize money from winning the largest prize b_1, as, for a choice of effort equal to x_i, this happens for given $c(x_i)$ with a probability of $(1 - F(c(x_i))^2)$ which is equal to the probability that the other two players' cost parameters c_j or c_k are higher than $c(x_i)$. If the other two players choose their efforts according to the equilibrium bid function $c(x)$, then $(1-F(c(x_i))^2)$ is also the probability that they both choose an effort that is smaller than x_i. Similarly, the second term is the expected prize money from winning the second prize, which happens if one of the other players has a higher cost parameter than i, and the other player has a lower cost parameter. The third term just denotes i's cost of choosing x_i. Using the first-order condition for a maximum of (4.1), the slope of the bidding function is obtained as

$$\frac{dx_i}{dc_i} = \frac{1}{c_i}\left[b_1 2(1 - F(c_i))(-F'(c_i)) + b_2 2(1 - 2F(c_i))F'(c_i)\right]. \tag{4.2}$$

A player i who has $c_i = 1$ knows that he has higher cost than both his competitors with probability 1 and will not expend positive amounts of effort. Accordingly, $x_i(1) = 0$. Using this property, the bidding function can be obtained by integration:

$$x_i(c_i) = \int_1^{c_i} \frac{1}{a}\left[b_1 2(1 - F(a))(-F'(a)) + b_2 2(1 - 2F(a))F'(a)\right] da, \tag{4.3}$$

which can be transformed, using $b_2 = 1 - b_1$, to

$$x_i(c_i) = 2b_1 \int_{c_i}^{1} \frac{1}{a}(2 - 3F(a))F'(a)da + 2\int_{c_i}^{1}(2F(a) - 1)F'(a)da. \tag{4.4}$$

This function can be used to explain why the expected sum of effort choices is an increasing function in b_1. Taking expecations, and inspecting this expected effort, Moldovanu and Sela (2001) show that, for general distributions, the expected effort is not lower for $b_1 = 1$ than for a different division of the prize. An increase in b_1 (and an implied decrease in b_2) makes effort more worthwhile to win the big prize, and it becomes less worthwhile to bid for the second prize. Why the first effect is stronger than the second effect is in general not obvious. The effect is straightforward for $n = 2$. Here the loser wins b_2 in any case. Shifting prize money from the winner prize to the loser prize reduces the difference in prizes (first effect) but has no countervailing effect, as neither of the two players makes positive bids for b_2.

Further results on the consequences of the prize structure for aggregate expected effort (and for the highest effort) are obtained in Moldovanu and Sela (2006). In particular, a partition of the contestants into smaller groups of players who compete for smaller prizes also does not induce more aggregate effort in expectation, provided that the cost of effort is linear in effort. Moldovanu and Sela (2001) carefully analyze the robustness of their results with respect to non-linear cost functions and find that convex effort costs may make multiple prizes optimal. Gavious, Moldovanu, and Sela (2002) also highlight the relevance of convex cost in the context of bid caps in the all-pay auction with incomplete information. Intuitively, with convex cost-of-effort functions, it is useful to induce many contestants to participate in the contest, as their first units of effort are not very costly to them, but they contribute fully to the aggregate amount of effort. Hence, even if the division of prizes into several prizes reduces the cost of effort that is expended by the contestants who are most interested in winning, the increase in effort made by contestants who attribute a lower valuation to winning the prize may overcompensate for this.[4]

Budget constraints will generally lead to results that parallel the results with convex cost. A linear cost up to a budget constraint is, in fact, a special case of a convex cost. With budget constraints, a reduction in the top prize need not reduce what the contestants with the highest valuation expend, if they expend their whole budget in any case. But the amount by which the prize is reduced can be used to establish a tournament among other less able or less eager contestants, who may expend something on contesting for this additional prize. To illustrate this, consider an all-pay auction with complete information in which four bidders compete to win. Let their cost be linear, that is, $C_i(x_i) = x_i$, but let them have different budgets, equal to $w_1 = 10$, and $w_2 = w_3 = w_4 = 1$. The contest designer has total prize money $b = 2$ and considers whether to make the bidders compete for one single prize of this size, or to establish two contests with equal prizes. The situation where there is only one big prize was considered in the subsection

[4] Kräkel (2006) further explores the implications of cost convexity in a tournament setup. He shows that splitting the group of contestants into several subgroups and allocating a prize to each subgroup is beneficial if the total prize money available can be chosen by the tournament organizer.

on constraints on effort in the section on the all-pay auction, and one of the equilibria has players 1 and 2 as the only players making positive bids. Using (2.13) and (2.14), total expected effort equals $Ex_1 + Ex_2 = 1$. Alternatively, if the contest designer chooses to establish two prizes $b_I = 1$ and $b_{II} = 1$, then one of the equilibria has players 1 and 2 compete for prize b_I and players 3 and 4 compete for prize b_{II}. The competition for each of the prizes is equivalent to the standard all-pay auction without budget constraints, as the budget constraints are non-binding. The expected efforts sum up to 2. Accordingly, the choice of multiple prizes increases total effort. The example illustrates a more general principle, according to which multiple smaller prizes may reduce or eliminate the effort-reducing effect of budget constraints.

A second important assumption that is potentially crucial for the strong results in Moldovanu and Sela (2001, 2006) is an ex ante symmetry between the contestants: players may differ in their actual cost of effort, but the parameter that determines their cost of effort is drawn independently from the same distribution. It is seemingly less clear whether the grand contest, in which all players are admitted and compete for one single prize, elicits more total effort than other prize structures if the cost-of-effort parameters of players (or their valuations of winning) are drawn from very different distributions.

The possible non-optimality of a single large prize for contests with complete information, even without cost convexities or budget constraints, can intuitively be illustrated with respect to a contest many of the readers of this book are aware of—the Nobel prize. The optimality of one single big prize would imply that, disregarding aspects of risk aversion, the optimal remuneration system for economists would be to make the Nobel prize somewhat bigger than it is now, and to scrap all minor awards and compensation for other scientific achievements, like wage increases for successful publishing, tenure as a function of publication success, including the remuneration from publication success that stems from peer group pressure. This system would obviously not work. The majority of economists in academia do not have a positive probability of winning the Nobel prize. And, disregarding intrinsic motivation for a second, they would stop publishing if all remuneration other than the Nobel prize ceased to exist.[5] This suggests that a structure of multiple prizes with an explicit or an implicit assignment of the set of competitors to these prizes may actually increase the aggregate effort.

[5] This consideration was brought to my attention by Kjell Erik Lommerud many years ago.

Suppose that there are 1,000 contestants with many different (commonly known) abilities, and that the only benefit of participating in a contest is one single prize of given size. In this situation, most of the contestants will be strongly discouraged and only a small group of top contestants will make a serious effort to win the prize. Accordingly, having several prizes of different sizes may overcome this participation problem. If, in addition, the set of contestants can be partitioned into subsets of contestants who concentrate on different prizes of different size, this can make the contest in each of these sets more homogeneous. But homogeneity of contestants increases aggregate equilibrium effort. An example that is not identical, but is in the spirit of Szymanski and Valletti (2005), who address this problem more formally, is as follows. Suppose there are four contestants with cost of making effort

$$C_1(x) = x_1, C_i(x_i) = 2x_i \quad \text{for} \quad i = 2, 3, 4. \tag{4.5}$$

These cost functions are publicly known. A contest organizer would like to allocate total prize money that is normalized to 1 either as one big winner prize, or as two prizes b_I and b_{II} with $b_I + b_{II} = 1$. If there are two prizes, contestants have to decide whether to make bids for one prize or the other. Finally, let the contest success function be characterized by (2.1).

If there is one big prize only, the effort-maximizing equilibria are those in which only contestant 1 and one further contestant make positive bids with positive probability. Let this contestant be $i = 2$. He would never bid more than $x_2 = 1/2$, implying that contestant 1 randomizes his choice of x_1 uniformly on $[0, 1/2]$, and contestant 2 chooses zero effort with probability 1/2 and, with the remaining probability, contestant 2 randomizes x_2 uniformly on $[0, 1/2]$. This yields expected aggregate effort

$$E(x_1 + x_2) = 3/8 \tag{4.6}$$

and $x_3 = x_4 = 0$ in the equilibrium.

If there are two prizes, for instance, $b_I = b_{II} = 1/2$, then one of the effort-maximizing equilibria is characterized by contestants 1 and 2 competing for prize b_I and contestants 3 and 4 competing for prize b_{II}. The equilibrium effort in the contest for b_I is equal to $E(x_1 + x_2) = 3/16$, which is half the size of (4.6), and the equilibrium effort in the contest for b_{II} is equal to $E(x_3 + x_4) = 1/4$. Summarizing these expected efforts yields

$$\frac{7}{16} > \frac{3}{8}. \tag{4.7}$$

The intuition for this result is related to the exclusion argument in Baye, Kovenock and de Vries (1993). If there is only one contest for a big prize, the players who are active contestants are very heterogeneous in this example. As a result, the aggregate effort is low. Splitting the big prize into two smaller prizes generates two smaller contests. One of these contests is among heterogeneous players and still does not generate very much effort. The second contest is among homogeneous players. This contest among the homogeneous players 3 and 4 generates more effort in expectation than the contest among the heterogeneous players 1 and 2, although player 1 has a much lower cost of effort than all other players. This increased effort in the more homogeneous contest causes the increase in overall effort. Note that the contest designer could do even better if he could exclude player 1 from participating in the contest and have only one contest for a big prize with completely homogeneous contestants. For the numbers in the example, this would generate expected effort equal to 1/2, which is even higher than 7/16. This may illustrate that the increased homogeneity among contestants at least partially drives the result.

4.3. Endogenous prizes

A major determinant in contests is the contest prize that is awarded to the contest winner. In artificially created contests, the prize may be chosen by the contest organizer. The organizers of sports tournaments choose the money prize(s) and the prize structure. In research tournaments, the winner prize is also a matter of choice.[6] In R&D races, the government can influence the size of the prizes by the choice of patent laws and patent regulation more generally. But even in contests that take place in environments that have not been carefully designed for the purpose of this type of competition, contest prizes are often endogenous. Moreover, it is often the contestants who can influence the size of the prize. In this section, I will consider cases in which the contestants themselves influence the size of the prize, and have two separate instruments, one of which influences the size of the prize and another of which influences the contestants' win probability. Then I will turn to cases in which one instrument influences both the win probability of a contestant and the size of the prize, and will distinguish between two situations. One situation depicts promotional competition where contest effort increases the prize. The other

[6] See, e.g., Windham (1999), who collected a large list of monetary prizes for major technological achievements.

situation depicts the opposite case, where an increase in contest effort implies a reduction in the total value of the prize at stake in the contest.

Prize moderation

Contestants who can choose both the winner prize and the loser prize prior to entering into a contest would typically like to move these closer together, if this does not reduce the sum of the two. Doing this will typically reduce the contestants' effort without reducing what is paid out in terms of total prizes. A similar logic applies if players cannot choose the difference between the winner and the loser prize, but contest for mutually exclusive, conflicting policy outcomes and each player can choose the policy outcome that is implemented if the player wins the contest. Both contestants may be willing to moderate their policy goals compared to their respective most preferred policies and choose policy targets that are closer together than their respective most preferred policies. Modifications of this result are derived by Leidy (1994), Epstein and Nitzan (2003a, 2003b, 2004), and Münster (2006c). Suppose there are two contestants who fight for different policies. These can be, for instance, free trade versus a tariff with effective protection in a contest between national consumers and domestic firms, or the governmentally regulated prize in the contest between a natural monopoly and consumers. In such a structure, both contestants may be willing to moderate their policy goals.

To illustrate the point, consider two contestants who have a conflict of interest: they care about the value of a variable z that is taken from the real numbers. Their bliss points are Z_1 and Z_2, with $Z_1 > Z_2$, and their utility from an actual policy choice z equals

$$b_i(z) = -(Z_i - z)^2. \tag{4.8}$$

Each contestant has to choose a policy z_i which he then has to fight for. Once these values z_1, and z_2 are given and observed, the contestants expend effort x_1 and x_2 in a Tullock contest. Either z_1 or z_2 is chosen, and the probabilities for these outcomes are $x_1/(x_1 + x_2)$ and $x_2/(x_1 + x_2)$, respectively. Contestant 1 values winning as the difference $b_1(z_1) - b_1(z_2)$, which is

$$(Z_1 - z_2)^2 - (Z_1 - z_1)^2 \equiv v_1(z_1, z_2), \tag{4.9}$$

and similarly for

$$(Z_2 - z_1)^2 - (Z_2 - z_2)^2 \equiv v_2(z_2, z_1). \tag{4.10}$$

The contest equilibrium for given prizes v_1 and v_2 is characterized in (2.44), and using $r = 1$ this yields payoffs as a function of valuations v_1 and v_2 as

$$\pi_1(v_1, v_2) = \frac{(v_1)^3}{(v_1 + v_2)^2} \quad \text{and} \quad \pi_2(v_1, v_2) = \frac{(v_2)^3}{(v_1 + v_2)^2}. \tag{4.11}$$

Calculating first-order conditions $d\pi_1/dz_1 = 0$ and $d\pi_2/dz_2 = 0$ yields

$$\frac{\frac{\partial v_1}{\partial z_1}}{\frac{\partial v_2}{\partial z_1}} = \frac{2v_1}{v_1 + 3v_2} \quad \text{and} \quad \frac{\frac{\partial v_2}{\partial z_2}}{\frac{\partial v_1}{\partial z_2}} = \frac{2v_2}{v_2 + 3v_1}. \tag{4.12}$$

Using the parametric versions of v_1 and v_2 as in (4.9) and (4.10), the left-hand side of the first-order condition for contestant 1 becomes

$$\frac{\frac{\partial v_1}{\partial z_1}}{\frac{\partial v_2}{\partial z_1}} = -\frac{2(Z_1 - z_1)}{2(Z_2 - z_1)} \tag{4.13}$$

and is positive due to the equality in (4.12). Accordingly, $Z_1 > z_1 > Z_2$ must hold. Both contestants choose values of z_i that are between their bliss points, but closer to their own bliss point than is the value chosen by their competitor.

The intuition for this moderation result is as follows. If contestant 1 departs from choosing his bliss point and chooses some z_1 slightly different from Z_1 in the direction towards Z_2, what he sacrifices if he wins compared to receiving Z_1 is of second order, as $b_1'(z_1) = 0$ at $z_1 = Z_1$. However, this departure has a positive effect that is of first-order magnitude. The move towards Z_2 reduces contestant 2's loss from losing the contest, and hence his stake in the contest by $b_2'(Z_1)$, which is strictly positive. Player 2 will then use less effort in the contest. Even if contestant 1 did not adapt his own effort to this lower effort of his competitor, contestant 1 would have a first-order gain.

The insight on moderation is important in many areas of conflict. Contestants may strengthen their position in a contest in terms of the stock of arms they accumulate, or by making choices and investment that increases their own ability to fight, but they have some tendency to moderate their own demands. In negotiations and bilateral bargaining with incomplete information, a buyer may try to hide his true willingness to pay and a seller may try to overstate his reservation prize. Hence, both ask for more than what they actually need in order to be compensated. In the contest, in the absence of incomplete information, the reverse might be true. There is a tendency to narrow the gap between the two conflicting players' unconstrained optimal policy choices.

A related trade-off is studied in Konrad (2002). This paper considers an incumbent who can choose how much to invest in a project if the project returns must be defended in a future contest between this incumbent and a challenger. High investment generates a high prize and causes a high future cost of defense. If the incumbent wants to avoid this, he needs to moderate his investment behavior. Unlike in a situation in which the investor receives the returns on his investment only with some exogenously given probability smaller than 1, as in simple expropriation problems with exogenous expropriation probabilities, the incentive to moderate investment here is much stronger. The investor knows he can avoid expropriation of the future returns by making defense expenditures in the future. The higher the investment (and its returns), the higher is the challenger's appropriation effort, and the more defense effort is needed to fend him off. Lower investment will reduce the required defense cost in the future. Put differently, future defense cost can be seen as being part of the investment cost, and has to be taken into consideration by the investor when he makes his investment effort.

Concordance between production and appropriation

In many instances, the contestants themselves influence the value of winning the prize. For instance, the analysis by Baye and Hoppe (2003) that was reported in section 2.3 shows that research activity influences both the probability of winning the contest and the expected value of the prize for winning the R&D contest. A similar example emerges in the context of promotional competition and has been recognized there. Promotional effort by a firm typically changes the size of the firm's market share, but also increases the total size of the market. Promotional effort has the usual negative contest externality as a contestant steals some market share from other contestants when increasing his promotional effort. But, by increasing the market size, the effort at the same time benefits all other competitors, and this is a positive externality. The marketing literature tries to distinguish between these two effects, and contest theory can be of help in deriving some hypotheses that are empirically testable.[7] Generally, if the prize is an increasing function in the efforts expended, the individual effort contributes to a public good (the prize) but it also has a negative externality, as

[7] Huck, Konrad, and Müller (2002) and Barros and Sørgard (2000), for instance, consider the profitability of merger between two firms in a market that is characterized by promotional competition.

it reduces the win probabilities of other contestants. Consider, for instance, a symmetric Tullock game among n players with payoffs

$$\pi_i(x_1,\ldots,x_n) = \frac{x_i^r}{\sum_{j=1}^n x_j^r} v_i\left(\sum_{j=1}^n x_j\right) - x_i \tag{4.14}$$

that is analyzed by Chung (1996). For $r = 1$ and $v' > 0$ and $v'' < 0$, imposing further regularity conditions on the problem that guarantee a unique equilibrium, he finds that the efforts chosen in the equilibrium are higher than the efforts that maximize the sum of the contestants' payoffs. He also discusses the fact that this 'overprovision' outcome is not robust to parameter changes, as becomes clear from considering $r = 0$. For this case, the problem turns into the standard problem of private provision of a public good as in Bergstrom, Blume and Varian (1986) and is typically characterized by too small contributions x_i.[8]

In these examples, an increase in contest effort typically increases the prize, and this gives a productive element to the contest activities. The reverse may also be true in other applications in which increased effort reduces the value of the prize, and this case is considered next.

Conflict between production and appropriation

An environment in which there is a trade-off between production and appropriation is studied by Skaperdas (1992). He considers individual decision-makers who are endowed with a given budget, for example, an amount of time that is available and used either for productive purposes or for appropriation, which means either trying to take from others, or trying to prevent others from taking, or a mixture of the two. Let there be two players 1 and 2. Each of them can use a share of his endowment to produce valuable consumer goods and the remaining share for military goods. The total output of consumer goods is consumed by the two decision-makers, but their consumption shares in total output are determined as a function of what they allocate to appropriation expenditure, that is that shares of their budget used for arms, military goods, or fighting effort more generally. Note that an increase in own appropriation expenditure will generally

[8] Morgan (2000) considers another case in which contest effort has a positive side-effect. He studies a lottery contest in which some of the revenue from the purchases of lottery tickets is used to award a monetary prize, and some of the revenue is used to provide a public good. This is discussed in the next chapter. Individuals who purchase lottery tickets do not directly increase the prize in the lottery as in Chung, but they contribute to a public good, and higher lottery purchases ameliorate the public good provision outcome.

affect (and typically reduce) the total prize, as fewer resources can be used for productive purposes. Each contestant will face the trade-off between generating a larger total output and receiving a larger share of the total output. However, the strategic situation is a bit more complicated. If a contestant decides to produce a further unit of output, this will weaken his military capacity and will also make it more attractive for the other contestant to expend appropriation effort.

To consider one aspect of the problem in Skaperdas (1992) more closely, one that is a variant of what is known as the 'paradox of power' (Hirshleifer, 1991), let each player be endowed with one unit of resource. Let $y_i \in [0, 1]$ be used for producing valuable consumer goods and let

$$x_i = 1 - y_i \tag{4.15}$$

be used for appropriation purposes. Write the total output of valuable consumer goods as $y = ay_1 + y_2$. Hence, the production amounts add up to total production, and each player has constant returns in this activity. Consider the two cases $a \in \{0, 1\}$. One case, $a = 0$, refers to the case in which contestant 1 has no specific ability for producing output, but the player can use his time as effectively as contestant 2 for the purpose of appropriation. For $a = 1$, the situation is perfectly symmetric. For ease of comparison, a linear contest success function will be used that is not very plausible, but is simple, such that

$$p_1(x_1, x_2) = \frac{1}{2} + \frac{x_1 - x_2}{2}. \tag{4.16}$$

Consider first the symmetric case. Contestant 1 maximizes

$$\pi_1(y_1, y_2) = \left(\frac{1}{2} + \frac{x_1 - x_2}{2}\right)(y_1 + y_2), \tag{4.17}$$

and similarly for $i = 2$. Maximization of this objective function yields first-order conditions that are just fulfilled at $y_1 = y_2 = \frac{1}{2}$, that is, for the case in which both contestants expend half of their resources on productive effort. It is interesting to compare this result with the outcome for the case $a = 0$. In this case, contestant 1 will not expend any effort on productive purposes, but will expend all effort on the contest. Contestant 2 will react to this and, hence, maximizes $\frac{x_2}{2}(1 - x_2)$, which, again, yields $y_2 = 1/2$ as the optimal choice. As a result, contestant 1 will earn a payoff equal to 3/8, and contestant 2 will earn a payoff equal to 1/8. Even though contestant 1 has an absolute disadvantage in producing consumption goods, the comparative advantage in fighting is sufficiently strong to turn this disadvantage into an advantage. Contestant 2 is more efficient at transforming input into consumable output and would be much richer in the absence of conflict than player 1. In the absence of property rights, this player expends a large share of his resources on producing consumer goods, and, hence, less on appropriation. In fact, in the parametric example, $x_2 = 1/2$ and $x_1 = 1$. Contestant 2's share in aggregate output is therefore smaller than that of contestant 1: $p_2 < p_1$. The player who is genuinely more productive can end up with lower consumption.

The implications of the players' trade-off between production and defense or appropriation in an environment without property rights protection have been explored in a number of directions, most notably by Skaperdas and several co-workers. Some of the results are in stark contrast to the standard economic results that are obtained with exogenously assumed well-defined property rights. For instance, Anbarci, Skaperdas, and Syropoulos (2002) consider the implications of future negotiations and the role of alternative cooperative solution concepts for investment in military capacity at an earlier stage. Skaperdas and Syropoulos (2001) consider trade between agents who later enter into a period of conflict. They show that trade based on comparative advantages is not necessarily a Pareto improvement. Intuitively, relative power matters for the outcome of the contest that determines the allocation of total output. But, while trade may enhance total output, it may also shift the balance of power, and, for the agent who loses power, this shift may overcompensate for the benefits of the increase in output.[9] Also in contrast to the more standard intuition in economics is the result that increased competition may decrease welfare. Skaperdas (2002) shows that, unlike the type of competition that brings asking prices and willingness to pay closer together, competition for the provision of protection, and, in particular, competition for territory or zones of influence that takes the form of a wasteful contest, mainly dissipates resources, and an increase in competition typically increases dissipation. Intuitively, this is a result of the increase in contest effort that typically goes along with an increase in this type of competition. Further surprising results can be found in Skaperdas (2003),

[9] Conflict is another instance in which relative position regarding some goods determines the allocation of absolutely scarce goods. Seen from this perspective, the result is reminiscent of relative standing comparisons in the literature on trade. If the country's relative standing enters into the country's welfare function, trade that improves all countries' consumption level may still reduce the welfare of those countries that gain only a little, and lose in terms of relative standing. The analysis of Skaperdas and Syropoulos (2001) can therefore also be seen as a new microeconomic underpinning for a concern for relative standing.

and Garfinkel and Skaperdas (2007) give a recent overview over this most dynamic area of research.

4.4. Summary

Contest organizers often have some control over the contestants' cost of effort and of the structure of prizes. They may use this control for their objectives. In section 4.1 it was shown that organizers of contests may influence the cost structure in a way that makes contestants more homogeneous, if they aim at an increase in overall effort.

The choice of the structure of prizes has been analyzed in section 4.2. If the participants in a contest are homogeneous with regard to their characteristics, and if their cost of effort is linear in their effort choices, contest designers may want to choose a simple prize structure with one big prize and $n-1$ identical loser prizes that are preferably small. This is a strong result and evidence on the prize structure in many contests that are carefully designed contradicts this result. The theoretical result is not robust, however. Cost convexities, caps or budget constraints on players' efforts, or appropriate types of heterogeneity among contestants, may make a more complex structure of multiple prizes optimal. Hence, these characteristics may contribute to explaining why the bold prize structure with one big single winner prize is rarely observed in contest applications, even if contest organizers care primarily about aggregate or maximum contest effort, and why contest organizers typically choose more complex prize structures.

The discussion has also highlighted the fact that contest organizers may be driven by further considerations, which may also require a different prize structure, and has shown that quite a number of research questions remain to be addressed. Some aspects will be addressed in subsequent chapters. For instance, contestants may be able to sabotage their co-players, and their incentives to do this depend on the structure of the prizes. Sometimes contestants will take part in many contests and the outcomes in the different contests interact. A particular prize may be valuable only in combination with some other prizes. There is again a wide range of examples of parallel contests with interdependent prizes. Fragmented property rights and the need for multiple patents for innovating a product has, for instance, been identified as a potentially important problem by Heller and Eisenberg (1998). Clark and Konrad (2008) study this problem in a formal context. They find that this type of complementarity may strongly discourage R&D effort. They also show that the possibility of inventing around single patents, an activity that is typically seen as reducing patent protection and, hence, discouraging R&D effort, may encourage R&D effort if the complementarity of patents is an important problem.

The size and the structure of prizes in contests is sometimes also determined or co-determined by the contestants. Contestants who contest for different policy outcomes may moderate their own goals. Instead of pursuing a policy that is identical with their bliss point, they may pursue a policy that is at some distance from their own bliss point and closer to the bliss point of their competitor. Such a choice reduces their adversary's incentives to fight and reduces overall contest effort. This example shows again that strategy in contests follows a logic that is different from other types of interaction, where players often have an incentive to build up an extreme position, for instance, before entering into negotiations.

Contestants may also affect the value of the contest prize by their contest efforts. The effect may go both ways. Advertizing expenditure served as an example of prize-augmenting contest effort. Military expenditure on arming served as an example of prize-reducing contest effort. The analysis of these cases showed that the endogeneity of the prize may cause counterintuitive outcomes such as the paradox of power.

5

Externalities

Contests are games in which the effort of one player typically imposes a strong externality on all other players. These mutual negative externalities could even be seen as the constituent element of such games. However, sometimes the nature of externalities in such games is more complex and more asymmetric, and in this chapter I will turn to some examples and applications.

5.1. State lotteries and financing public goods

Entries on 'lottery' or 'lotto' in Wikipedia[1] suggest that the fundamental principle of allocating a prize by way of an organized lottery or raffle is very old and very popular. It traces back to the Han Dynasty (205–187 BC) in China and has existed for a long time in many other parts of the world. Moreover, while lotteries are often private, governments often engage actively not only in regulating and taxing lotteries, but also as their organizers. The Wikipedia article on 'lottery' lists nine national lotteries in the Americas, 32 national or European lotteries in Europe, and the institution is also popular in other continents and with their surpluses contributes to financing public expenditure. Lotteries may initially have been invented by private individuals. However, the public sector quickly discovered this source of revenue, and often used its power to regulate to impose restrictions in the private sector and favored state lotteries. The income obtained from lotteries is considerable.[2] Morgan (2000) provides an explanation for why the government may want to use lotteries to finance public

[1] <http://en.wikipedia.org/wiki/Lottery>; <http://de.wikipedia.org/wiki/Lotto>.

[2] Turnover in the German Lotto was roughly 5 billion Euro in 2005. About half of this amount is returned as prizes. The other half is mainly used for particular types of public expenditure, a general lottery tax revenue, and a small share is needed to cover the transaction cost (*Frankfurter Rundschau*, October 7, 2006, p. 2).

goods, even though the government has other means of collecting funds at its disposal. His explanation relies on a specific external effect that plays a role if the payments to a lottery are used to finance something that benefits all individuals who participate in the lottery. If this is the case, the cost of buying a lottery ticket is less than the actual amount paid: the buyer anticipates that the purchase of a lottery ticket will increase the state income from lottery tickets and will, therefore, improve the supply of public goods. Surprisingly, this seemingly small additional benefit that emerges if the proceeds of the lottery are used for this purpose may, in some cases, become sufficient to implement fully efficient financing and provision of a public good.

This insight can be illustrated using the simplified approach in Morgan and Sefton (2000). They consider the symmetric standard Tullock lottery contest among n contestants with one modification: the sum of contest efforts $x_1, \ldots, x_n$, measured in monetary units, is used to finance a monetary prize of size R, and the returns of the lottery that exceed this prize are used for public expenditure. Each unit of this public expenditure contributes to a public good and yields a constant marginal benefit equal to $\beta \in (0, 1)$ to each contestant. Accordingly, a player i's payoff becomes

$$\pi_i(\mathbf{x}) = w - x_i + \frac{x_i}{X}R + \beta(X - R), \tag{5.1}$$

where $X \equiv \sum_{j=1}^{n} x_j$ is total lottery expenditure, and w is a given amount of endowment or initial wealth that characterizes the maximum that i can expend in the lottery. Morgan and Sefton also assume that $n\beta > 1$, such that the provision of $(X - R)$ is a socially efficient activity.

The Samuelson optimum would be characterized by a corner solution with $x_i = w$ and $R = 0$, as any further increase in X financed by a uniform increase in all x_i by one unit increases the utility of each player by $(n\beta - 1)$. This is the normative benchmark for evaluating the welfare properties of the non-cooperative equilibrium which is considered next.

In the non-cooperative equilibrium, each player i chooses x_i for given anticipated x_j by other players in order to maximize (5.1). This maximization yields n identical first-order conditions

$$\frac{X - x_i}{X^2}R = 1 - \beta. \tag{5.2}$$

Summing up both sides of (5.2) for $i = 1, \ldots n$ yields $\frac{n-1}{X}R = (1 - \beta)n$. This, in turn, yields

$$X - R = \frac{n\beta - 1}{n(1 - \beta)}R \tag{5.3}$$

provided that $x_i \leq w$ is non-binding. Otherwise $x_i = w$ may emerge. Condition (5.3) shows that the incentives to participate, and expend money, in the lottery yield positive contributions to the public good if $n\beta > 1$. Moreover, a higher lottery prize R and a larger number n of players induces higher net contributions to the public good.

In this example, it was assumed that the marginal social benefit of the public good is always above its marginal cost. Therefore, the outcome in (5.3) does not describe the first-best Samuelson optimum if R is redistributed as money and privately consumed by the players, unless a corner solution is approached. However, the incentives work similarly if the marginal social benefit of the public good is decreasing, and it can be shown that the size of R can be used to induce the optimal amount $(X - R)$ of the public good. Intuitively, the lottery contest itself is welfare neutral: some players receive a private surplus, others are left with a loss in private income, but all expenditure and the prize are in units of money. Given the linear preferences, this redistribution is neutral from a welfare point of view. However, if the expenditures that exceed the value of the prize are used for the public good, the sum of these expenditures exceeds the value of the prize. Hence, the lottery can be used to finance the provision of the public good. Moreover, the size of the lottery prize can now be used to fine-tune the problem such that an optimal amount of government revenue results.

The general insight that tournament prizes can induce a certain type of desirable behavior has other applications. Kolmar and Wagener (2007) and Kolmar and Sisak (2007) consider related questions, allowing for asymmetries between the contestants on the one side, and allowing for fine-tuning of the probability process that awards prizes to the participants, and of the prize structure. Lange, List, and Price (2007) allow for risk aversion and multiple prizes. As shown in Goeree et al. (2005), an all-pay auction without noise can also generate a surplus for financing a public good in a context of incomplete information about the players' private valuations of winning the prize. The all-pay auction may even be designed to generate a surplus for an efficient provision of a public good.

Also in these frameworks, the preferences of individuals regarding the public good are known to the designer of the auction. The fundamental problem of preference revelation regarding the public good is absent in this context. It can be argued that complete information about willingness to pay for the public good leaves the government and the private sector a large number of alternatives for an efficient, more direct provision of public goods. These alternatives include, for instance, lump-sum taxes and efficient provision choices by the government. The particular benefit of using a lottery as a financing device is therefore not immediately obvious. However, these mechanisms are interesting for several reasons. First, financial contributions are made voluntarily. Hence, the lottery or the all-pay auction may save the transaction costs of tax collection and enforcement that accrue if the public good is financed by lump-sum taxes or other taxes. Second, the analysis by Goeree et al. (2005) reveals an important difference between winner-pay and all-pay auctions in the context of financing public goods, showing that the all-pay auction is more suitable for raising revenue for the provision of public goods than a winner-pay auction. This insight is also of more general interest. Third, the financial surplus that may be generated by the lottery itself is a surprise, given the standard results on dissipation rates in the Tullock lottery contest. Lottery revenue exceeding the value of a monetary lottery prize emerges only if the surplus does not end up in the hands of a group other than the lottery participants. If lottery tickets do not finance a public good that is valued by the lottery participants ($\beta = 0$), then the problem becomes equivalent to the standard Tullock problem, and total expenditure fall short of the value of the prize, as has been seen in section 2.3. A participant's expenditure in the lottery yields two types of benefit to him: an increase in his probability of winning the lottery prize, and his own benefit from the increase in public expenditure. This second motive is an additional motive for expending resources in the lottery. It increases a player's incentives to buy lottery tickets and drives up his own expenditure. Moreover, if purchases of lottery tickets are strategic complements, the general equilibrium effect further increases aggregate lottery expenditure and further contributes to the public surplus.

5.2. A loser's preference about who wins

Players who participate in a contest typically want to win the prize for themselves. If a player does not win, however, the player need not be indifferent about who among the other players wins. A player who loses in the contest may attribute a higher own payoff to the winning of one opponent than another. Such externalities are very common and have been studied in the theory of standard auctions. Jehiel, Moldovanu, and Stacchetti (1996), who also analyze the efficiency properties of standard auctions in environments with externalities, mention mergers and other ownership changes among firms, the allocation of patent rights, and licensing of patents among a set of rival competitors, the location of environmentally hazardous enterprises or of international organizations as some of the examples.

Such externalities may also occur if valuable objects or prizes are awarded in all-pay auctions or contests. For instance, in the context of war and of military conflict, a defeated party may care about who is the winner of the war, anticipating that the identity of the winner has implications for the country's payoff that eventually results from a peace treaty. Externalities are also very common in sports, because the outcome of a particular tournament or competition affects participants' ranking or position in a grand contest. Tennis players, for instance, care about their rank in the ATP ranking. If a player loses a particular tournament, the implications for the player's ranking may depend on the performance of the closest competitors. In Formula I races, if there are two drivers A and B who are the close contenders for the world championship and if driver A drops out early in the race, A may prefer B to also drop out or be defeated by some, or even several, other drivers, rather than see B win the Grand Prix, because the performance of B in this given Grand Prix affects the competition for the world championship.

The problem of externalities has been addressed in general terms by Linster (1993b), who attributes a monetary payoff to each player as a function of each respective player who may win a Tullock contest. Suppose players A, B, and C take part in a Tullock lottery contest where A and B are brothers, and C is a stranger. Player A's willingness to expend a further unit of effort may be lower if A knows that his brother holds the major share of the remaining lottery tickets than if these are owned by the stranger. The general equilibrium solution of the problem is structurally straightforward, but, except for some special cases, it does not lead to simple closed form solutions.

Konrad (2006) analyzes the externalities that emerge if one firm owns shares in another firm, assuming that several firms compete for business contracts and that this competition follows the rules of an all-pay auction without noise. Ownership cross-holdings change the owning firm's incentives to become the winner of the all-pay auction. The firm that owns a share in another firm is no longer indifferent about who, among the other firms, wins the prize. A possibly preferred outcome is that the firm itself wins the prize. The second most preferred outcome is that the firm wins the prize in which it has a minority ownership share. Less preferred outcomes are that some of the other firms win the prize. The change in a firm's objectives that is induced by cross-holdings of shares suggests a change in firms' incentives. Therefore, firms can also use shareholdings strategically in order to change their incentives in the competition.

To illustrate this by way of an example, consider firms $i = 1, 2, 3$ who are solely owned by persons 1, 2, and 3. These three firms may compete to win a business contract. Each firm may make bids in an all-pay auction to win a business contract in the standard all-pay auction described in section 2.1, with a contest success function (2.1) and linear costs of effort. Firms may differ, however, regarding their valuations of winning the contract. For instance, each firm may have different costs when completing the contract, which leads to differences in firms' operating profits from winning the contract. In the example, let these profits be $v_1 = 210$, $v_2 = 200$ and $v_3 = 170$, respectively.

If the three firms compete independently for the contract, the results in section 2.1 can be used straightforwardly to characterize the equilibrium. Firm 3 will abstain from participating in the auction. Firm 1 and firm 2 will make positive effort choices as in (2.2) and (2.3). Only firm 1 has a positive payoff equal to $210 - 200 = 10$ in this equilibrium. Now let firm 1 purchase a 40 percent share in firm 2, and let firms behave in a way that maximizes their payoff, which consists of the sum of their operating profit and their income from ownership shares in other firms. Suppose that firm 1 quits and expends zero effort. The contest will then be between firms 2 and 3. Applying the results on the equilibrium of the standard all-pay auction without noise, this will earn firm 3 an expected operating profit of zero, and firm 2 an expected operating profit of $200 - 170 = 30$. This expected profit is distributed between the owners of firm 2 according to their shareholdings. Firm 1 will therefore receive 12 in expectation, which is more than the 10 received without the shareholdings, and firm 2 will receive an operating profit of 30, which exceeds the profit of zero obtained without these shareholdings. The initial owner, person 2, will receive 18 units of the operating profit of firm 2, as he sold a share of 40 percent in firm 2 to firm 1, which already exceeds this owner's returns in the equilibrium without cross-holdings. To this payoff, person 2 may add any revenue from selling the 40 percent share to firm 1. For this outcome to emerge, however, it was assumed that firm 1 indeed abstains from making a strictly positive bid. Whether this abstention describes equilibrium behavior by firm 1 will generally depend on the three firms' valuations of winning, and on the size of the minority share which firm 1 acquired in firm 2. For the respective case in which the firm with the highest valuation purchases a minority share θ_{12} in the firm with the second highest valuation, Konrad (2006) shows that the condition that makes firm 1 abstain from bidding for the contract is

$$\theta_{12} > \frac{v_1 - v_3}{v_2 - \frac{v_3}{2}}. \tag{5.4}$$

Note that this condition is fulfilled for the values assumed here, as the critical share determined by this condition would be 0.34783. Hence, abstention by firm 1 and the mixed strategies as in a standard all-pay auction between firms 2 and 3 with valuations v_2 and v_3 are indeed mutually optimal replies.

This example is another illustration of the importance of heterogeneity in contests. Heterogeneity may well be in the interest of the contestants if the reduction in equilibrium effort that it may cause does not change the prize that is allocated between them. Contestants may have some means of influencing their heterogeneity by creating external effects between them. Among firms, cross-ownership shares can have this purpose. In the example, the minority shareholdings shift the identity of the active contestants and induce contestants who are more heterogeneous to be active.

5.3. Personnel economics and sabotage

Competitors in a tournament or contest may expend effort on improving their own performance. However, they may also expend effort on activities that reduce the performance of one, or some, of their competitors. This latter possibility has attracted the attention of researchers in personnel economics. Edward Lazear (1989), who had previously laid the ground for a theory of relative reward schemes in personnel economics jointly with Sherwin Rosen, was also the first to recognize the important counterproductive role of such incentive devices if players can sabotage each other. He illustrates the negative implications of the option of sabotaging another player in a tournament for the efficiency properties of the tournament as an incentive instrument. The option of sabotage may cause poor performance of tournaments as incentive devices, particularly if the cost of the sabotage effort that reduces the competitor's performance is low compared to the cost of the effort that enhances a player's own performance. This leads to insights about possible counter-measures that contest designers more generally, and firms in particular, may take. Pay compression, or a reduction in the spread between the payment for the winner and the loser, typically reduces the incentive to expend both the effort that enhances own performance and the effort that sabotages other competitors. Hence, wage compression may increase internal harmony and efficiency. However, as wage compression also reduces the stimulus to improve own performance, such pay compression runs counter to the idea of a tournament as an incentive instrument.

Lazear suggests that firms could try to hire employees who are not very good at sabotaging others but who are very productive at turning own effort into own output. Such employees will not engage much in sabotage.[3] Lazear (1995) also reports empirical evidence that firms may chose a structure for the tournament that reduces sabotage. First, before the breakup of AT&T, the president of the corporation was usually chosen from the group of presidents of the various subsidiaries of the company. As there was some geographic distance between these subsidiaries and not too much direct exchange and communication, it was physically difficult and costly for one of them to sabotage an other, much more difficult than sabotage between various vice presidents working alongside each other within the headquarters of the company. Dow Chemical Corporation is used as a second example. According to Lazear, in this company, competition for the top headquarters jobs also took place between people in (typically different) field operations who had less opportunity to compete with each other. Third, sabotage, or the lack of cooperation which is a weaker form of sabotage, may also be reduced among the employees within a firm by competition from outside: if unsatisfactory performance by the firm may cause the firm to go out of business, or if the unsatisfactory performance of a unit triggers competition from outside, then sabotage has an additional cost. If promotion is the main incentive for providing effort, the firm owner may want to appoint someone from outside if the firm performance as a whole is not sufficiently good (Chan, 1996).[4]

More formally, sabotage is a costly effort for one player and reduces the performance of another player. Hence, if there are more than two players, the sabotage activity also affects the payoffs of players who are neither sabotaging nor being sabotaged. These external effects of sabotage make it a particularly interesting phenomenon. Consider, for instance, players $i = 1, \ldots n$ in a modified version of a Tullock lottery contest with sabotage. Let the prize of winning be $v_i = 1$ for all $i = 1, \ldots n$. Let the win probability of the players be determined by the lottery contest success

[3] The use of sabotage in tournaments and contests has also been explored experimentally, e.g., by Harbring et al. (2004) and Harbring and Irlenbusch (2008).

[4] See, e.g., Tsoulouhas, Knoeber, and Agrawal (2007) for a recent re-consideration of several trade-offs regarding strong competition for successorship inside the firm and the potential role of outsiders.

function as in (2.39) for $r = 1$. Without sabotage, players can exhibit only one type of effort, which is considered to be productive or desirable from the point of view of the contest organizer. The (non-negative) quantity of this effort is denoted as y_i and the player i's cost of this effort is denoted $C(y_i) = y_i$. Hence, the problem is identical to the standard Tullock lottery contest, and $y^* = (n-1)/n^2$ is the equilibrium value of contest effort for all players.

To allow for sabotage, assume that players have the option of sabotaging other players. Let $S_i \equiv \sum_{j \neq i} s_{ij}$ be the total amount of sabotage by player i, and s_{ij} the amount of sabotage by player i towards player j. Assume that player i's cost of an amount of sabotage S_i is $\Psi(S_i)$ with $\Psi(0) = 0$, $0 < \Psi'(0) < 1$ and $\Psi'' > 0$. Let us further assume that a player's own productive effort y_i and the total sabotage $s_i = \sum_{j \neq i} s_{ji}$ which other players use against player i determine this player's effective net effort, that is,

$$x_i = \max\{y_i - s_i, 0\}. \tag{5.5}$$

For the case of two players, with both players having the option of sabotaging the respective other player, assuming symmetry and an interior solution, the problem in which each player $i \in \{1, 2\}$ chooses his own efforts in productive effort y_i and sabotage $s_{ij} = s_j$ to maximize his own payoff can be solved explicitly. The first-order conditions for players yield

$$\Psi'(s_i) = 1 \tag{5.6}$$

and

$$y_i = \frac{1}{4} + s_i \tag{5.7}$$

and these characterize an equilibrium, provided that the payoffs of both players are positive for these values of effort.

For larger groups, sabotage exhibits an interesting externality. Suppose for simplicity that only player 1 has the option of choosing positive amounts of sabotage. For given effort levels of all other players $i = 2, \ldots, n$, player 1's maximization problem is

$$\max_{y_1, s_{12}, \ldots s_{1n}} \frac{x_1}{x_1 + x_2 + \cdots + x_n} - y_1 - \Psi(S_1). \tag{5.8}$$

The marginal cost of the first unit of sabotage is equal to $\Psi'(0)$. The marginal benefit of sabotage for the first unit of sabotage, given the equilibrium values of productive efforts as in the standard Tullock lottery contest, is equal to $1/(n-1)$. Returning to the problem with n players, and focusing on player 1's option of sabotaging, the first unit of sabotage effort has a higher cost than benefit for player 1 if

$$\frac{1}{n-1} < \Psi'(0). \tag{5.9}$$

This shows that sabotage ceases to be a useful option if many similar players compete for the prize. This result generalizes in an obvious way to the case in which all players have the option of using sabotage, similarly to player 1: for any player i, if all other players do not use sabotage, but use productive efforts according to the Nash equilibrium in the ordinary Tullock lottery contest, then sabotage does not pay for player i if (5.9) holds.

Intuitively, if there are many players and player 1 sabotages player 2, then this reduces 2's relative performance and improves 1's relative performance, but it also improves the relative performance of all other contestants $3, 4, \ldots, n$ by as much as it benefits player 1 himself. This public good aspect of sabotage makes sabotage less desirable if there are many contestants. With sufficiently many contestants, an equilibrium with very little or no sabotage becomes likely (Konrad, 2000a).

Sabotage causes further interesting outcomes if contestants are heterogeneous. Shubik (1954) was probably the first to study heterogeneity of contestants in a problem that is related to sabotage in a game theory model of a contest. In a paper entitled 'Does the fittest necessarily survive?', he considers three shooters of different quality. They shoot at each other in a randomly determined sequence. The shooters are of heterogeneous quality. In the numerical example that follows, their hit probabilities when shooting at an adversary are $p_A = 0.8$, $p_B = 0.7$ and $p_C = 0.6$. Shubik considers sequential shooting and shows that the most able shooter need not survive with the highest probability. Suppose C gets a first chance and can choose whether to shoot at A or B, and hits with the specified probabilities. If C hits, then there is a duel between the remaining shooters. In the rules of this duel, they shoot simultaneously, and hit with the respective probabilities. Accordingly, C is better off if he uses his early shot against A. If he eliminates A, his survival probability is higher than if he eliminates B. If C does not hit, we may assume that a first shot is randomly assigned between A, B and C. Accordingly, if C does not hit, it does not matter whether he has tried to hit A or B. This shows that, choosing between the two alternatives, if shooter C tries to hit, C will try to hit the stronger of the two possible targets. Note that this choice of target is independent of C's own ability to hit. Whoever gets an early chance to eliminate one of the adversaries may use his shot to try to eliminate the stronger of the adversaries. Shubick's rules of shooting between the three players is different, but he comes to similar conclusions. The main mechanism that underlies the example above, and also Shubick's example, is the same: it is more advantageous to eliminate a strong future adversary than a weaker one. This makes the lives of stronger adversaries more dangerous.

Shubick's example reveals a more general mechanism that is explored further by Chen (2003) and Münster (2007a). The latter shows that the availability of sabotage activities in a contest environment has a strongly equalizing property. The contestants who are most productive in turning effort into own output will attract the largest amount of sabotage, so that sabotage leads to an equilibrium in which the probabilities of winning are compressed compared to a world in which sabotage effort is not feasible. Intuitively, if a contestant considers whether to expend additional effort, he has a number of options. He can increase his own performance, or reduce the performance of others. If his first unit of effort has a high marginal effect along all possible dimensions, and if the marginal effect of effort is decreasing sufficiently strongly, then the player will choose his effort such that the marginal cost of an additional unit of effort generates the same marginal benefit along the different types of expenditure. If the player is very strong in turning effort into own output, the player will expend a lot of effort on this, and little effort on sabotaging. Less productive players or players who have a comparative advantage in sabotage activities will expend a larger share of their effort on sabotaging. Moreover, as the most productive player ('the favorite') is the most dangerous competitor, sabotaging him is more effective than sabotaging a player who is likely to lose in any case.

Similar concerns emerge in elimination tournaments when players can try and influence the outcomes of contest rounds that determine their future competitors. If a player A knows he will be in a pairwise contest between players B and C and C is the stronger player, then A may have an incentive to increase B's chances of winning the competition between B and C. Such problems are analyzed in Amegashie and Runkel (2007).

The arguments here about who would prefer to sabotage whom partially rest on the assumption that the contest has one (or few) winner prizes. Different types of contests with other prize structures can yield different results. The incentives for sabotage may change considerably if, for instance, the best $n - 1$ contestants receive a prize. In this case, players try not to be the player with the worst performance, and players may coordinate on sabotaging one player, making it very likely that this player picks the loser prize (see, e.g., Kräkel, 1998; Münster, 2007a).

5.4. Information externalities and campaigning

Contest effort may affect the informational status of players. For this reason, such effort has the potential to exhibit information externalities. In this section I study one type of information externality that may emerge in the context of electoral campaigns. Interest groups may try to affect electoral outcomes and policy choices of elected parties or politicians by making campaign contributions. Also, rival politicians may compete to elicit campaign contributions. Campaign expenditure may affect both the decision whether to vote and the decision about whom to vote for (see, e.g., Rekkas, 2007), and there are multiple channels by which campaign expenditure may affect voters' choices whether to vote, and for whom to vote. Many of these aspects may also interact with one another, and also with other aspects of political competition, which makes political competition a complex matter. However, taken in isolation, all three types of competition have elements of contests. Much like persuasive advertising, campaign contributions may buy favors from politicians, and campaign expenditure may buy vote shares, and some of the literature has adopted this view (see Stratmann, 2005, for a survey). This contest perspective considers the transmission mechanisms from expenditure to decision-making as a black box, and the mechanisms in section 2.3 may yield a partial microeconomic foundation that may underlie this black box.

More detailed views on campaigning and the relationship between campaign effort and election outcomes take into consideration issues such as candidates' ability to raise funds as a function of their ability, ideology and behavior, the distribution of voters regarding their information, their ideology etc. and many other things. Campaign resources may also be used to alter the distribution of information in a voter population, and this may affect the electoral outcome. If, for instance, a party has a superior policy platform or the more able candidate, it may simply try to provide the voters with this evidence, and this may cost effort. However, in a competitive environment it is unlikely that one party platform is simply superior to that of another. Party platforms often differ 'horizontally' in the sense that the platform of party A benefits different voter groups than does the platform of party B. In this case, an interesting paradox can emerge. Parties or candidates may sometimes find it in their interest to expend their campaign money on informing voters that some voter group will be better off if the rival party or candidate wins the election.

An example of this type of behavior emerged in the Presidential election campaigns in 2000 in the USA. The Republicans were planning a change in the tax and transfer system that would benefit a relatively small group of rich citizens. The Democrats pointed out this in the Democratic National Platform (2000: 5): 'The Bush tax slash ... is bigger than any cut Newt Gingrich ever dreamed of. It would let the richest one percent of Americans afford a new sports car and middle class Americans afford a warm soda.' Why would the Democrats like to inform rich voters and high-income earners that they gain substantially from voting for the republicans? Wouldn't this inform this group of voters about a major advantage of voting Republican, and eventually make them vote for the Republicans? This is likely to be the case. But the information revealed about the benefits of the high-income earners also has a second effect. It informs all non-high-income earners that the Bush government will implement a redistributional program that benefits high-income earners. Unless there are major efficiency benefits from such a program, the gains of the rich will imply that some of the non-rich will lose from this program; maybe not all of them, but on average they will lose. If this group is large, the Democrats may win more votes by this information than they lose by informing the very rich about their advantage of voting for Bush. Hence, informing the public about the small group of winners from the Bush redistribution program has an information externality for voters who are not part of this group, but learn something about what the program implies for them in expectation.

The problem can be formalized as follows. Suppose there are only two parties A and B who compete in an election and are purely office motivated. The payoff functions of the parties are given by (1.2), with $v_A = v_B = 1$, and they have constant unit cost of effort. Suppose now that the parties have chosen different policy platforms a and b, and these platforms have different implications for the different voters. Let there be 100 voters, each represented by a square in the large square in Figures 5.1 and 5.2, with the number in the square being the actual payoff difference for this voter from party A being elected, compared to the outcome in which party B is elected. Let 51 among these 100 voters gain 1 unit of income from party A (and not B) being elected, whereas 49 voters lose 1 unit of income. Let us assume further that each voter knows this distribution of gains and losses, but is ignorant about whether he belongs to the group of 51 winners or to the group of 49 losers.

1	1	1	1	1	1	-1	-1	-1	-1
1	1	1	1	1	-1	-1	-1	-1	-1
1	1	1	1	1	-1	-1	-1	-1	-1
1	1	1	1	1	-1	-1	-1	-1	-1
1	1	1	1	1	-1	-1	-1	-1	-1
1	1	1	1	1	-1	-1	-1	-1	-1
1	1	1	1	1	-1	-1	-1	-1	-1
1	1	1	1	1	-1	-1	-1	-1	-1
1	1	1	1	1	-1	-1	-1	-1	-1
1	1	1	1	1	-1	-1	-1	-1	-1

Figure 5.1 All voters are uninformed. Each uninformed voter has a probability of 0.51 of being one of the voters who gain 1 unit from party *A* being elected, and of 0.49 of being one of the voters who lose 1 unit.

The (at least partial) ignorance of voters about their own benefit or loss from one or the other platform is a key assumption, and also plausible. Thinking, for instance, about complex tax reform proposals with many changes, of which some may benefit and some may harm a particular person, and taking the complex general equilibrium repercussions of such a reform into consideration, the voter's uncertainty about whether he gains or loses from the reform is not unlikely. This is particularly true if the tax reform has mainly redistributional consequences and no major efficiency effects. Moreover, the voter's incentive to invest major research effort to resolve his own ignorance is very small: rational ignorance of voters is a well-known feature in political science.[5]

The decision problem for a representative voter can be illustrated using Figure 5.1. If a risk-neutral voter knows he is one of the voters in the grid in Figure 5.1, and has a payoff of either -1 or $+1$, respectively, if party *A* wins rather than party *B*, the voter will calculate his expected payoff for both outcomes and conclude that he is better off by voting for party *A*, as the expected payoff if *A* wins is higher by 2/100. Accordingly, without

[5] These assumptions are not uncommon in the literature on electoral competition; see, e.g., Fernández and Rodrik (1991).

1	1	1	1	1	1	-1	-1	-1	-1
1	1	1	1	1	-1	-1	-1	-1	-1
1	1	1	1	1	-1	-1	-1	-1	-1
1	1	1	1	1	-1	-1	-1	-1	-1
1	1	1	1	1	-1	-1	-1	-1	-1
1	1	1	1	1	-1	-1	-1	-1	-1
1	1	1	1	1	-1	-1	-1	-1	-1
1	1	1	1	1	-1	-1	-1	-1	-1
1	1	1	1	1	-1	-1	-1	-1	-1
1	1	1	1	1	-1	-1	-1	-1	-1

Figure 5.2 Three voters who gain are identified (the ones in the grey boxes). This changes the distribution of gains and losses for the remaining 97 uninformed voters.

any campaigning, party *A* will win the election with 100 percent of the votes.

Consider now party *B*'s incentives to use a particular version of advertising which could be called 'inverse campaigning': let party *B* have the option of identifying a few voters, find out about whether they gain or lose from party *A* winning the election, and be able to inform these voters and a greater public about these findings. Then, if party *B* can identify three voters who gain 1 unit from party *A* being elected, and can credibly publicize this information to all voters, this will change voting behavior. These three voters will now vote for party *A*, as they are sure to be better off if party *A* wins the election. However, all other voters will reconsider their decision. Their expected benefit from voting for party *A* is no longer 2/100, but turns into a negative value, equal to $-1/97$. All 97 uninformed voters will then vote for party *B* and party *B* will win the election.

Of course, the choice of *B* to use inverse campaigning for only three voters is not the equilibrium of this game, as party *A* will optimally react to party *B*'s inverse campaigning. It is straightforward that the equilibrium of this game cannot be in pure strategies. If B decides to inform three voters, then party A may decide to inform two voters who would gain from party B being elected. Of course, then party B would rather like to inform five voters who benefit from A being elected. The reasoning is similar to that describing the all-pay auction without noise, with the units of effort chosen by party A being the number of voters whom party A informs that they gain from voting for B and vice versa. Note also that this mechanism works only as long as the remaining set of uninformed voters is sufficiently large, such that a shift in the voting behavior of this uninformed majority changes the voting outcome. The functioning of this mechanism therefore requires that it is too expensive for one party to inform very large groups of voters. If, for instance, party A could costlessly inform all voters who benefit from A being elected, inverse campaigning could never occur. Konrad (2004c) establishes sufficient conditions for the existence of voting equilibria with inverse campaigning. He uses a continuum of voters, rather than a finite set, to avoid the discontinuity in efforts. Also he discusses instances in which the distribution of benefits of voters from one party winning is more skewed. Intuitively, if this is the case, the groups which gain most or lose most are the prime targets of inverse campaigning if it is known that the difference between party platforms is not a large difference in total output, but rather in how this output is distributed between the groups of voters. If this is the case, the party B particularly gains in terms of shifting support from uninformed voters if it can identify a group of voters who gain very much if party A wins, as this is the most effective means of changing all other voters' expectations about what they can gain or lose from party A's policy.

5.5. Inter-group contests and free riding

A different type of externality emerges if the prize that can be gained by winning a contest is a public good for a well-defined group of recipients. Examples of this can be found in the federalism context. For instance, when a public facility has to be located in some municipality and generates a benefit or a cost to each member of this municipality, the municipality will then fight for or against becoming the location of this facility, depending on whether having the facility is a public good or a public bad for the inhabitants of the municipality where the facility is to be located. Other examples are groups of national producers and consumers who compete with each other about whether an import tariff should be enacted or not, or team sports where teams compete to win the tournament. Everyone in the team who wins will receive the same winner prize, but may value it differently.

Homogeneous groups

Contests for a public good between groups have been analyzed by Katz, Nitzan and Rosenberg (1990) more formally as follows.[6] Let there be two groups 1 and 2. Let n_1 and n_2 be the respective numbers of members of the two groups, and let all group members within each group be identical. The two groups enter into a contest, and one group wins a prize. The prize is a public good that yields each member of the winning group the same benefit that is equal to v_1 and v_2 in the two groups. Each group member can choose to contribute non-negative contest effort to the aggregate effort that is expended by his group, and x_{ij} denotes the effort expended by member j in group i. The individual contributions are summed up to aggregate group effort and the ratio between a group's aggregate effort and the sum of aggregate efforts from both groups equals the group's probability of winning the prize, that is,

$$p_1(...x_{ij}...) = \begin{cases} \frac{\sum_{j=1}^{n_1} x_{1j}}{\sum_{j=1}^{n_1} x_{1j}+\sum_{j=1}^{n_2} x_{2j}} & \text{if} \quad \max\{\ldots x_{ij}\ldots\} > 0 \\ \frac{1}{2} & \text{otherwise.} \end{cases} \tag{5.10}$$

Contestants care about their expected benefit from winning and about their cost of effort. Their payoff is

$$\pi_{ij}(\ldots x_{ij}\ldots) = p_i(\ldots x_{ij}\ldots)v_i - x_{ij}. \tag{5.11}$$

Maximization of (5.11) yields first-order conditions

$$\frac{\partial \pi_{ij}}{\partial x_{ij}} = \frac{\sum_{j=1}^{n_{-i}} x_{(-i)j}}{\left(\sum_{j=1}^{n_1} x_{1j} + \sum_{j=1}^{n_2} x_{2j}\right)^2} v_i - 1 = 0 \tag{5.12}$$

where $-i$ denotes the group other than group i.

The solution of these $n_1 + n_2$ first-order conditions yields a unique solution for the aggregate amounts of effort which are expended by each group in the equilibrium. However, as can be seen from each of these first-order conditions, they do not determine how the aggregate effort of each group is

[6] For related formal analyzes see also Gradstein (1993) and Ursprung (1990).

allocated among the members of the group. Accordingly, the equilibrium is unique as regards group efforts and the winning probabilities of groups, but a multiplicity of equilibria emerges as regards individual contributions to group effort. As all first-order conditions for n_i contestants within a group i are fully identical (and not just symmetric), this reduces to a system of two equations which determines $x_1 \equiv \sum_{j=1}^{n_1} x_{1j}$ and $x_2 \equiv \sum_{j=1}^{n_2} x_{2j}$ and the groups' equilibrium win probabilities as in a contest between two contestants 1 and 2 with valuations of the prize equal to v_1 and v_2. The aggregate effort of a group and its win probability in the equilibrium are hence determined by the valuations v_1 and v_2, and are fully independent of the number of members in the two groups, or the group's relative group size.

This result is in contrast to the fact that the benefits of a group from winning the contest are twice as large if the size of the group doubles. One interpretation of this result is that free riding intensifies if groups grow larger, and that the increase in free riding just compensates for the additional incentives of the group to win the prize. However, this interpretation is misleading, as can be seen when modifying one of the assumptions made in the analysis.

Heterogeneous groups

Consider the following modification in the analysis by Katz, Nitzan and Rosenberg (1990), which is discussed more formally by Baik (1993). Let the groups consist of heterogeneous members, all of whom value the public good differently, and let $v_{ij} > 0$ be the valuation of the prize by member j in group i. Carrying through the same equilibrium analysis leads to $n_1 + n_2$ first-order conditions like (5.12), but with v_i replaced by the individual valuations v_{ij}. It is not possible to fulfill all these conditions for all ij if there are at least two members of the same group whose valuations of winning the group prize differ. Given the valuations of the prize by members of group i, let

$$v_i^* \equiv \max\{v_{i1}, \dots v_{in_i}\}$$

define the highest among these valuations. If all members of a group differ in their valuation of winning the group prize, then the equilibrium is described by

$$x_{1k} = x_1^* = \frac{v_2^* v_1^* v_1^*}{(v_1^* + v_2^*)^2} \quad \text{for } k \text{ with} \quad v_{1k} = v_1^* \tag{5.13}$$

and

$$x_{1k} = 0 \quad \text{for all } k \text{ in group 1 with} \quad v_{1k} < \max\{v_{11}, \dots v_{1n_i}\} \tag{5.14}$$

and analogously for group 2, with '2' replacing '1' in (5.13) and (5.14) and vice versa. Accordingly, if the group members differ in their valuations of the public good, only the members with the highest valuation make contributions to the inter-group contest. This is a known result from the theory of public goods when the payoff functions of the voluntary contributors to the public good are linear in income, as is assumed in the context here. The result also reveals the appropriate intuition for the results in Katz, Nitzan and Rosenberg (1990). The aggregate amount of effort is independent of group size. It is determined by what the group member with the highest valuation of the prize would be willing to expend if he were the only contestant. As long as the group size does not change the member with the highest valuation of the prize, it does not affect the aggregate group effort in the equilibrium.

Other contest success functions

The outcome that makes only the group member who likes the public good most contribute to group effort (or to a group-specific public good more generally), as in the case considered by Katz, Nitzan and Rosenberg (1990) or in the case with a heterogeneous group, can be extended to the larger class of contest success functions in which the probability that group i wins is a function $p_i(x_1, x_2)$ of the aggregate group efforts of the various groups. Nti (1998) considers the special case $p_i(x_1, x_2) = \varphi(x_i)/(\varphi(x_1) + \varphi(x_2))$ for $i \in \{1, 2\}$.

The result is also robust with respect to the case in which the group that makes the highest group effort wins with probability 1. This is illustrated by Baik, Kim, and Na (2001). Consider, for instance, two groups 1 and 2 with n_1 and n_2 members and valuations v_{ij}, respectively, and let the size of the valuations within a group be sorted so that $v_{i1} > v_{i2} \geq \cdots \geq v_{in_i} \geq 0$. Assume further that $v_{11} > v_{21}$. Each individual can choose his own contest effort. All group members' contest efforts add up to x_1 and x_2, respectively. Replacing the Tullock contest success function as in Katz, Nitzan and Rosenberg (1990) with the all-pay auction as in (2.1) leads to an equilibrium in which $x_{ij} = 0$ for all $j \neq 1$ and in which group members 1 in the two groups choose mixed strategies with their efforts x_{11} and x_{21} according to the equilibrium strategies (2.2) and (2.3). Hence, if two groups bid for the allocation of a group-specific public good and each group's members make their contributions in a non-cooperative fashion, the problem reduces to a contest between the set of members who have the highest valuation in their group. All other group members choose zero effort.

The intuition for the result is as follows. Consider the equilibrium strategy for aggregate group effort that is described by $F_1(x_1)$ as in (2.2), with v_2 replaced by v_{21}, making use of $v_{21} = \max\{v_{21}, \ldots v_{2n_1}\}$. For this choice, consider the member of group 2 who has the highest valuation v_{21}. If this individual anticipates that all other group members will make zero contributions, he is just indifferent about effort choices from the interval $[0, v_{21}]$ and may just randomize on this interval according to $F_2(x_2)$ as in (2.3), again with v_{21} replacing v_2 and v_{11} replacing v_1. All other individuals would not choose any positive effort given $F_1(x_1)$ as they have a lower valuation of the prize than v_{21}. This establishes that $F_2(x_2)$ with $x_{21} = x_2$ and $x_{2j} = 0$ for all $j > 1$ is an optimal reply to $F_1(x_1)$.

The argument for why this equilibrium $F_2(x_2)$ makes player $j = 1$ in group $i = 1$ just indifferent regarding a choice of effort from the equilibrium support $[0, v_{21}]$ and makes all players $j > 1$ in this group strictly prefer $x_{1j} = 0$ follows analogous lines.

The discussion in the section of the all-pay auction without noise suggests also that this solution generalizes to more than two groups which compete for the prize, and for cases in which there is one or several groups in which there is more than one member who has the highest valuation within this group.

Making the 'group' size meaningful

The result, according to which group size does not matter and effort is determined by the group members who value the public good most highly, is sensitive to, for instance, the linear cost assumption. This has been highlighted, for example, in Konrad (1993: 70–72), Esteban and Ray (2001) for the case of convex cost, and by Riaz, Shogren, and Johnson (1995) for the case of increasing marginal opportunity cost of individually devoting additional resources to the group contest. If, for instance, $C_i(x_i) = C(x_i)$ with $C' > 0$ and $C'' > 0$, this leads to first-order conditions

$$\frac{x_2}{(x_1 + x_2)^2} v_{1j} = C'(x_{1j}) \quad \text{and} \quad \frac{x_1}{(x_1 + x_2)^2} v_{2j} = C'(x_{2j}) \tag{5.15}$$

for individuals $1j$ and $2j$ in groups 1 and 2. This makes interior solutions feasible for all group members, even if they differ in their valuations of the group prize. Moreover, suppose the group effort x_1 of group 1 is given and consider an increase in the size of group 2. Let $x_2^*(x_1)$ be the aggregate effort that group 2 would expend when anticipating x_1 by group 1 in the Nash equilibrium. Then x_2^* would typically be an increasing function of group 2's size. To see this, consider the simple case in which the group size increases from $n_2 = 1$ to $n_2 = 2$, and let the new group member have the same valuation of the group-specific public good. Suppose both group members were to stick to the same aggregate quantity x_2^* that was optimal for $n_2 = 1$, implying that both would have to contribute only $x_2^*/2$. If the first-order condition (5.15) was fulfilled for x_2^* and $n_2 = 1$, then

$$\frac{x_1}{(x_1 + x_2^*(x_1))^2} v_2 > C'(x_2^*/2) \tag{5.16}$$

would result. Both group members would like to increase their contributions until the new aggregate equilibrium effort by group 2 is reached.

In the inter-group contest, the individual effort contributions to the aggregate group effort are contributions to a public good, where the quantity of the public good could be defined as $p_i(x_1, x_2)$, the probability of winning the contest, and $p_i(x_1, x_2)v_{ij}$ are the individual valuations of the public good. For given (or anticipated) aggregate effort of the competing group, the voluntary contributions of effort are therefore equivalent to the problem of voluntary contributions to a public good, one which has been carefully studied.[7] The assumption of additivity, or of perfect substitutability of individual contributions, has a prominent role in this literature. However, this literature has also emphasized that contributions to a public good could follow different patterns. For instance, Hirshleifer (1983) discusses the additivity assumption and illustrates its crucial aspects for the equilibrium results by considering the cases in which the aggregate provision level is determined by the smallest or the highest contribution within the group. More generally, imperfect substitutability of contest efforts is a possible channel through which the group aspects of inter-group contests for public goods become meaningful.

Group size may also be important if the prize is a congestible public good, that is, if the prize is a common property resource. Nitzan and Ueda (2008) consider this case, essentially using the framework of Esteban and Ray (2001), and replacing the pure group public good by a common property resource with open access. The common property is overused by the members of the winning group. This reduces the value of winning the prize, compared to a situation in which the winning group chooses an efficient exclusion mechanism to implement efficient usage of the common property resource. As the group values winning less highly, the members of the group engage less actively in the inter-group conflict.

[7] See, e.g., Bergstrom, Blume, and Varian (1986), Cornes and Sandler (1986), and Batina and Ihori (2005).

Moreover, the amount of overuse of the common pool resource depends on group size. Accordingly, larger groups may have an advantage in terms of aggregate contribution cost, if each group member's contribution cost is strictly convex, but group size may also be disadvantageous, as it drives down each single individual's benefit from winning, due to the crowding externalities.

5.6. Summary

In this chapter five types of externalities that add to, or interact with, the fundamental mutually negative externalities of efforts in contests have been considered.

First, if the surplus that is generated in a lottery contest is used to finance a public good, then a player's contest effort has several effects for other players: it reduces other players' win probabilities, but other players also benefit from the higher amount of resources available for public good provision. As an outcome, a lottery contest may generate a surplus, and by suitable design, this surplus can be made very large.

Second, a contestant typically prefers winning the prize in a contest. However, if a contestant does not win the prize, he or she may have a preference about who of the other contestants wins the prize. This generates another type of externality, as a player A who prefers that player B wins rather than player C gains from player B's additional contest effort. Section 5.2 studied a framework in which such externalities emerge naturally: where firms hold ownership shares in other firms. As a result, such share cross-holdings may influence the equilibrium in which firms compete for business contracts in a contest.

Third, contestants may expend effort that sabotages the performance of some of their competitors. If sabotage is feasible, this has implications for the design of contests. In a contest with one prize, if there is a favorite, this player will be a prime target of other players' sabotage. In a contest with many winner prizes and only one or very few loser prizes, some of the weakest players may become the prime target of sabotage effort. Also, sabotage is more likely to occur if the group of contestants is small, as sabotage effort by one player harms one other player, but also benefits the players who were neither sabotaging nor the target of sabotage.

Fourth, contest effort may have information externalities. This was shown in section 5.4 for a problem of electoral competition. Campaign spending in elections that inform voters about their own advantages from one or the other electoral outcome may reveal important information for the voters who are not directly approached.

Fifth, a player's contest effort may have positive externalities for other players if these players belong to the same group and if groups complete for a prize that benefits all members of the winning group. In this case, the member who contributes to his group's contest effort makes a contribution to a group-specific public good. This problem was studied in section 5.5. The analysis shows that contest effort that can be mobilized in a non-cooperative equilibrium of inter-group contests is low compared to the values at stake if the groups are large and homogeneous.

6

Nested contests

Conflict often takes place between groups, and examples of this have been discussed in section 5.5 on inter-group contests for public goods. Such conflict ends once the inter-group contest has determined a winner if the prize that is awarded to the winning group is a good that all group members can consume or if the allocation of the good within the group cannot be influenced by group members. In many cases, the inter-group contest is about private goods, and the conflict does not necessarily end once the contest prize is allocated to one of the groups, or once its shares are allocated to the different groups.

Examples come from war, politics, sports, federalism, corporate governance, and other areas of conflict. Consider, for instance, the coalition of the US, Russia, France, the UK, and others who joined forces to defeat Germany, Japan, Italy and other members of the 'Axis' in the Second World War. Once the Second World War was over, the US and the Soviet Union emerged as super powers and started to struggle over how to divide the world between them. War and pillage is another illustrative example. Consider a medieval army that tries to conquer a city. This is a contest between two groups: the attacking army and the city population. Once the army has succeeded in conquering the city, the members of the victorious army may have pillaged the city and divided the spoils among themselves. In politics, leading figures inside a political party often join forces prior to an election, trying to get their party into power. Once this goal is achieved, they may start struggling about who will obtain which office, or who will eventually become the party leader. The first and second triumvirates in ancient Rome is another example. The coalitions that were formed initially helped the triumvirate to win power collectively. Later, each member of the triumvirate tried to increase his own share of this power, or to become the sole leader. Sports contests provide further examples. Many types of sports contests take place between teams. This implies that a team player's own effort benefits himself only if it improves his team's performance. A football player can win the world championship only if his team wins the football championship. However, the winning team in a championship is not fully homogeneous. Not only do players have a different, more or less charming appearance and their own personality; they also differ visibly in their contribution to their team's success. Accordingly, they do not all get the same prize from winning the championship, and it is probably true that, within teams, there is rivalry about who receives higher recognition and can earn higher benefits from media attention, sponsoring and ego rents. Wärneryd (1998) suggests federal structures as another example, in which players within regions may join forces to try to obtain some share in the global budget, and once a region succeeds, there is a struggle about how to allocate it between them. Other examples comprise corporate governance issues as in Inderst, Müller, and Wärneryd (2005) and Müller and Wärneryd (2001).

It seems plausible that the rules that govern the allocation of the prize will affect the group members' efforts in winning the battle. A number of different cases do need to be distinguished, but a unified framework will be used to describe them, building on the notation introduced in section 5.5, and both the Tullock contest and the all-pay auction case will be considered.

6.1. Exogenous sharing rules

If two groups compete and the group members make contributions to the group's effort to win the inter-group contest, these very contributions may also influence the allocation of the prize inside the winning group.[1] To illustrate, if parties compete for power, party members may engage actively in speeches or other promotional activities, and their effort may indeed be rewarded by a higher share in the rents accruing to such members if the party gets into power. More formally, let there be two groups 1 and 2 with n_1 and n_2 the respective numbers of members of the two groups, and let the members within each group all be identical. The two groups enter into a contest for which of them wins a prize. The prize is of size v and awarded to the group as a function of aggregate efforts of the group members; that

[1] This analysis is closely related to Nitzan (1991a).

is, the contest success function for the inter-group contest is

$$p_i(\ldots x_{ij}\ldots) = \begin{cases} \dfrac{x_i}{x_1+x_2} & \text{if} \quad \max\{x_1, x_2\} > 0 \\ \dfrac{1}{2} & \text{otherwise,} \end{cases} \tag{6.1}$$

where $x_{ij} \geq 0$ is the effort contribution of member j in group i, and $x_i \equiv \sum_{j=1}^{n_i} x_{ij}$. Once group i wins the contest, the distribution of the prize v between the group members is also determined. Member j in group i receives a share

$$q_{ij} = \begin{cases} (1-\alpha)\dfrac{x_{ij}}{x_i} + \alpha\dfrac{1}{n_i} & \text{if} \quad \max\{\ldots x_{ij}\ldots\} > 0 \\ \dfrac{1}{n_i} & \text{otherwise.} \end{cases} \tag{6.2}$$

One interpretation of the rule (6.2) is that the prize is allocated according to 'merit' with a probability $1-\alpha$ inside the group, and according to a random mechanism that gives each group member the same chance of winning with the remaining probability α. In the 'merit' regime, each group member wins the prize with a probability that equals his own share in the aggregate group effort.

Nitzan (1991a) describes the equilibrium by the first-order condition for maximizing the objective function of contestant j in group i,

$$\pi_{ij}(\ldots x_{ij}\ldots) = p_i q_{ij} v - x_{ij}, \tag{6.3}$$

and the first-order condition for $i = 1$ is

$$(1-\alpha)v\frac{x_1 + x_2 - x_{1j}}{(x_1+x_2)^2} + \alpha v \frac{x_2}{(x_1+x_2)^2}\frac{1}{n_1} - 1 = 0, \tag{6.4}$$

and analogously for a player j from group $i = 2$.

For $\alpha = 0$, use of symmetry of players inside a group yields

$$x_{ij}^* = \frac{n_1 + n_2 - 1}{(n_1+n_2)^2}v. \tag{6.5}$$

This effort is the same as emerges in the equilibrium in a standard Tullock lottery contest among $n_1 + n_2$ identical contestants. This structural equivalence is due, and sensitive to, the specific choice of the contest success function in the inter-group contest and how it corresponds to the sharing rule that applies in the winner group. The result also follows directly from consideration of (6.3) if p_i and q_{ij} are replaced by their actual values as in

(6.1) and (6.2), as x_i cancels out and the payoff function as in the standard Tullock contest remains.

For $\alpha = 1$,

$$x_1^* = \frac{n_2}{(n_1 + n_2)^2} v \quad \text{and} \quad x_2^* = \frac{n_1}{(n_1 + n_2)^2} v. \tag{6.6}$$

For $n_1 = n_2 = n$, each group's aggregate effort becomes $x_i = v/(4n)$. The aggregate effort levels are thus identical to those in a contest between two players for a prize of size v/n, which is indeed the prize that each contestant competes for in this problem.

Note also that the individual effort levels are undetermined for $\alpha = 1$. This result resembles the case of inter-group contests for the allocation of a prize that is a group-specific public good, or the result for the private provision of a public good with homogeneous contributors with quasi-linear preferences who all have constant marginal contribution cost. Indeed, given the fixed and perfectly symmetric sharing rule, the prize is like a public good that benefits all members of the winning group equally, and here the contribution cost is assumed to be strictly linear. Moreover, if the contributors in the group had different, but constant marginal opportunity cost of effort, or had equal and constant marginal opportunity cost of effort, but value winning the prize differently, the contributor with the least cost of contributing within a group, or with the highest valuation of the prize, would become the only contributor. As in the context of private provision of a public good, these strange features of the equilibrium outcome disappear once the marginal opportunity cost of effort is no longer constant, as has been discussed in the context of strategic aspects of public good contests between groups.[2]

6.2. The choice of sharing rules

One can now ask what happens if groups have different sharing rules or can choose the weights they would like to give to merit or to pure chance in the intra-group allocation of the prize.[3] Suppose groups can choose their own α_i in (6.2) prior to each group member's effort choice. The first-order conditions need not be suitable for describing the equilibrium in the

[2] Priks (2002) considers an interesting application of the inter-group contest structure to the competition between firms. Firms constitute teams that may contest with each other for contracts. The governance structure inside the firms and their size have implications for the firms' competitiveness.

[3] These questions are addressed in Nitzan (1991b) and Lee (1995).

inter-group contest if the two groups have chosen sufficiently different weights α_1 and α_2. To give an example, let $\alpha_1 = 0$ and $\alpha_2 = 1$. In this case there is an equilibrium with

$$x_2 = 0 \quad \text{and} \quad x_1 = v\frac{n_1 - 1}{n_1} \tag{6.7}$$

if $n_1, n_2 \geq 2$. To see this, consider the contribution incentives in group 1 if the members of group 2 do not contribute. Their contribution incentives are the same as in a simple symmetric Tullock contest with n_1 contestants. Accordingly, the aggregate contributions made by group 1 will be $x_1 = v\frac{n_1-1}{n_1}$. For these contributions of group 1, consider now the individual incentives for members in group 2 to contribute. Suppose that all members $j = 2, \ldots n_2$ contribute zero. In this case, the objective function for group member 1 in this group 2 is

$$\pi_{21} = \frac{x_{21}}{x_{21} + x_1}\frac{v}{n_2} - x_{21} \tag{6.8}$$

Now,

$$\frac{\partial \pi_{21}}{\partial x_{21}} = \frac{x_1}{(x_{21} + x_1)^2}\frac{v}{n_2} - 1. \tag{6.9}$$

Inserting (6.7) yields

$$\frac{\partial \pi_{21}}{\partial x_{21}} < 0 \quad \text{at} \quad x_{21} = 0 \quad \text{if} \quad n_2 n_1 > n_1 + n_2. \tag{6.10}$$

Davis and Reilly (1999) characterized these corner equilibria that emerged in the problem studied by Nitzan (1991b). Their analysis highlights the importance of corner solutions in contest games with asymmetry.[4] In many instances, contestants would be wise to stay out of the contest if other contestants enter who are more motivated, either by a higher prize or by a lower cost of effort. In the case studied by Nitzan, the contestants in the group that allocates the winning prize according to 'merit' are far more motivated to expend effort than those in the group in which the prize is allocated according to some egalitarian rule. Members of this group contribute to two contests simultaneously when making contributions to group effort. They make it more likely that their group will win, and they increase their own share in the prize if their group does win. This latter incentive is strong enough to induce high effort choices that also count for the group's effort in the inter-group effort, even though the group does not really face any serious competition from the other group.

[4] For an analysis of possible corner solutions, see also Ueda (2002).

6.3. Intra-group conflict

That group members' contributions to the inter-group contest influence the intra-group allocation of a prize once the prize is allocated to a group may be seen as being in line with some broad views on equity. Moreover, from the perspective of the group, it is advantageous to use such a rule as an incentive mechanism to make the group members contribute. It is often more plausible, however, that group members will struggle about the intra-group allocation of the prize. For this internal struggle, it may then be of secondary importance whether a member contributed much or little to the inter-group conflict. As shown by Baik and Lee (1998), a group may prefer an exogenous, egalitarian sharing rule compared to an intra-group contest, but this need not be a matter of choice, and the intra-group contest may simply be the time-consistent outcome. The intra-group allocation can then be seen as the outcome of an intra-group contest in which the members' contributions to the inter-group contest are sunk and irrelevant to the intra-group allocation of the prize. The example of the conquest of a city and the pillage and plundering that may occur once a city has been conquered may illustrate this. Other examples that are more closely related to standard topics in economics have also been used to study this problem. The first paper on this topic in which the group prize is contested among the members of the winning group once the winning group has been determined is Katz and Tokatlidu (1996). They analyze this type of problem and provide the comparative statics with respect to group size.

This hierachical structure may expend less effort in total than a one-stage contest in which no group structures exist and the prize is allocated in a single Tullock contest with all members of all groups competing simultaneously in a grand contest. A more hierarchical structure can, hence, be advantageous or disadvantageous, depending on whether contest effort is undesirable or desirable. Wärneryd (1998) focuses on a situation in which contest effort is wasteful, in an application with regions in a federation defining the groups in the inter-group conflict. Müller and Wärneryd (2001) consider the role of outsiders in the ownership of a firm and show that the mere existence of such a group and its incentives to expend effort in trying to appropriate some share in the earnings may mitigate the distributional conflict between the insiders in the firm. Inderst, Müller, and Wärneryd (2005) identify similar structures in the context of allocating free cash flow for investment between divisions inside the firm.

I will illustrate the role of a hierarchical structure for the overall contest effort compared to the grand single stage contest between all contestants, as in Wärneryd (1998), and then turn to the analysis of asymmetries, focusing on the all-pay auction.

Contest effort moderation by hierarchies

Consider a prize that all contestants value equally as v.[5] Suppose there are $n \geq 2$ groups that compete for the prize in an inter-group conflict. For simplicity, let each group consist of m homogeneous members. Let x_{ij} be j's contribution to group i's effort in the inter-group conflict as before. Let y_j be the effort of member j in the winning group in the intra-group contest that emerges once the group is victorious in the inter-group conflict. These intra-group conflict efforts are chosen only after the inter-group conflict has been decided. These efforts y_j determine the allocation of the prize inside the group according to the rules of a Tullock lottery contest (2.39) with $r = 1$. Further, let the contest success function in the inter-group conflict be of the same functional form as (6.1) with inter-group efforts $x_i = \Sigma_{j=1}^{j=m} x_{ij}$ that are chosen independently of intra-group efforts.

Solving the problem recursively, suppose group i was the victor and received the prize. The contest among the group members that emerges is identical with the standard Tullock contest, and individual and aggregate effort and payoffs are

$$y_j^* = \frac{m-1}{m^2}v, \quad \sum_{j=1}^{m} y_j^* = \frac{m-1}{m}v, \quad \text{and} \quad \pi_j^* = \frac{v}{m^2}. \tag{6.11}$$

Note that the members of the winning group use up considerable resources in the intra-group conflict, compared to a peaceful allocation inside the group. This reduces the value of winning the prize for each group member from v/m to v/m^2 and for the whole group from v to v/m.

Turning to the inter-group conflict, when thinking about his effort choice in the inter-group conflict each of the members of group i considers what is at stake for him. As in a game of voluntary contributions to a public good, each member chooses his own inter-group conflict effort so as to increase his group's aggregate effort to the amount he considers individually optimal, or abstains from making a positive effort and leaves it to others to compete, if what the others contribute is above his individually optimal threshold level. Symmetry will cause all members of group

[5] This analysis is a variant of Wärneryd (1998), who considers the case with two groups of different sizes.

i to prefer the same aggregate group effort x_i, and the objective function that guides their choices is

$$\frac{x_i}{\sum_{k=1}^{n} x_k} \frac{v}{m^2} - x_{ij}. \tag{6.12}$$

Taking into consideration that $\partial x_i / \partial x_{ij} = 1$, this yields aggregate group efforts and win probabilities in the equilibrium as in the standard Tullock contest with $\pi_j^* = \frac{v}{m^2}$ as the winner prize. Hence,

$$x_i^* = \frac{n-1}{n^2} \frac{v}{m^2}, \quad \sum_{i=1}^{n} \sum_{j=1}^{m} x_{ij}^* = \frac{n-1}{nm^2} v. \tag{6.13}$$

Taking into consideration the equilibrium efforts in the continuation game in the winner group, the aggregate payoff that is not dissipated in the two-stage contest is

$$\left(1 - \frac{n-1}{nm^2} - \frac{m-1}{m}\right) v. \tag{6.14}$$

The payoffs that result for the grand single-stage contest in which all nm contestants compete with each other in a single stage, assuming that the random mechanism that determines the winner in this contest is the same lottery contest success function, is simply

$$\left(1 - \frac{nm-1}{nm}\right) v. \tag{6.15}$$

Comparing (6.14) with (6.15) reveals that

$$1 - \frac{n-1}{nm^2} - \frac{m-1}{m} - 1 + \frac{nm-1}{nm} = \frac{(m-1)(n-1)}{nm^2}. \tag{6.16}$$

The numerator of (6.16) is strictly positive if there is more than one group and more than one player in each group. Hence, the hierarchical structure dissipates less effort in total than the grand simultaneous contest.

There are several forces at work explaining why the hierarchical structure may dissipate less rent. The most important effect that also emerges if the groups in the inter-group contest are not of equal size, is a collective action problem. Groups do not compete according to what the group gets as rent if the group wins the contest, but decisions are made by each single group member. Each member of a group considers what he or she expects to win if the group wins, and considers whether it is in this member's interest to expand the amount of contributions that others make by own contributions. For instance, if one group member j already expends the inter-group effort that characterizes his group's equilibrium effort, then all other group members would not like to further increase it, but rather free-ride on this contribution. This is one possible equilibrium. But there is a whole continuum of equilibria, all characterized by the same group efforts in the inter-group conflict, but composed of different vectors of individual group members' contributions. If all other group members' contributions sum up to less than the contribution that is optimal from the perspective of a single group member j who—by his own contribution that adds to the contributions of others—chooses aggregate group effort, then j increases the group contributions filling up the difference between what is optimal for j and what the other group members had already contributed. For instance, if groups consist of two players, the rent that can be gained by the group as a whole in the inter-group contest is $v/2$, which takes into consideration that half of the prize v is dissipated in the intra-group conflict that takes place if the group wins the prize in the inter-group contest. However, the group members behave non-cooperatively inside the group, adjusting the group effort such that the marginal additional effort is just optimal from their individual perspective. The group's aggregate effort in the equilibrium is the same as that which would result from coordinated group effort for a group prize of size $v/4$. Hence, the free-rider problem shelters some of the later rents from competition. For instance, if all groups in the final stage are of size $m = 2$, this will shelter one-quarter of the total rent from competition. For this group size, this is a lower bound on dissipation for the Tullock contest with $r = 1$, regardless of how many groups compete with each other in the first stage, and how many players are involved in total.

In this framework, the effort that is expended in the inter-group contest does not increase or diminish players' ability to compete in the intra-group contest, as the cost of effort in the intra-group contest does not depend on the effort that has already been expended. This simplifies the exposition, but also assumes away an important channel for further interaction between the two types of contest. Münster (2007b) considers a framework in which all players have an exogenously given budget which can be used only for investing in production, as intra-group conflict effort and as inter-group conflict effort. Contributing an additional unit to the group's aggregate effort in the inter-group contest then typically increases a player's opportunity cost of intra-group effort. Changes in the nature of the inter-group conflict that induce higher effort in this contest will then typically decrease effort expended in the intra-group contest.

Asymmetric valuations

If members of a group individually choose their contributions to the group's effort in a conflict with another group, these efforts are contributions to a group–public good. This does not imply that all members of the group gain similarly if the group wins the conflict. Moreover, different group members may have a different opportunity cost of making contributions. Such asymmetries are known to play an important role in the theory of private provision to a public good. As has been emphasized in this literature, players who gain more or have a lower contribution cost than others overproportionally contribute to the public good.[6] The role of asymmetry among contestants with respect to their valuations of winning the prize or effort cost differences therefore matter for how the members share in the burden of aggregate group effort, but also for the aggregate effort that results.

The effects of asymmetry are most pronounced and easiest to derive in conflicts in which small differences in effort are decisive, that is, if the contest success function is given by (2.1). Konrad (2004b) studies the role of asymmetry among players in this framework. In order to find closed-form solutions, he replaces the contest success function (2.39) in the framework above with (2.1). The main insight can be obtained from the following example. Consider the set of all players from all groups. Let players differ in their valuations of the prize, but let all have the same constant marginal cost of effort. Let the elements of the set of players be renumbered according to their valuation of the prize, with $h = 1$ the player with the highest valuation, and player $h = nm$ the player with the lowest valuation of the prize. Assume further that strict inequality applies, that is, $v_h > v_{h+1}$. This strict inequality eliminates some cases with multiple equilibria and simplifies the exposition. Consider first the grand single-stage contest among this set of players. This is the all-pay auction with nm players that has already been studied in section 2.1. It will give a positive payoff only to player 1, who has the highest valuation of the prize among all players, and this payoff will be equal to the difference between his valuation v_1 and the valuation v_2 of player 2. Moreover, it will elicit effort which, in expectation, sums up to $\frac{v_2}{2}(1 + \frac{v_2}{v_1})$ in the unique equilibrium. If, instead, the players are allocated to n groups of size m, consider the incentives of players to contribute to an inter-group contest if they know that this contest is followed by an intra-group contest within the group of players that wins the prize.

[6] For a survey see Batina and Ihori (2005).

Players in each group know that, once their group wins the inter-group contest, only the player with the highest valuation will win some positive expected payoff in the intra-group contest for this prize, and this player in group i knows that his payoff will be equal to $v_{i1} - v_{i2}$, that is, the difference between his own valuation v_{i1}, and v_{i2}, which is the second highest valuation of the prize in this group i. Accordingly, all players in a group who do not have the highest valuation in their group have nothing to gain if their own group wins the prize. Therefore, they will not contribute to their group's effort in the inter-group contest. Concentrating on subgame perfect equilibrium, the equilibrium behavior in the continuation game reduces the inter-group contest to a contest between the players who have the highest valuation in their respective group, and defines their valuation of their group winning the inter-group contest as the respective difference $v_{i1} - v_{i2}$ for groups $i = 1, ...n$. This sets the stage for the inter-group contest. If one assumes, for convenience, that the groups are numbered such that the differences $v_{i1} - v_{i2}$ are descending in i and that, in addition, $v_{21} - v_{22} > v_{31} - v_{32}$ holds strictly, the inter-group contest becomes essentially equivalent to the all-pay auction with complete information between players 11 and 21, who compete for prizes of size $v_{11} - v_{12}$ and $v_{21} - v_{22}$.

The outcome in the hierarchical contest has interesting implications. One implication is that even the bidders who have the highest valuation of the prize may have a zero probability of winning the prize. Consider the following numerical example. Let there be six players who value prizes as $1001, 1000, 12, 10, 3, 1$, and let them be sorted into groups $G_1 = \{1001, 1000\}$, $G_2 = \{12, 10\}$, $G_3 = \{3, 1\}$. Note that the players in group G_1 will not actively bid in the inter-group contest. The player who has the highest valuation in this group wins a payoff of only 1 unit in the intra-group contest if his group wins the prize. The players with the highest valuations in groups G_2 and G_3 win a payoff equal to 2 if their group wins the inter-group contest. Hence, the prize will end up with group G_2 or G_3, and, by the choice of the numbers, it will end up in each of the two groups with equal probability. Once G_2 or G_3 wins the inter-group contest, the members of the respective group will compete in an all-pay auction without noise to win the prize. This shows that even the contestant with the smallest valuation of the prize has a considerable probability of 1/12 of winning the prize. The players with the highest valuations of winning never win the prize in this numerical example.

6.4. Summary: a strategy analysis of nested contests

Group competitions for prizes involve several strategic aspects. Groups would like to overcome the free-rider problem when making contributions to group effort. Groups must also solve the problem of how to allocate a given prize among its members in case the group wins the prize. The incentives of group members to contribute effort to the contest between groups depends on their expectations about the aggregate effort that is provided by the other group, their expectations about other group members' contributions to group effort, and on their own expected benefit from their own group winning the prize. This latter aspect causes a close link between intra-group allocation processes and a group's competitiveness in inter-group competition. A group member's willingness to expend effort is typically increasing in the benefit which the individual player expects to gain from the player's group winning the contest.

If groups can choose a peaceful intra-group allocation of a prize that makes each player's reward a function of all group players' efforts, groups may have incentives to choose a rule that provides incentives for players to contribute more, in order to overcome the free-rider problem. A merit rule, for instance, will provide higher group effort than an egalitarian rule. In finding the optimal rule, many aspects may play a role. Among these are asymmetries among players inside a group. Strategic considerations may also play a role. If the division rule is observed by rival groups, the rule may play a role as a commitment device. Considerations similar to the ones on the commitment value of delegation would become relevant.

The group's coordination problem in the inter-group contest is less easy to solve if the group suffers from a time-consistency problem and cannot commit on an exogenous intra-group distribution rule. In this case, group members anticipate that what their group wins is worth less than the value of the prize, because they will dissipate part of this prize when competing internally about its distribution inside the group. Winning the prize becomes less valuable in such a context, and this explains why inter-group contest effort is reduced in such a framework.

The intra-group contest shelters some of the rent that is allocated between the groups from being competed away in the inter-group contest. This may sometimes be beneficial from a welfare point of view, if contest effort is wasteful, as the aggregate contest effort in the inter-group contest and the intra-group contest combined may be lower than in a single-stage grand contest. From the strategic perspective of a single group, what might be socially beneficial is to the group's disadvantage. In the inter-group contest, a group collectively suffers from lack of commitment: the looming intra-group contest weakens the group and does not allow the group to mobilize much group effort.

A further result concerns the efficiency of conflict with respect to allocating the prize to those contestants who value it more highly. In this respect, a conflict hierarchy with an intra-group contest following an inter-group contest may introduce a major distortion. If the competition is particularly strong within groups with players who value the prize very highly, and less strong in groups with players who value the prize not highly, then the inter-group contest may allocate the prize to a group with players who value the prize not highly, and eventually the prize may end up with a contestant who values it much less than other contestants.[7]

The analysis leading to these results was carried out assuming that group efforts add up to a group's aggregate effort. The aggregation of effort in a conflict between groups may follow very different rules. Hirshleifer (1983) suggested that the aggregation of individual provisions to a public good need not be additive, nor even continuous. He provided a number of examples for which the aggregate group effort is essentially determined by the highest effort that is expended by a member of the group; he called this case *best shot*. He also provides examples in which the aggregate effort is essentially determined by the smallest effort that is made by a member from the group; he referred to such situations as cases of *weakest link*. Not much is known about the strategic interaction between and inside groups if the group effort is determined by such functions.

[7] Our discussion of this topic was in the context of a full information framework. Hierarchical contests in the context of incomplete information are a challenging field for future research: the outcome in previous conflict stages may reveal some information about the players' strength or their desire to win. Depending on what is actually observed in previous contest stages, this leads to strategic considerations of information revelation which are absent in a complete information framework.

7

Alliances

The analysis of nested contests has taken the composition of groups in the inter-group contest as exogenous. If more than two players compete for a prize, one or several subgroups of players may, but need not, form such an alliance. The formation of such groups is a very widespread phenomenon in politics, business and in the context of military conflict. The alliance between the USA and Russia during the Second World War, for instance, has been mentioned as an example already. The alliance emerged voluntarily, suggesting that it was perceived as useful for the Allied Forces in their goal of defeating Nazi Germany. When the end of the war came closer, however, a divergence of interests among the Allied Forces became visible. It was not difficult to anticipate that the alliance might break up after the defeat of Germany and that a conflict between the two large victorious countries might emerge. Rational politicians in the respective countries might therefore have anticipated what is now known as the Cold War. The conferences that took place prior to the termination of the war (e.g., the Moscow Conference, October 1944, and the Yalta Conference, February 1945) may partially be seen as attempts to reach an agreement regarding the division of the gains of winning the war, in order to reduce the scope of conflict between the members of the Allied Forces. Part of the agreement, for instance, was the division of the defeated regions into spheres of influence. As is well-known now, these attempts have been only partially successful. The agreements were seemingly not time consistent. They did not solve the fundamental conflict and competition about political dominance, and about which was to be the future social and economic world order.

Nevertheless, the looming conflict between some of the Allied Forces obviously did not prevent them from fighting jointly in an alliance, which included sacrificing own resources, sharing resources with allies, and voluntarily transferring resources to another member of the alliance, coordinating military actions, etc., and they reached the common goal of winning the war against Germany.

Once alliances have formed, the structure of the game becomes similar to the problems that have been analyzed in Chapter 6, with a contest between groups that constitute the alliance, possibly followed by a contest within the victorious group or alliance. When alliance members choose their efforts in the inter-group conflict, each player has a free-rider incentive and the problem of collective action reappears. Also, when alliance members anticipate the breakup of the alliance once their common enemy has been defeated, this further weakens the alliance members' incentives, as they anticipate that what they win net of future fighting effort may be fairly small. Alliances are common in practice, despite these strategic considerations, and this constitutes a puzzle.

This chapter first illustrates this puzzle more formally, showing why the formation of an alliance may have several strategic disadvantages, similar to Esteban and Sákovics (2003). Then some factors that may make alliances more useful are discussed. These may explain why alliances are so frequently observed.

7.1. The alliance formation puzzle

To illustrate the strategic problems caused by alliance formation more formally, consider a set of three players $N = \{A, B, C\}$ who compete for a prize that is valued equally by all three players. The value can be normalized to be equal to 1 here. Two of the players may form an alliance against the third player. For the purpose of this example, these are players B and C.[1]

Once the alliance has formed, two groups $\{A\}$ and $\{B, C\}$ compete with each other. Let the effort choices of A, B, and C in the inter-group contest (stage 1) be x_A, x_B, and x_C. Let the allies' efforts add up to the effort of the alliance, and let the contest between A and $B\&C$ be determined as the outcome of the Tullock lottery contest, with

$$p_A = x_A/(x_A + x_B + x_C) \quad \text{and} \quad p_{B\&C} = 1 - p_A. \tag{7.1}$$

Once the price is allocated to one of the groups, the game proceeds as follows. If group $\{A\}$ wins the prize, the game ends, as there is no further

[1] Alliances formation is typically a voluntary process, bringing up the question of who forms an alliance with whom. This problem of endogeneity of alliance formation is disregarded here. For analyzes of this question in the context of contests, see Bloch, Sánchez-Pagés, and Soubeyran (2006) and Sánchez-Pagés (2007), and the short literature survey there.

problem of dividing up the prize inside the group, as the group consists of one player only. If the alliance $\{B, C\}$ wins the prize, given the non-cooperative nature of the problem, B and C allocate the prize among themselves according to another contest. A Tullock lottery contest success function (2.39) determines the winner among $\{B, C\}$, with y_B and y_C the efforts in this contest.

Note that this game is equivalent to the nested contest in the previous section, with two groups, with one player in one group and two players in the other group. The winning group is determined in a first stage, and an intra-group contest follows if the winning group consists of more than one player. Solving backwards, standard results on the Tullock contest can be used: In the subgame in which B and C fight for the prize in stage 2, each of the players B and C expend $y_B = y_C = 1/4$, and each of them has an expected payoff in the equilibrium of the subgame equal to $1/4$. These payoffs determine the valuations of winning which B and C have when entering into the inter-group contest. Each member of the alliance values winning the inter-group contest in stage 1 by $1/4$. Player A values winning the inter-group contest in stage 1 by the full value of the prize, that is, by 1.

Straightforwardly applying the logic of the inter-group conflict in the previous section for the Tullock lottery contest success function yields the equilibrium efforts as

$$x_A^* = \frac{4}{25} \quad \text{and} \quad (x_B + x_C)^* = \frac{1}{25}. \tag{7.2}$$

In turn, the equilibrium payoffs are

$$\pi_A^* = \frac{4}{5} - \frac{4}{25} = \frac{16}{25} \quad \text{and} \quad \pi_B^* + \pi_C^* = \frac{3}{50}. \tag{7.3}$$

Note that the linearity in the effort contributions of B and C again causes a multiplicity of pairs of equilibrium contributions of effort by B and C. Only the sum of their contributions, and, therefore, their joint payoffs, are uniquely determined. Independently of how B and C share the burden of the equilibrium contest effort $(x_B + x_C)^*$, comparing payoffs of the groups shows that B and C suffer from being in the alliance, whereas A gains from formation of the alliance between B and C, although A is not a member of the alliance.

Each player in the alliance would rather be in the position of player A than in an alliance with another player, and the alliance members would rather resolve the alliance. Intuitively, there are two main reasons why the alliance is not attractive to its members. First, the members of the alliance may turn against each other once they have defeated their joint enemy. Because of this dissipation of rent, the alliance members attribute a lower valuation to winning the inter-group contest. In the example, their valuation of winning the inter-group contest is only one-quarter of the valuation of winning for the solo player. Both B and C value winning the prize at $1/4$. This lower valuation of winning reduces the alliance players' willingness to expend effort, compared to the solo player. A second effect further reduces the effort that is chosen by members of the alliance. Note that the aggregate valuation of winning for B and C is equal to $1/2$. However, when making their effort choices, they face a classic collective action problem. As the non-cooperative outcome, their aggregate effort is equal to the effort that would also be expended by a single player who values the prize at $1/4$.

These disadvantages of an alliance are compounded if the alliance is even larger. A larger alliance faces an even stronger collective action problem. Also, a larger alliance is likely to have more difficulties in solving the distributional conflict inside the alliance. It is possible that a large alliance that wins the prize will disintegrate into disjoint subsets of players, that is, into a subset of alliances, until the prize finally ends up with one player. The results on nested contests in Chapter 6 showed that this may, but need not, further reduce individual alliance members' expected benefit from a victory of the alliance.

The strategic disadvantages of alliance formation are revealed also in numbers by comparing the payoffs in (7.3) with the outcome in the absence of an alliance. For the three-player example with linear cost functions and homogeneity of players, the symmetric Tullock lottery contest with $n = 3$ that may describe the situation without an alliance yields

$$x_A = x_B = x_C = \frac{2}{9} \quad \text{and} \quad \pi_A = \pi_B = \pi_C = \frac{1}{9}.$$

A comparison of the payoffs in this outcome with the outcome after formation of an alliance shows: both the payoff of A is higher if the alliance $\{B, C\}$ is formed than if not and the payoff of B and C is lower if the alliance is formed.[2]

Whether the grand contest is a suitable point of reference compared to what happens if B and C form an alliance is not obvious and depends

[2] The results in Esteban and Sákovics (2003) establish the inferiority of alliance formation in more general terms in a slightly modified formal structure. They consider a modified version of the alliance game (namely with a cost function $C_i(z) = z^2$ and possibly different fighting productivities) and compare the payoffs in the alliance game with the players' payoffs if they do not form an alliance and simply fight in a grand simultaneous contest.

on the institutional framework. The simultaneous grand contest between three players is conceptually a different contest from what happens with coalition formation. For instance, the contest success function need not follow the rules of a lottery contest with three players. An alternative point of reference could be the situation in which two players are randomly chosen to compete in stage 1, and the winner has to compete with the remaining player. In this case, stage 2 is a symmetric lottery contest between the winner in the stage-1 contest and the player who did not fight in stage 1. It yields payoffs equal to 1/4 to each player who is admitted to the subgame. Accordingly, in stage 1 the players who are randomly selected to compete against each other fight to be admitted to stage 2 in a standard lottery contest for a prize which they value at 1/4. Standard results yield that each of these players expends effort equal to 1/16. The total effort of all players in stages 1 and 2 sums up to $\frac{2}{16} + \frac{2}{4} = \frac{5}{8}$. From an ex-ante point of view, when players do not know whether they are drawn to fight in stage 1 or get free admission to the final contest in stage 2, the expected payoff of each player is equal to 1/8. Hence, alliance formation is also not an advantage for members of the alliance if the point of reference is an elimination contest in which the players in the first round are randomly drawn.

The aggregate payoff for all three players is higher if an alliance is formed than in either of the two points of reference. The players A, B, and C may find the formation of an alliance desirable from a collective point of view. Each of them, however, prefers that the other players form the alliance.

The disadvantage of alliance formation is not due to the contest success function in the lottery contest. The disadvantage is even more striking if the prize is allocated not according to a Tullock lottery contest success function, but according to a contest success function that has even higher marginal effectiveness of effort. Suppose, for instance, that the contest follows the rules of an all-pay auction without noise, as in (2.1). With fully symmetric players, if B and C form an alliance, they anticipate that they will dissipate the prize competely in the intra-group contest in stage 2 if this alliance should win the prize in stage 1. Accordingly, they value winning the prize in stage 1 at zero, and none of the players is willing to make any positive effort. Player A does not face a similar problem with winning the inter-group contest and values winning the prize in the inter-group contest at 1. As a result, group $\{A\}$ wins the inter-group contest with probability 1 and with zero effort (or with negligible effort, depending on the tie-breaking rule that applies) in stage 1.

These considerations suggest that the formation of an alliance involves a strategic cost.[3] The members of an alliance anticipate future wasteful conflict within the alliance, should the alliance be successful against its enemy, and, in addition, its members face free-rider incentives. Also, it is likely that an increase in the group size of an alliance will increase these problems, rather than solving it: larger groups typically dissipate a larger share of a given amount of resources if these resources are allocated in a contest among the group members. Also, free-riding incentives tend to be stronger in larger groups. Summarizing this discussion, joining forces in an alliance has some obvious drawbacks. The pervasiveness of alliances in politics, business and in military conflict therefore comes as a surprise. Section 7.2 will suggest some reasons why alliances may generate some benefits that may outweigh these disadvantages.

7.2. Solutions to the alliance formation puzzle

Several dimensions are missing from the picture of alliance formation in the previous example. For instance, if alliance formation allows the building of institutions inside the alliance that make a peaceful allocation of the alliance's revenues feasible, this can eliminate one of the major drawbacks of alliances.[4] Applying the results that have been described in Chapter 6, the formation of an alliance is more profitable if the members share revenue peacefully. The alliance may even overcome the collective action problem if it can implement a suitable sharing rule. In Chapter 6, a merit rule was shown to overcome the collective action problem. However, the development of institutions that induce such sharing rules and eliminate

[3] The negative side-effects of 'joining forces' are well known from many other contexts. These include Harsanyi's bargaining paradox (1977) and the merger paradox by Salant, Switzer, and Reynolds (1983). The forces that make alliances less attractive in a contest environment are different, however, from the forces that make joining forces less attractive in a bargaining context or in a Cournot game.

[4] Bloch, Sánchez-Pagés, and Soubeyran (2006), for instance, study alliance formation under such conditions. The grand coalition becomes attractive under these conditions, as it avoids conflict completely. They also carefully review the literature. Peaceful sharing inside the alliance is also assumed by Sánchez-Pagés (2007). Both contributions concentrate on problems of endogenous coalition *formation*. Noh (2002) also discusses alliances. In his framework, the intra-group conflict is assumed to be less pronounced. The alliance can use less resource-wasteful rules that govern how the members of the alliance share in the total revenue. He assumes that they may even choose the sharing rule that is most beneficial to the alliance. He also addresses the problem of enforceability of the sharing rule, building on a possible relationship between applying the sharing rule on the one hand, and the alliance members' effectiveness in their conflict effort towards the alliance's enemy. Garfinkel (2004) allows for internal conflict inside alliances and analyzes the importance of the rules of this conflict for the stability of coalitions.

wasteful conflict inside the group is not a trivial matter, particularly in a fully non-cooperative environment in which the enforcement of contracts is notoriously difficult.

The threat of internal conflict may solve the collective action problem

A fully non-cooperative mechanism for overcoming both the collective action problem of the alliance in the inter-group contest and the redistributive conflict inside the alliance is suggested by Konrad and Leininger (2007b). They consider an alliance that consists of a group of n players, and an external conflict between this alliance group and another player E, followed by possible conflict inside the alliance. More precisely, they consider a game which has a time structure that is illustrated in Figure 7.1. In stage 1, the alliance fights with an enemy in an all-pay auction without noise. The enemy can be considered as a single person who values winning the prize at 1 and has some given cost function of contest effort x_E, but can also be a more complex entity; however, the microstructure of this entity is not further analyzed. The members of the alliance must choose their individual contest contributions. If the sum of their contributions falls short of the aggregate effort that is chosen by the enemy, then the alliance wins zero, the prize goes to the enemy, and the game ends. All alliance members who contributed to the alliance's aggregate effort bear the cost of their contributions privately. If the alliance's contributions exceed the contributions chosen by the enemy, then the alliance wins the prize. In this case, the game continues, as the alliance must determine the allocation of the prize.

The continuation is as follows. There is one member of the alliance who is called 'big-man'.[5] The identity of the 'big man' is already known at the beginning of stage 1. This player is the most able fighter inside the alliance, or, if there are several, equally able fighters, he is a member of this set of most able fighters. The big man can hand out non-negative gifts to each of the other members of the alliance. These hand-outs are unconditional monetary transfers. The choice of these gifts establishes and completes stage 2 in Figure 7.1.

Once these hand-outs are made, the intra-group contest problem emerges in which the members of the alliance may fight internally about the division of the prize in an all-pay auction without noise. Unlike in the example of the alliance puzzle in section 7.1, Konrad and Leininger (2007b) allow for endogenous timing of effort. Recall, from section 3.1, that the

[5] They borrow this name from Sahlins (1963), who observed and described the existence and behavior of leaders in the organization of Melanesian tribes.

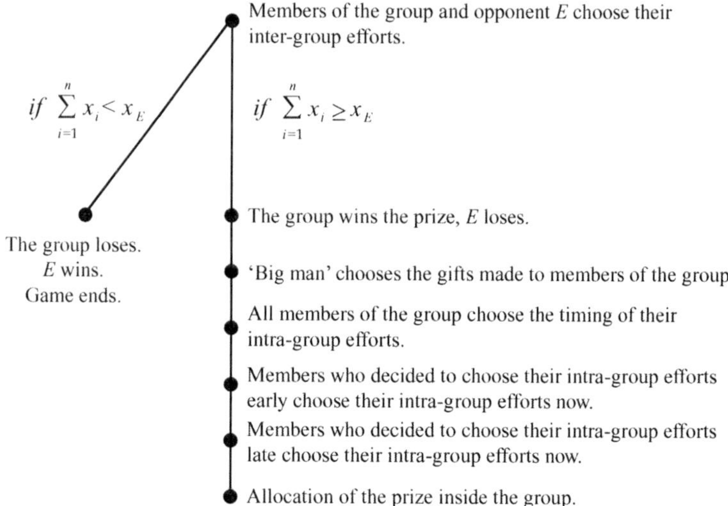

Figure 7.1 The Konrad–Leininger mechanism to overcome the free-rider problem and to avoid internal conflict.

option of endogenous timing may generate multiple equilibria in this all-pay auction, some of which are completely peaceful and allocate the full prize to the player with the highest fighting power: all players except for the strongest player receive a zero payoff in the simultaneous all-pay auction without noise. For instance, if they have an option to commit to not making any contributions, they are indifferent ex-ante about whether to exercise such an option. Endogenous choice of the timing of own contributions essentially provides such an option. Hence, if all alliance members except for the strongest player commit to choosing their effort early and the strongest player chooses his effort once their efforts are chosen, an equilibrium emerges in which the strongest player wins effortlessly. Other equilibria are more resource wasteful and lead to a smaller prize net of contest effort for the player with the highest fighting ability, and to zero payoffs from the all-pay auction for all other members of the alliance. All players except for the player with the highest fighting ability are indifferent regarding which of these equilibria is chosen. The player with the highest fighting ability strictly prefers the peaceful equilibrium, as it gives him the highest net payoff in this all-pay auction.

One can now see how the intra-group distribution problem and the multiplicity of equilibria in this intra-group competition may be used to induce an equilibrium of the whole game in which the alliance members overcome the collective action problem when fighting the external enemy, and coordinate on a peaceful equilibrium inside the alliance. The key for reaching efficiency is that the choice of the equilibrium for intra-group redistribution may depend on the behavior of alliance members in the external conflict, and on the size of gifts that the big man makes to the other members of the alliance. Suppose the group coordinates on the most wasteful equilibrium in the intra-group contest if the group members do not choose the first-best efficient fighting effort in the external conflict. Suppose further that the strongest fighter (the 'big man') may make suitable gifts to the group members, if all members of the alliance choose efficient contribution levels. Suitability means that the expectation of this gift to be received by a member of the alliance outweighs the cost of his effort contributions to the external conflict, when these contributions are chosen. Suppose also that the equilibrium selection for the internal distributional conflict also depends on the gifts made by the most able fighter. If these gifts deviate from such suitable amounts, then, again, the group coordinates on the most conflictual, most resource wasteful equilibrium in the intra-group contest. However, if the members of the alliance make efficient effort choices in the external conflict, and, in case the group wins against the enemy, the most able fighter in the group makes suitable gifts, then the group coordinates on the peaceful equilibrium. If the fighting ability of the enemy group is not too high, this set-up yields a subgame perfect equilibrium in which all members of the alliance can expend efficient effort levels, the alliance wins a positive amount net of effort cost in the inter-group contest, all members of the alliance are (at least) compensated for their contributions by generous gifts if the group wins the contest, and the alliance finally coordinates on the peaceful equilibrium which gives the prize to the strongest player without any cost of fighting.

The equilibrium in Konrad and Leininger (2007b) has several interesting features. First, there is no visible violence or fighting inside the alliance, even though there is a distributional conflict inside the alliance and such fighting would not be ruled out. Second, unconditional gifts are observed in the equilibrium. These gifts are positively correlated with alliance members' fighting efforts. Looking at the alliance from the outside, not knowing the game which they play, this looks like reciprocal behavior: the ordinary alliance members on the one side make efficient contributions to the collective good. The most able fighter in the alliance on the other side hands out gifts. Finally, the alliance peacefully awards a share of its income to the strongest fighter who made the gifts. This sequence of contributions and gifts may look like reciprocity from the outside, possibly sustained by preferences for reciprocating. In fact, the behavior is not based on such preferences, but can be explained as the outcome of the non-cooperative interaction between players who are perfectly selfish, narrowly defined. Third, fully efficient collective action emerges for the group in the contest with the external enemy, although the group public good that is produced is not a discrete public good. Unlike the equilibrium of private provision to a public good as in Bergstrom, Blume, and Varian (1986), in which each player chooses a contribution such that the cost of an additional marginal contribution just equals his own marginal benefit from increased public good provision, the alliance members can coordinate on fully efficient contributions.

This structure overcomes the strategic pitfalls of alliance formation: the collective action problem is avoided. Moreover, the potential violence and resource-wasteful conflict inside the alliance is turned into something positive: the threat of this potentially looming conflict induces the members of the alliance to choose efficient contributions to collective action.

The reasoning so far explains how the shortcomings of alliances that establish the alliance puzzle can be overcome in a strictly non-cooperative framework. It does not explain why alliances are superior to individual action. In the framework by Konrad and Leininger (2007b), each alliance member has a strictly convex cost of effort in an external conflict. This makes a larger group more effective in external conflict, as it gives the alliance as a whole a cost function with lower marginal cost than each single alliance member. This possible cost advantage completes the picture and makes the alliance strictly favorable.

Apart from such efficient non-cooperative structures, there are further aspects that may make the formation of an alliance more attractive for its members. In what follows, the role of budget constraints, complementarities in fighting and strategic benefits from resource transfers inside the alliance are discussed.

Budget constraints

Players may often like to expend more resources in a contest than they have. Being resource constrained in this absolute sense can represent a major disadvantage in contests. We have seen in section 2.1 for the all-pay auction that the more resource-constrained player ends up with a payoff equal to zero in the (otherwise symmetric) all-pay auction without noise. Alliances may enable the group of players inside an alliance to expand their group effort above the effort that each group member would be able to expend. This is illustrated in work by Konrad and Kovenock (2008b). They consider the example with three players, A, B and C, with B and C forming an alliance, and the following two-stage structure.

In a first stage (stage 1), the group $\{B, C\}$ competes against $\{A\}$. Players' non-negative efforts are x_A, x_B and x_C. Each player i can choose $x_i \in [0, m_i]$, and has a cost equal to this effort. Hence, m_i is some exogenously given cap on individual effort, for instance, a budget constraint, where they assume that $2m_B > m_A \geq m_B = m_C$. The contest success is determined by the contest success function of the all-pay auction without noise, that is, A wins if $x_A > x_B + x_C$, and vice versa. In a second stage (stage 2), the game ends if $\{A\}$ is the winner of the inter-group contest, as A does not have an internal distribution problem. If $\{B, C\}$ wins, the members of the winning alliance fight about the distribution of the prize among the alliance members. This internal fight is also an all-pay auction without noise. Their effort choices are y_B and y_C, with $y_i \in [0, m_i]$ for $i \in \{B, C\}$, and the cost of effort is, again, linear in this effort.

Let $2m_B$ be small, compared with the size of the overall prize that is normalized to 1, for instance, $2m_B < 1/2$. Amounts of resources that are not used up in the inter-group contest are non-transferable to the intra-group contest or vice versa. As B and C formed an alliance, they are able to expend an amount equal to $x_B + x_C \in [0, 2m_B]$ in the contest between $\{A\}$ and $\{B, C\}$ in stage 1. Solving this game by backward induction, Konrad and Kovenock (2008b) show that, for $1/2 > 2m_B$, an equilibrium exists which has the following properties. Each B and C has an expected payoff from participating in the contest if the alliance wins the prize, equal to

$$v_{BC} \equiv (1/2) - m_B. \tag{7.4}$$

Intuitively, they both expend their whole budget in the intra-group contest, but as the sum of these budgets does not exhaust the value of the prize, (7.4) describes their value of winning the inter-group contest. Turning to stage 1, this contest is described by one player A, who values winning at this stage at the value of the prize, which is 1, but cannot expend more effort than m_A, and a group $\{B, C\}$ of players each of whom values winning this stage 1 contest at $(1/2)-m_B$ but who can jointly make an effort x_B+x_C from the interval $[0, 2m_B]$. The problem combines the contest problem studied by Che and Gale (1997) with several players who have different budgets that fall short of the valuation of the prize, and Che and Gale (1998) who consider a budget cap for players with different valuations. It further adds to this problem the fact that B and C face a public good problem when it comes to making contributions.

As is shown in Konrad and Kovenock (2008b), if B and C can coordinate their non-cooperative actions using a randomization mechanism (as described and used also in Konrad and Leininger, 2007b) that is observable to them but not to outsiders such as player A, an equilibrium exists that generates for them an expected payoff equal to $v_{BC} - m_A > 0$. If the players do not form an alliance, player A's payoff is $1 - m_B$ and the payoffs for B and C are zero in an all-pay auction without noise in which all players A, B, and C play simultaneously. The payoffs of B and C are also zero in a sequential game with two players randomly chosen in a first stage, and the winner playing against the player who has not been chosen for the first-round contest. This establishes that sufficiently tight budget constraints can make alliances profitable for the members of the alliance, and reduce the payoff for the non-member of the alliance, even if a winning alliance enters into internal distributional conflict. The case for alliance formation can be made, even if the distributional conflict inside the winning alliance takes place.

Intuitively, if players would like to expend more than they have in an all-pay auction, the player who has a higher budget than his competitor can simply make a bid that is slightly higher than his competitor's budget, and this guarantees that he himself wins the prize (and this also determines the equilibrium payoff in the mixed strategy equilibrium). An alliance may increase the range of possible effort, compared to players' options in a stand-alone situation. The formation of an alliance may allow the group to outbid budget-constrained competitors. This is a potential advantage from joining forces. On the other hand, an alliance has been seen as being detrimental for its members when it comes to the later conflict between these members, as they may internally dissipate the whole prize. With sufficiently low budget constraints, however, this disadvantage is not a serious matter. Even if the members of the alliance start fighting with each other as severely as possible in the intra-group contest, this does not waste much resources if they have only few resources for fighting. Hence, the beneficial budget enlargement effect of forming an alliance may outweigh the harmful effect of intra-alliance fighting once the alliance has reached its primary goal and won the prize.

Resource transfers in multi-front conflict

The problem of resource constraints is closely related to a solution to the alliance puzzle that has been offered by Kovenock and Roberson (2008) in a Colonel Blotto game with multiple fronts. The Colonel Blotto framework differs from the types of contest that were analyzed in Chapter 2 with the assumption that all players always expend their whole stock of resources which they can use for contest effort; hence, the choice of contest effort is exogenous, and the problem is how to allocate this effort across different battle fronts. Their results are based on a theorem in Roberson (2006) and the solution to the multi-battle problem with the all-pay auction without noise is not straightforward. The intuition of the result can be illustrated, however, using a very simple example and the Tullock lottery contest.

Suppose there are three players, A, B, and C. Player A can be attacked by players B and C. This constitutes two contests. In each of these contests a prize of size 1 is awarded to the winner. Each player has a total stock of weapons, troops or arms equal to m_A, m_B and m_C. In this example B and C have no choice. They just use their resources in their respective battle with A, hoping that they will win. In other words, their payoffs are equal to

$$\pi_B = \frac{m_B}{m_B + x_{AB}} \quad \text{and} \quad \pi_C = \frac{m_C}{m_C + x_{AC}} \tag{7.5}$$

where $x_{AB} \geq 0$ and $x_{AC} \geq 0$ are the efforts which A uses against B and C, respectively, with $m_A = x_{AB} + x_{AC}$. The payoff of A is

$$\pi_A = \frac{x_{AB}}{m_B + x_{AB}} + \frac{(m_A - x_{AB})}{m_C + (m_A - x_{AB})}, \tag{7.6}$$

and for given exogenous m_B and m_C, A allocates his resources in a way that maximizes the expected number of battle wins. This leads to the marginal condition

$$\frac{m_B}{(m_B + x_{AB})^2} - \frac{m_C}{(m_C + m_A - x_{AB})^2} = 0 \tag{7.7}$$

which equalizes the marginal probability impact of the last resource in both battlefields. Corner solutions with $x_{AB} = 0$ or $x_{AB} = m_A$ are also feasible. For instance, if $m_B >> m_C$, then A may give up in the contest with B and may expend all resources in the contest with C.

This is the point of departure for introducing an alliance that allows a resource transfer between B and C. If B transfers 1 unit of contest resource to C, if this happens prior to A's decision about how to divide m_A on the two battlefields and is observable for A, this transfer will typically change A's allocation of effort. As a reaction to a resource shift from B to C, player A may shift an amount of resources from the battle with B to the battle with C as to make (7.7) again fulfilled. As a result, B has fewer resources but faces an enemy with a smaller army, C has more resources but also faces an enemy with a larger army. Surprisingly, this transfer can be advantageous for both

B and C. For instance, calculating this example for $m_A = 10$, and $m_B = 11$ and $m_C = 1$ initially, the equilibrium payoffs are $\pi_B = 0.65076$ and $\pi_C = 0.19621$. If B transfers 1 unit of military resource to C and A optimally adapts to this change in military endowments, the payoffs become $\pi_B = 0.65782$ and $\pi_C = 0.29419$.

The intuition as to why both B and C can gain from the transfer is related to the general insight on asymmetry. If B is much better endowed with weapons than C, in order to maximize their joint win probabilities, they would be better off with a more balanced stock of weapons on both frontiers. This does not explain, however, why B gains from transferring weapons to C. The reason for this is that, starting from a situation in which C has (almost) no weapons, a small transfer makes C a much more serious competitor. This induces A to shift an amount of weapons from the battlefield with B to the battlefield with C. Player B benefits more from this reduction in A's effort on the battle front between A and B than B suffers from the reduction in own resources for fighting.

Complementarities and increases in fighting power

Alliances may have a number of effects not captured in the previous examples. For instance, alliances may change the fighting technology that is available for players inside an alliance. This may occur due to a transfer of technology among alliance members, or by way of transfers of specific resources. In a military alliance, for instance, a wealthy member of the alliance may endow the soldiers provided by other allies with weapons and equipment. In more general terms, the resources that can be contributed by different allies can be complements, making it less expensive to reach a given level of fighting power, or the combination of resources may enhance fighting power over and above the fighting power which the allies could achieve with given resources in isolation. This can be formally described by a contest success function that is not simply a function of the sum of allies' efforts. For a contest success function that is supermodular in the allies' contest efforts, as in Skaperdas (1998), the alliance provides a technological benefit for the group of allies, and this may be an important reason why the formation of an alliance can be attractive. Skaperdas considers several three player contest problems in which players have exogenously given contest resources that are not depleted during a contest. In the simplest case, players can enter an all-against-all simultaneous contest directly, or two players may decide to join forces and turn against the third player, and, if they jointly win the prize, fight it out between themselves. Two players may gain from the formation of an alliance if their cost-efficiency advantage from joining forces in the inter-group contest is sufficiently high to outweigh the disadvantages from collective action and from the looming distributional conflict inside the winning alliance.[6]

7.3. Summary

Summarizing this discussion, joining forces in an alliance has some obvious drawbacks. Teaming up in an alliance causes two problems. First, the alliance members need to overcome the collective action problem to be effective regarding their common goals. Second, wasteful conflict is looming once the alliance has achieved its primary goal. The pervasiveness of alliances in politics, business and in military conflict therefore comes as a surprise. It suggests that alliance formation is overall advantageous for its members, despite of these problems.

Some mechanisms may be at work that neutralize alliances against these problems, even in a fully non-cooperative framework. One of these mechanisms may be particularly plausible: the threat of conflict inside the alliance may induce alliance members to contribute efficiently to the overall goal of the alliance. This happens if a failure to resolve the collective action problem causes more wasteful conflict inside the alliance. If, in addition, the efficient collaboration of alliance members is technically superior to individual actions, for instance, due to scale effects, individual budget constraints or complementarities, the alliance formation puzzle is resolved.

[6] Tan and Wang (1997) also consider synergies among members of an alliance. They analyze coalition formation with more than three players. They also assume that winning alliances of multiple players need to continue to fight internally.

8

Dynamic Battles

In a contest, a group of players expend efforts up-front, trying to win some prize. The process by which the efforts translate into success probabilities is often considered a black box, and much of the analysis in previous chapters follows this spirit. However, if one looks at contest games with some high-resolution spectacles, they often reveal a finer substructure and can be decomposed into a number of smaller battles or component contests, with the overall outcome generally being a function of the outcomes in these component contests.[1] A related type of dynamic interaction emerges if players can subsequently add further effort to the effort they have already committed for a number of rounds, with the final amounts of effort entering into a contest success function and determining who wins a given prize.[2] The dynamics of contests are often surprising and counterintuitive. Among the many relevant dynamic structures, elimination tournaments, a race, the tug-of-war and different types of dynamic incumbency fights will be considered.

[1] Reseachers in the R&D context noted that R&D is not a single, one-shot event (see, e.g., Harris and Vickers, 1985, 1987). Dynamic contest problems emerge, and have been analyzed also in the contexts of political campaigns (Klumpp and Polborn, 2006), violent conflicts for power, resources or territory (Mehlum and Moene, 2004; McBride and Skaperdas, 2006) and, with a multiplicity of applications in mind, by Gradstein and Konrad (1999), Amegashie (1999, 2000), McAfee (2000), Fu and Lu (2007), Moldovanu and Sela (2006), Groh et al. (2003), Konrad and Kovenock (2005, 2008c, 2008a), and Matros (2006). Mehlum and Moene (2004), Polborn (2006), and Aidt and Hillman (2008) consider repeated contest games in which there is an incumbent and a rival in every period and these may change roles from one period to the next as an outcome of the respective contest in the period contest. Hillman and Katz (1987) consider a hierarchical chain of players granting favors in rent-seeking contests. Gradstein (2004), Gonzalez (2007), Gonzalez and Neary (2004), and Eggert, Itaya, and Mino (2006) consider appropriation games with an infinite time horizon and with discrete and continuous time periods, respectively.

[2] These dynamics are analyzed in Leininger and Yang (1994) who assume that the increases in players' effort commitments occur sequentially.

8.1. The elimination tournament

One of the motivating examples of a contest in the Introduction was the tournament which Jack Welch staged to determine his successor as CEO of General Electric (GE). Welch (2001) claims he was looking for a strong leader with further personal characteristics and abilities that are most suitable for this position; he did not want to lose highly talented and highly performing managers at GE during the finding process; he wanted to limit harmful competition or sabotage among the competitors. And these were only the most important goals from a long list. Formally, the tournament lasted for six years, and at least three selection rounds could be identified, as depicted in Figure 8.1. In a first round a shortlist of 23 persons was selected. The competition narrowed this group down to eight. From these eight, three persons were finally selected. At this point, the candidates were told that they were in a contest for the successorship, and who were their competitors. Finally, one of the three candidates was chosen to become the new CEO; the other two contestants had to leave GE. Whether a candidate learns whether he is a candidate in the race, whether he knows the

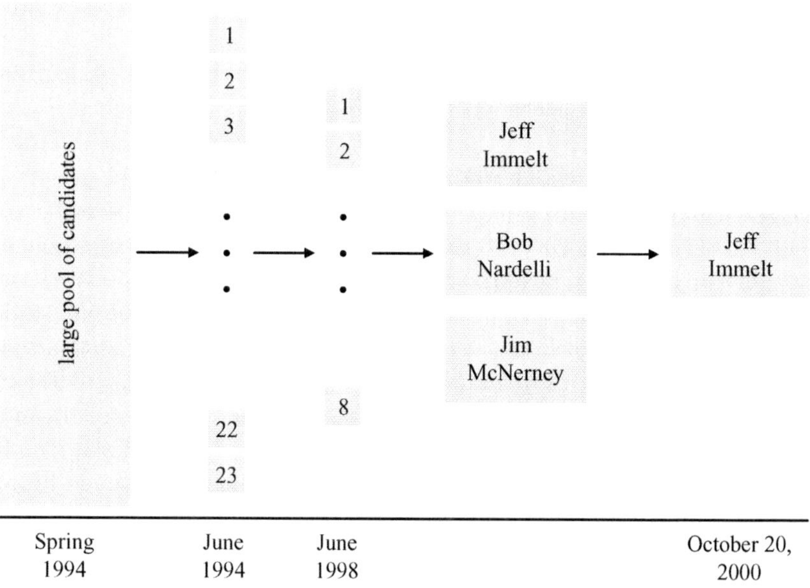

Figure 8.1 The elimination tournament to determine the successor of Jack Welch as the CEO of General Electric.

size of the group of competitors or even their identities, at which stage this information is revealed, the sequencing in which candidates are dropped as candidates, what happens to them once they drop out of the contest, and whether they know what happens to the ones who do not win the race, are some of the parameters that can be influenced by the designer of this contest.

Jack Welch searched for his successor among the group of managers inside GE. Other selection procedures include the option to hire a new CEO from outside. This is also a dimension of possible design choice. Multiple other dimensions play a role when making design choices. For instance, Welch reports that a defined sequence of managerial tasks in different sections of GE had been designed for each candidate. All these decisions affected transparency, firm output, the precision of quality signals obtained from the contestants, and the growth of their managerial competence over the period of the competition.

It has also been discussed in the introduction that selecting winners who are likely to be most suitable for a particular task is only one of the possible goals which the designers of multi-round tournaments may pursue. Many types of sports competition follow the structure of an elimination tournament, but the purpose of the tournament is not to hire the winner of the final contest for some particular job. The principal who organizes sports tournaments is often interested in making the tournament attractive to viewers, and to acquire their willingness to pay by selling broadcasting rights, or selling entry tickets. Figure 8.2 looks familiar to everyone who occasionally watches soccer or tennis championships. A number of 2^n players are in a grand contest. First, players are pairwise matched and compete in battles in a first round. The winners of these first-round battles enter into the second round. These 2^{n-1} players are again pairwise matched and compete in battles. Again, the winners are promoted to the next round. This process of battles and eliminations continues up to the final. In the final, the winners from the two semi-finals compete for the prize that is awarded to the winner of the final. Various assumptions can be made about the nature of the battles, players' types, their information status etc. Examples in the literature also include cases in which more than two players are matched in a battle, and in which more than one player proceeds to the next round.[3]

[3] The first person who studied this structure systematically and formally was Rosen (1986). More recent contributions are Gradstein and Konrad (1999), Amegashi (1999, 2000), Fu and Lu (2007), Harbaugh and Klumpp (2005), Groh et al. (2003), and Konrad and Kovenock (2008a).

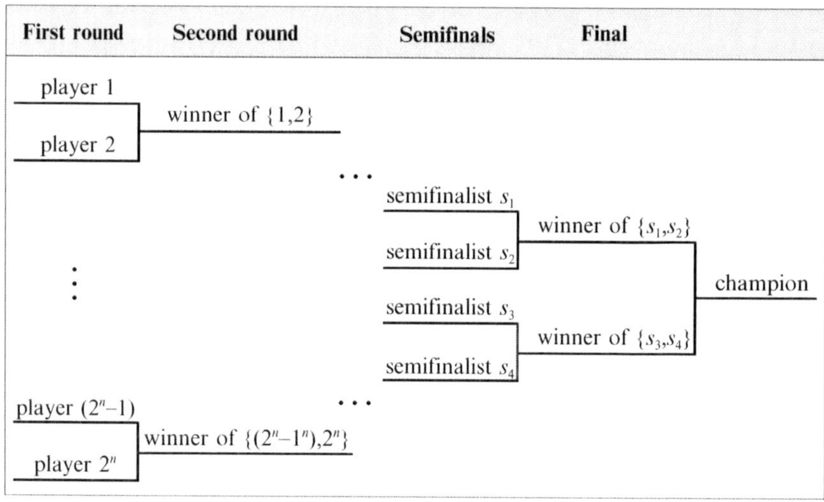

Figure 8.2 A general elimination tournament with pairwise competition.

The properties of the structure in Figure 8.2 have been studied more formally by Rosen (1986).[4] He distinguishes between players who are homogeneous in their abilities and heterogeneous players, and, in the latter case, between a situation in which all players know each other's abilities, and in which they do not. The most clear-cut results emerge for the case with homogeneous players. Many more or less plausible hypotheses about the goals of the principal who organizes such tournaments can be made. Rosen, for instance, considers the structure of prizes awarded to the losers at each stage, and to the final winner of the final stage if the contest designer wishes to keep the effort of each contestant in each round at a constant level.

More formally, let there be 2^n players.[5] They are teamed up pairwise in group contests with groups of two players each as in Figure 8.2. The losers in each of these contests receive a loser prize of zero and exit. The 2^{n-1} winners receive the period prize W_n and are again teamed up in groups of two players who compete in a contest for promotion to the next round. The losers again receive zero and exit. The winners receive W_{n-1} and are again teamed up, etc. This process continues for n rounds with W_{n-k+1} being the

[4] Similar structures have been discussed in biology as knockout conflicts, e.g., by Broom, Cannings, and Vickers (2000, 2001).

[5] This follows the analysis by Rosen (1986), using a simplified contest success function.

prize money for the winner in round k. Let $W_1 \geq W_2 \geq \ldots \geq W_n$. Suppose further that the win probabilities between two contestants i and j who are teamed up at round k are determined by their contest efforts x_{ik} and x_{jk} as in a lottery contest, that is, as in (2.39) with $r = 1$. Their cost of effort is again assumed to be equal to this effort.

The game can be solved backwards. The final contest follows the rules of a symmetric lottery contest for a prize of size W_1. The equilibrium efforts are $x_1^* = W_1/4$, and the expected payoffs of both finalists are equal to $V_1^* = W_1/4$. Assuming equilibrium play in the continuation games, in the semi-finals each player competes with his opponent for the prize $W_2 + V_1^*$. Hence, applying the results of the lottery contest,

$$x_2^* = \frac{W_2 + V_1^*}{4} = \frac{W_2}{4} + \frac{W_1}{4^2} \tag{8.1}$$

and the expected payoff V_2^* from being admitted to the semi-final is also equal to $(W_2/4) + (W_1/4^2)$. More generally,

$$x_k^* = V_k^* = \frac{1}{4}\sum_{s=1}^{k} \frac{W_s}{4^{k-s}}. \tag{8.2}$$

Backward induction reveals that $x_k^* = x_1^* = \frac{1}{4}W_1$ for all $k > 1$, if

$$W_k = \frac{3}{4}W_1. \tag{8.3}$$

This example is slightly less general than the analysis in Rosen (1986), as Rosen allows for non-linear cost of effort and for a more general contest success function. However, it reveals the main result in Rosen: In order to induce constant effort across all rounds of the specific elimination tournament that is depicted in Figure 8.2, the winner prizes in all rounds except for the last round develop according to a simple rule. In the specific example, they are even constant. However, the winner prize in the final round needs to be higher. Intuitively, in all rounds prior to the final, a winner in round k wins W_k, and in addition, he wins the right to continue in the contest. In the final, the winner prize consists of W_1 only. As the right to continue to participate is typically valuable, the prize for winning is higher than W_k in all rounds with $k > 1$. But as the valuation of winning (compared to losing, which yields a payout of zero) determines the equilibrium effort, the prize in the final needs to be increased compared to prizes in earlier rounds to make the valuation as high as in these earlier rounds.

It is not clear why the principal who organizes an elimination contest should be interested in inducing the same effort by all participants in all stages of the contest. However, it illustrates the different incentives of players who win a prize in an intermediate round plus the value they attribute to the right to continue in the next round, and of players in the last round in which the value of winning consists only of the winner prize itself.

Amegashie (1999) and Gradstein and Konrad (1999) consider a different objective: maximization of overall contest effort. They also allow the principal to choose the structure of the contest: he can choose whether to team up only two contestants in pairwise contests, or to choose larger groups competing internally. The latter show that the effort-maximizing structure depends on the marginal probability impact of effort in the contest success function. If the contest success function is given by (2.39) then either a contest in which all contestants compete in an 2^n - player simultaneous contest or the structure with the largest number of rounds with pairwise elimination contests as in the Rosen framework maximizes effort, depending on whether $r > 1$ or $r < 1$.[6]

As suggested by the example of the tournament described by Jack Welch which was designed to find his successor, organizers of elimination contests may have multiple objectives, and candidate selection may be particularly important. Such questions cannot be studied within a framework with perfectly homogeneous contestants, or with complete information. Rosen (1986) had already discussed questions of heterogeneity of players, and the consequences of incomplete information about own and other players' types. This leads to interesting and, to a large part, unexplored questions in a dynamic context, particularly if contestants are able to observe each other's efforts. One aspect that is likely to be robust is a *discouragement effect* in dynamic contests. Players anticipate that, by winning a preliminary stage of an elimination contest, this will mainly admit them to another contest. If promotion to the next round only leads to participation in another contest, the fact that much of the prize that is awarded at the end in this contest is dissipated in further rounds of the contest reduces their incentive to expend much effort when trying to win the component contest in early rounds. In Rosen's elimination contest, if $W_j = 0$ for all $j \neq 1$, that is, if the only non-zero prize that is awarded is the winner prize

[6] Fu and Lu (2007) analyze a further dimension of choice. They allow for loser prizes at intermediate rounds and also allow for more than one player being promoted from each single group contest into the next round. They maintain the assumptions of homogeneity of players and complete information. They find that a series of grand contests can be optimal in which the elimination of players is slower than in the structure considered by Rosen.

in the final round, then the effort in each round is

$$x^*_{n-k+1} = \frac{W_1}{4^{n-k+1}} \tag{8.4}$$

and becomes very small in the early rounds of elimination tournaments.

This discouragement effect is a key feature of dynamic contests. It will emerge in many other structures as well.

8.2. The race

A second, empirically relevant dynamic structure is the 'race'. Klumpp and Polborn (2006) identify a race, for instance, in the context of the primaries that anticipate the US presidential elections. Here a given number of candidates enters into a dynamic contest which consists of a finite series of primary elections across all states of the US. The party candidate who receives most votes in a state gains the party delegates of this state, and the candidate who first accumulates a majority in the total number of delegates will typically be nominated as presidential candidate for the respective party.

Suppose, for instance, there are just three primary elections and two candidates. Abstracting slightly from reality, which is more complicated due to the different size of states, loyalties, and other institutional features, let each of these elections be equally important. This means that the number of delegates for the winner of the state primary gets the same number of delegates for each of these states. In this case, the contest is over as soon as one of the contestants has accumulated two victories, and his competitor may exit from the game at this point. This structure has been found to be relevant in many other contexts. Many sports games follow this pattern. For instance, in male tennis championships, the final often has a maximum of five sets. Accordingly, the player who first accumulates three win sets also wins the match. It is easy to enlarge the list of examples in sports. Harris and Vickers (1985) were the first to identify similar structures in the context of R&D and to study this structure more formally. They argued that R&D competition may be a dynamic contest in which an innovation requires a given number of components that are innovated sequentially. In this case the player who first accumulates the required number of components wins the payoff from patenting the innovation.

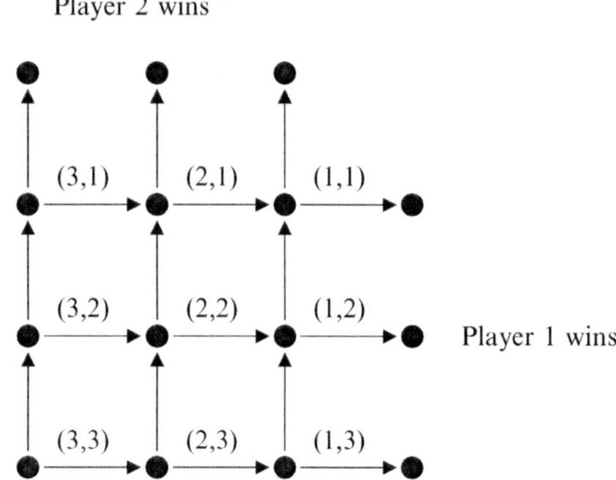

Figure 8.3 A race with $(n, m) = (3, 3)$: The player who first wins three battles wins the contest.

A simple race between two players is depicted in Figure 8.3. Both players start at state (3,3). The player who first wins three battles wins the race. For instance, a battle at state (3,3) determines whether player 1 wins, which moves the game to state (2,3), or whether player 2 wins, which moves the game to state (3,2). At (2,3), a further battle takes place. If player 1 wins again, the process moves to (1,3). If player 2 wins, the game moves to state (2,2). Similarly, the game continues from (3,2), when player 2 wins the first battle. If state (1,1) is reached, a final battle takes place, and the winner of this battle wins the grand contest. The grid in Figure 8.3 could be expanded and a race could start further to the lower left, with more battle wins required for the players, and the required number of battle wins could be asymmetric such that the starting state is some state (n, m). There could also be more than two players, and various assumptions can be made about the nature of the single battles at each state,[7] about possible intermediate prizes from winning single battles, budget constraints, etc.

Some of the key features of this structure can be illustrated in this simple example. Let the two players be 1 and 2, and their efforts at nodes (i, j) be $x_1(i, j)$ and $x_2(i, j)$. Let the effort cost be equal to effort chosen. Let the

[7] For instance, Harris and Vickers (1987), Klumpp and Polborn (2006), Ferrall and Smith (1999), and Leach (2004) consider races with noise, and Konrad and Kovenock (2008c) consider the case in which each battle is an all-pay auction. Malueg and Yates (2006) consider a set-up that is very similar to a race.

monetary prize of winning the dynamic overall contest be of size $v = 1$ and the same for both players. Finally, let the winner at each node (i, j) be determined as a function of the contest efforts as in the lottery contest. Solving the problem recursively, the subgame at $(1, 1)$ is equivalent to a simple static lottery contest. Equilibrium efforts $x_i^*(1, 1) = 1/4$, and these are also equal to the payoffs in this subgame for $i = 1, 2$. Turning from there to $(1, 2)$, player 1 wins a prize that is equal to the difference between the continuation value from winning (=1), and the continuation value from losing (=1/4); hence, the prize of winning at $(1, 2)$ is $3/4$. Player 2 wins a prize at $(1, 2)$ that is only as high as $1/4$. Winning by player 1 ends the game and awards this player the prize. Winning by player 2 brings the game back to a state of symmetry at $(1, 1)$, and each player values reaching $(1, 1)$ only by $1/4$. Accordingly, at $(1, 2)$ the asymmetric implications from winning for player 1 and for player 2 make the contest at $(1, 2)$ asymmetric. Player 1's valuation of winning is three times the valuation of player 2, and this asymmetry greatly benefits player 1, as is known from the analysis of the Tullock contest in section 2.3.

The example shows that the race favors the player who gained a lead in terms of the number of victories. This advantage typically causes a drift along the equilibrium path of the continuation game. Intuitively, the disadvantaged player can win only by moving the game back to a state at which both players are more symmetric again. But at this state much of the total rent that is allocated in the dynamic contest is dissipated. This effect discourages the disadvantaged player from expending much effort, trying to tilt the balance again in his favor.

Konrad and Kovenock (2008c) solved this game more generally for cases in which each component contest is described by an all-pay auction without noise. If each component contest follows the rules of an all-pay auction without noise, the equilibrium solution even pronounces the qualitative properties of the solution just derived. Note that the continuation values for both players of reaching $(1, 1)$ are zero in this case: at $(1, 1)$ they both enter into a fully symmetric all-pay auction without noise. As has been seen in section 2.1, the payoffs of both players are zero in this case. Hence, the benefit of winning for player 2 at $(1, 2)$ is zero. Player 2 is indifferent about winning or losing the component battle at $(1, 2)$. Player 1, instead, receives the value of the final prize, normalized to 1, if player 1 wins the all-pay auction at $(1, 2)$. If player 1 loses at $(1, 2)$, he wins the continuation value at $(1, 1)$, which is zero. Hence, the contest at $(1, 2)$ is between two extremely asymmetric contestants: player 2 does not care about winning, and essentially gives up; player 1 cares a lot about winning and has a high stake in winning this component contest, but will win this component contest with minimal effort. In turn, at (2, 2), the contest between the two players would again be fully symmetric, and both players would be willing to expend considerable effort in winning; essentially, the local equilibrium efforts at (2, 2) turn out to be identical to the ones at (1, 1). As Konrad and Kovenock show more generally, allowing for an arbitrarily large number of required battle victories and for asymmetries between the players, there is a very narrow area of states (i, j) in which players compete fiercely which are systematically ordered in a larger grid than in Figure 8.3. However, once the process left this set of intense fighting, the competition slackens off, more or less completely, and one contestant essentially gives up.

The dynamics of competition and the uncertainty involved in the process as to which path through the grid of states as in Figure 8.3 materializes also causes a wide dispersion in the actual amount of contest resources expended. Consider, for instance, the all-pay auction without noise as in Figure 8.3, and let this auction start at (2, 2). Suppose further that the contestants are almost symmetric regarding the valuation of finally winning the multi-battle contest, of $v_2 = v$ and $v_1 = v_2 + \theta$, with $\theta > 0$ but small. Then the competition at (2, 2) is very strong, and almost dissipates the lower of the two values of the prize, v, in expectation. One of the contestants wins and the process moves to (1, 2) with a probability slightly higher than 1/2, and to (2, 1) with a probability slightly smaller than 1/2. Suppose the process moved to (2, 1). Then player 2 has a considerable advantage. Player 2 values winning at (2, 1) at v_2, whereas player 1 still has a small but strictly positive expected value $v_1 - v_2 = \theta$ from winning the component contest at (2, 1), as this brings the contest to (1, 1), and the expected payoff of player 1 at (1, 1) is the difference θ between the valuations of the prize for the two players. Hence, the process is likely to move from (2, 1) to (2, 0), with player 2 winning and terminating the multi-battle contest. However, there is a small chance that player 1 wins the component contest at (2, 1), which brings the contest back to an almost symmetric state (1, 1) at which both contestants are willing to expend considerable efforts to try to win and, for small θ, again almost dissipate v in expectation. Past expenditures at (2, 2) and (2, 1) are sunk once the process reaches (1, 1). As shown in Konrad and Kovenock (2008c) more generally, this logic extends to a starting point at (n, n) for larger n and may cause (with a small probability) contestants to follow a path $(n, n-1)$, $(n-1, n-1)$, $(n-2, n-1), \ldots$ (1, 1) with expected efforts at each symmetric state (j, j) almost equal to v_2. The probability that the stochastic process follows this trajectory is small, and the expected aggregate equilibrium effort does, of course, not exceed the value of the prize. But the stochastic nature of the multi-battle contest makes trajectories possible for which aggregate effort is a multiple of the value of the prize.

8.3. The tug-of-war

A third type of contest that consists of a series of single battles, with final success or failure as a function of the sequence of battle outcomes is the 'tug-of-war' that receives its name from the game in which two parties pull a rope from the two opposite ends, and each party tries to pull the rope and the rival team across a given line. As the rope-pulling typically occurs in waves, moving the rope in discrete steps, each of these waves can be seen as a little battle which may bring one or the other team closer to victory. This structure is underlying a large number of contest problems. Military conflict can, for instance, be of this type: if two countries fight against each other over a long time and can replenish their military resources over time, a battle victory may shift some power or resources to the victorious country, but if the next battle is lost, this may eliminate the advantage gained with the previous victory. Final victory may require that one country wins a considerable majority in a sequence of battles, changing the balance of power across a critical point. Similar examples can be found in sports. In tennis, for instance, the rules in a tie-break require that one of the players needs to lead by at least two points in a game in order to win the game. Again, Harris and Vickers (1985) were the first to address the tug-of-war more formally, within the context of innovation contests.[8]

The formal structure of a tug-of-war between two players is depicted in Figure 8.4. The game starts at some state j, for instance, $j = 0$. At this

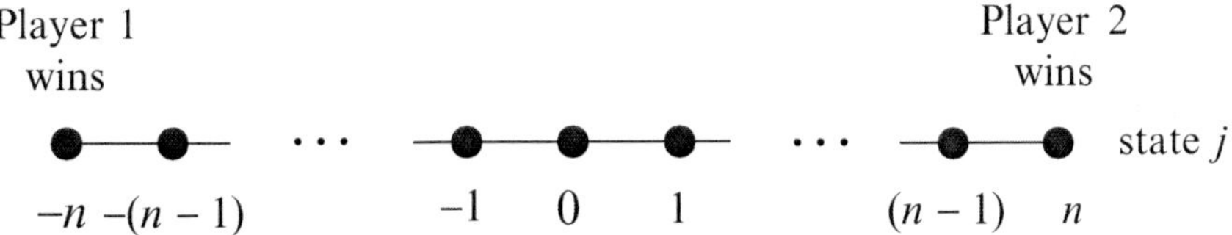

Figure 8.4 A tug-of-war with symmetric starting state 0 and $2n+1$ states. State $-n$ is a terminal state in which player 1 finally wins. State n is a terminal state in which player 2 finally wins.

[8] Further examples in the literature are McAfee (2000), Konrad and Kovenock (2005), and McBride and Skaperdas (2006).

state, a battle takes place that follows the rules of an all-pay auction, and the game moves either to state $j = -1$ or $j = 1$, depending on whether player 1 or player 2 is the winner of the battle. Players expend effort at each state, and a contest success function determines who wins the contest as a (possibly probabilistic) function of these efforts. At the new state, a new battle takes place, moving the process one step further to the left or to the right. This process continues until the game reaches one of the terminal states $j = -n$ or $j = n$. At the terminal states, players receive prizes. Once a terminal state n or $-n$ is reached, prizes are allocated and the game ends. At $j = -n$, player 1 receives a (monetary) winner prize $b_W > 0$ and player 2 a (monetary) loser prize $b_L < b_W$, which may be positive, zero or negative. When the terminal state $j = n$, then b_W is received by player 2 and b_L is received by player 1. Players are impatient and discount effort in a future period or a delay in the distribution of prizes with a discount factor $\delta \in (0, 1)$ per period.

As it is possible that a terminal state is never reached, the tug-of-war is a game with a possibly infinite horizon, making the construction of a formal set-up for studying the properties of equilibrium in the tug-of-war a cumbersome task, and I refer the reader to McAfee (2000) and to Konrad and Kovenock (2005). However, it is possible to sketch the structure of the game and characterize properties of equilibrium that emerge if the set of strategies is constrained to stationary Markov strategies without developing this formal apparatus.

Let us assume that players choose their efforts at any given interior state j from intervals $[0, k]$, with k being large, but finite. Then, a stationary Markov strategy for player 1 is a local mapping that maps each interior state j into an effort choice $x(j) = x_j \in [0, k]$, for all $j \in \{-(n-1), \ldots, -1, 0, 1, \ldots, (n-1)\}$. Similarly, the mapping $y(j) = y_j \in [0, k]$ that assigns effort $y(j)$ to an interior state for all $j \in \{-(n-1), \ldots, -1, 0, 1, \ldots, (n-1)\}$ describes a stationary Markov strategy for player 2. Mixing shall be allowed, with F_j and G_j the cumulative distribution functions denoting such mixed (local) strategies for the two players at the respective states. The actual effort choices at a given state j determine whether the process moves to $j-1$ or $j+1$, depending on whether x_j is larger or smaller than y_j. If $x_j = y_j$, different tie-breaking assumptions will be convenient depending on whether b_L is non-negative or not. For $b_L < 0$, it will be convenient to assume that the process stays in the same state if $x_j = y_j$, and for $b_L \geq 0$, the assumption will be made that the process moves to a state further away from state 0 if $x_j = y_j$. This does not define the direction of movement for $j = 0$, but any tie-breaking rule for $x_j = y_j$ if $j = 0$ is equally convenient.

For a given sequence of efforts for player 1, $\{x(t)\}_{t=0,\ldots t_T-1}$, starting at $t = 0$ and with a terminal state $-n$ or n being reached at period t_T, the payoff of player 1 is

$$\delta^{t_T} b_W - \sum_{t=0}^{t=t_T-1} \delta^t x_t \quad \text{if the terminal state is } -n \tag{8.5a}$$

$$\delta^{t_T} b_L - \sum_{t=0}^{t=t_T-1} \delta^t x_t \quad \text{if the terminal state is } n, \tag{8.5b}$$

and analogously for player 2.

A particularly interesting type of equilibrium behavior emerges if loser prizes b_L are negative, as in McAfee (2000). The nature of this equilibrium behavior can be illustrated most straightforwardly for cases in which the absolute values of the loser prizes exceed the size of the winner prizes. To illustrate what happens, let, for instance, the winner prize for player 1 (2) for reaching $-n$ (n) be equal to $b_W = v$, and the loser prize be $b_L = -(v+\theta)$ for some positive θ. Recall that the tie-breaking rule for $x_j = y_j$ requires that the process stays still at j. A Markov perfect equilibrium has $x_j = y_j = 0$ for all $j \in \{-(n-2), \ldots, +(n-2)\}$. Also, there is no effort to be chosen in the terminal states $-n$ or n. Finally, at the states $-(n-1)$ and $(n-1)$ that immediately neighbor the terminal states, both players expend positive effort in expectation. Here both players randomize as in a static all-pay auction without noise for prizes δv for the player who wins if the tug-of-war moves to the neighboring terminal state, and $\delta(v+\theta)$ for the player who loses $v+\theta$ if the tug-of-war moves to this terminal state. More formally, the equilibrium effort choices are stated as

$$x_j = y_j = 0 \quad \text{for all} \quad j \in \{-(n-2), \ldots, +(n-2)\}, \tag{8.6}$$

$$G_{-(n-1)}(z) = F_{(n-1)}(z) = \frac{z}{\delta v} \text{ for } z \in [0, \delta v] \tag{8.7}$$

with $G_{-(n-1)}(0) = F_{(n-1)}(0) = 0$ and $G_{-(n-1)}(z) = F_{(n-1)}(z) = 1$ for $z \geq \delta v$, and

$$F_{-(n-1)}(z) = G_{(n-1)}(z) = \left(1 - \frac{\delta v}{\delta(v+\theta)} + \frac{z}{\delta(v+\theta)}\right) \text{ for } z \in [0, \delta v] \tag{8.8}$$

with $F_{-(n-1)}(z) = F_{(n-1)}(z) = 0$ for $z < 0$ and $G_{-(n-1)}(z) = F_{(n-1)}(z) = 1$ for $z \geq \delta v$.

To confirm that this behavior describes a Markov perfect equilibrium, one can calculate the continuation values for both players for each state, assuming that they behave according to these local strategies for all others states, then invoke the one-stage deviation principle, and then consider why the local strategies are optimal, given the continuation values that are derived from future play according to the candidate equilibrium. The continuation values that result from the behavior in (8.6), (8.7), and (8.8) are zero for all states $-(n-2), \ldots, (n-2)$. The continuation values are equal to zero for player 1 and $-\delta v$ for player 2 at state $(-(n-1))$ and zero for player 2 and $-\delta v$ for player 1 at state $n-1$. Now, effort choices as in (8.6), (8.7), and (8.8) describe equilibrium behavior. This can be obtained from considering first what happens once the tug-of-war enters a state neighboring a terminal state, assuming that the continuation values for both players are zero at all states $-(n-2), \ldots, (n-2)$. Suppose the current state is $-(n-1)$. Then player 1 would like to push the process to state $(-n)$ and take the winner prize δv, instead of moving to $j = -(n-2)$, where his continuation value is zero. Player 2 would rather like to avoid the move to $(-n)$, as player 2 loses $\delta(v+\theta)$ by moving to this terminal state, but receives a continuation value of zero from moving to $(-(n-2))$. The difference between winning and losing at this state is (δv) for player 1, and $(\delta(v+\theta))$ for player 2. Accordingly, invoking the results on an all-pay auction without noise and prizes (δv) for player 1, and $(\delta(v+\theta))$ for player 2, they will randomize as in (8.7) and (8.8) and the payoffs from winning in this component all-pay auction are zero for player 1 and $\delta\theta$ for player 2. This can be used to consider state $-(n-2)$. The benefit of moving from $(-(n-2))$ to $(-(n-1))$ is equal to zero for player 1 and equal to $-\delta^2 v$ for player 2. None of the players would actually like to move to the state next to the terminal state. This explains why it is an equilibrium for them to expend zero efforts and just stay where they are for all interior states that do not neighbor a terminal state. For all further interior states j, the argument is more straightforward. Given the zero continuation values at neighboring states, both players are indifferent about whether they should move to one of these neighboring states or stay at j, which makes $x_j = y_j = 0$ mutually optimal replies.

The equilibrium that is described here suggests that there are situations in which players avoid areas of conflict, even though the stakes and the prizes allocated in these conflicts can be high. Players stay in some range of states in which contest effort does not pay, and in which they do not fight. They delay the resolution of the conflict into the infinite future. They know that, should they ever move close to an area in which one player is sufficiently advantaged such that he would be willing to force a victory, the other player would expend considerable effort trying to avoid defeat. This defense effort would be so high that the advantaged position would not lead to a positive payoff. Hence, once they approach the conflict zone, they are induced to fight, although the fight does not yield an expected gain to one of the players. This makes it preferable for then both to stay away from the conflict zone.

Konrad and Kovenock (2005) consider the tug-of-war for positive winner prizes and loser prizes equal to zero, assuming that each battle follows the rules of an all-pay auction. The non-negativity of the value of the prize given to the loser changes the nature of the equilibrium. It turns out that the players expend positive effort in expectation only at the symmetric state $j = 0$, or, for a more asymmetric tug-of-war, at most at two states, and these states ought to neighbor each other. Outside this area of conflict, one of the players essentially gives up, and the other player wins in the following sequence of battles that leads straighforwardly to a terminal state. The intuition for this result is again the discouragement effect: Consider a fully symmetric tug-of-war as depicted in Figure 8.4. Let the winner prize be $b_W = v > 0$ and the loser prize be $b_L = 0$. They show that the following local strategies describe a Markov perfect equilibrium: at all non-terminal states $j \neq 0$ both players choose efforts equal to zero and (by assuming the respective tie-breaking rule) the process moves further to the nearest terminal state. At $j = 0$, both players choose their efforts from mixed strategies that are described by the equilibrium for the symmetric all-pay auction with two players for prizes $v_1 = v_2 = \delta^n b_W$.

To confirm that these local strategies and the continuation values they imply for the two players for each possible state constitute a Markov perfect equilibrium, invoking the one-stage deviation principle, it is sufficient to show that players have no incentives to unilaterally deviate from their local equilibrium strategies. Key to the argument is the following consideration. Suppose the tug-of-war reaches a state $j = -1$. At this state player 2 could try to win the battle and move the tug-of-war back to the fully symmetric state $j = 0$. However, at state $j = 0$ both players are in a fully symmetric contest. They expect that whoever wins the battle at this state will win the tug-of-war in $n - 1$ further, essentially effortless battle contests. The continuation values for both players at $j = 0$ are zero. Therefore, nothing can be gained by player 2 through moving from state $j = -1$ to state $j = 0$. But then it does not make sense for this player to expend positive contest effort at state $j = -1$ by trying to move the process to state $j = 0$, and similarly for other states to the left of $j = -1$. Given the assumed tie-breaking rules for $x_i = y_j = 0$ for $j \neq 0$, the process moves effortlessly from there towards $j = -n$. For states $j = 1, \dots (n - 1)$ the argument is similar, but players 1 and 2 switch their roles.

8.4. Iterating incumbency fights

An important class of dynamic tournaments that depict a variety of empirically observed behavior can be viewed as iterated tournaments with a particular type of asymmetry. Suppose there is an incumbent player in an initial period $t = 0$. A challenger may show up. The two players fight in a contest. The winner of the contest receives the reward b_0 in this period, and is also the incumbent for the next period $t = 1$. In all future periods, this period game may repeat. The period reward may, but need not, be the same in each period or for each possible winner in a given period. Also, the rules of the continuation games that result for different possible winners in a given period may, but need not, be identical. Depending on the different applications one can have in mind, a defeated incumbent may return as a challenger, as in applications by Mehlum and Moene (2004), or may disappear forever, with new challengers emerging in the future. Similarly, the challenger who is defeated in period t may return as a challenger in period $t + i$, or may disappear with some reservation utility forever.

Structures of this type can be found in many contexts. Perhaps the most obvious example comes, again, from sports. Champions, for instance, obtain a flow of rents while they are champions. They receive payments from their sponsors, and fees for promoting consumer products in commercials, and presumably they also receive a rent from the status or prestige of being the champion. However, champions can be challenged by newcomers from time to time, and may lose the title of champion to the challengers. Biology provides many other examples. Particularly among animals living together in herds, some leader or leaders receive a particular benefit from preferential access to food and to opportunities to reproduce. But these advantages only last until they are successfully challenged by newcomers. Politics also provides examples. Rulers, party leaders or parties in power more generally must defend their leadership against many types of threats. Rulers of a territory may have enemies or enemy groups inside their own jurisdiction who would like to take over, or external enemies may wage a military attack, trying to conquer this territory. Party leaders face competition from party members who represent different power groups inside the party, or just from the next generation of politicians. And in the context of party competition and elections, iterating incumbency fights are even more formalized, regulating the intervals in which incumbents can enjoy their incumbency rents, and the point of time of elections, which are the events when rival parties challenge a party's or a coalition's incumbency.

An early analysis of one of these structures is by Stephan and Ursprung (1998). They consider an infinitely iterated incumbency fight in which the probability that the defeated challenger may return is somewhere between zero and unity. Modifications of this set-up are also possible, particularly regarding the role of a challenger who defeated the incumbent. Depending on the empirical application one has in mind, a new incumbent may be threatened by future challengers, or may enjoy more secure property rights than his predecessor. Another dimension that deserves consideration is the particular structure of the incumbency contest. Incumbents may be technologically advantaged or disadvantaged in this fight, or particularly vulnerable. Their capability of fighting may follow a deterministic pattern, as in Stephan and Ursprung (1998), or may follow a stochastic pattern. In the most simple stationary version of this problem, an incumbent meets a new entrant in every period; entrants who fail to overthrow the incumbent or incumbents who are defeated receive a zero payoff for all future periods and never return as a challenger. Let the period rent that is allocated to the winner of the incumbency fight in a given period be normalized to unity and let $\delta \in (0, 1)$ be the common and time-invariant discount factor. Finally, let the incumbency fight follow the rules of a Tullock lottery contest. Considering a simplified version of Stephan and Ursprung (1998), let x_t and y_t be the fighting efforts by the respective incumbent and entrant in period t, let $p(x_t, y_t)$ be the probability that the incumbent wins this fight given these efforts. Then, focusing on Markov perfect equilibrium in stationary strategies, let u^* be the value of being an incumbent at the beginning of a period. The objective function of an incumbent then becomes

$$u_t(x_t, y_t) = p(x_t, y_t)(1 + \delta u^*) - x_t. \tag{8.9}$$

The incumbent expends fighting effort equal to x_t, which cannot be recovered, regardless whether he wins or loses the period contest. If the incumbent loses the period contest, he disappears and receives zero in this and all future periods. This happens with probability $(1 - p)$. However, the incumbent wins with a probability p, and in this case the incumbent receives the period payoff from being the winner in this period that has been normalized to 1, and also he is the incumbent in the next period. Assuming equilibrium behavior in the next period, this advantage is worth u^* at the beginning of the next period and needs to be discounted when calculating the payoff in the present period t.

The objective function of the entrant is

$$\omega_t(x_t, y_t) = (1 - p(x_t, y_t))(1 + \delta u^*) - y_t. \tag{8.10}$$

The interpretation is similar. The challenger has a fighting cost that is equal to y_t. If the challenger loses he receives zero in this and all future periods. This happens with probability p. The challenger wins with probability $(1 - p)$. He then receives the period payoff that is normalized to 1, plus the discounted value of being the incumbent in the next period, δu^*.

Focusing on Markov perfect equilibrium, if the problem is well-behaved and if $p(x_t, y_t)$ is symmetric in both arguments, the first-order condition $\frac{\partial p}{\partial x}(1 + \delta u^*) = 1$ together with $x_t^* = y_t^*$ and the stationarity property $u_t(x_t^*, y_t^*) = u^*$ characterize the period efforts in a stationary Markov perfect equilibrium. For instance, for the lottery contest, the continuation value as incumbent becomes $u^* = 1/(4 - \delta)$, and the equilibrium efforts in each period are $x^* = y^* = 1/(4 - \delta)$. If $\delta = 0$, this outcome reproduces the static Tullock contest. If the players are more patient, then they also value the position as an incumbent in a future period and, for this reason, they are willing to expend more effort in fighting. However, the total effort expended in each period is far below the value of the (uncontested) total prize, which is $1/(1-\delta)$, because the players anticipate that any incumbent will be challenged and will have to expend effort in the future.

As discussed, many problems fit well into the structure of iterated contests and readers may consider themselves whether incumbents or challengers have a second chance, whether these incumbency fights are asymmetric, whether the situation is stationary and perpetuates forever or not, and what are the other specific characteristics in the different specific situations that are described more generally as iterated contests. In the formal framework analyzed here, it was assumed that a contest takes place in every period. Whether or not an incumbent has to fight a new challenger in a given period may, however, be an endogenous outcome. In some instances, such as some applications in sports or politics, the period contest is deterministic, follows strict rules and is part of the design of the game. In other cases, the outbreak of conflict between two rival leaders may not be inevitable. The outbreak of conflict in a given period may, instead, depend on rivals' absolute or relative strength in a given period and on many other aspects. This leads to a further class of dynamic problems.

8.5. Endogenous fighting

In a static conflict about resources, players often have two options. They can fight or abstain from fighting. In a dynamic situation, a further option can emerge: players have to decide on the timing of a conflict. The question of why actual fighting should take place and the timing of actual fighting has generated much interest among political scientists in the field of international politics who study military conflict. Indeed, knowing about the enormous social cost of war, in terms of lives sacrificed, the destruction of property and the loss of income due to redirecting the use of resources from producing butter to producing guns, the outbreak and the long duration of military conflict is puzzling. In the light of the Coase theorem, one might think that a small number of players should be able to negotiate a deal, moving from the inefficient status of military conflict to a less inefficient status of peace. Similar questions emerge in any dynamic framework. Within a political party, a firm or another type of organization, leadership positions are typically contested for, and an incumbent leader usually expends some time and effort trying to prevent attempts by rivals' who may try to replace them, or to make such attempts unsuccessful. In such frameworks, the same types of questions emerge: why should rivals enter into a wasteful incumbency fight rather than negotiating a deal, and if a wasteful fight is eventually inevitable, what is the optimal timing of attack?

What makes violent fighting inevitable?

Political scientists and economists addressed the first question and came up with several reasons why a resource-wasteful contest may be inevitable.

The first answer invokes an information argument. War or other types of resource-wasteful conflict may be the outcome of incomplete information. Uncertainty and misperceptions regarding the strength of a possible adversary, or misperceptions about how an adversary evaluates certain goals pursued in negotiations may play an important role.[9] Also, in the context of military conflict, some political economy reasons have been put forward to explain the outbreak of war. An important argument in this context is by Hess and Orphanides (1995). They argue that a political leader may wage war for reasons of reelection: A leader who performed poorly in some policy areas and developed a reputation of having low competence in these areas may wage a war with another country, hoping that his competence in the field of military conflict turns out to be high, and that he might be re-elected on the basis of this high competence, given that a high competence is important for the welfare of the country in an ongoing international military conflict.

[9] See Fearon (1995) for a survey of this type of reasoning in political science, and Bester and Wärneryd (2006) for an analysis along the lines of mechanism design.

Other reasons causing resource-wasteful contests have to do with incomplete contracts and lack of credible commitment. Two examples can illustrate this. In one example, fighting today may be the only option for one player to change the balance of power in his favor tomorrow. In the second example, fighting today may be a means for a player to select a preferred equilibrium among a set of multiple equilibria that may prevail in the continuation game in a dynamic framework.[10]

The first example draws on Garfinkel and Skaperdas (2000). A simplified version of their argument is as follows. Suppose that a prize of size 1 is allocated between players A and B in the second of two periods $t = 1, 2$. Suppose that, without military intervention in period 1, the military strength of the players is determined by their capacities for weapon production in the respective periods, and let these be exogenously given and equal to $x_1 = 10$ and $y_1 = 1$ in period 1 and $x_2 = 1$ and $y_2 = 10$ in period 2. Invoking the logic of contest theory for a given contest success function with win probability $p(x_2, y_2)$ for player A and $1 - p(x_2, y_2)$ for player B in period 2, if they fight in period 2, these are the win probabilities, and their expected prizes are these probabilities multiplied by the prize. For instance, p could be the contest success function of the lottery contest. If the players reach period 2, they may fight and find out who receives the prize. In this case, they face a real cost of contest effort, and possibly other welfare losses from collateral damages of fighting. They may as well save their resources and avoid such damages and divide the prize among them. They may, for instance, use a sharing rule in which the win probabilities resulting from their fighting abilities in period 2 define their respective shares. Given that player B is very strong in period 2, player 1 receives only a small share in the prize, defined by $p(1, 10)$ in this case. Players may already anticipate this period-2 outcome in period 1. In period 1, player A is much stronger than player B. Player A may threaten player B with military action in period 1 and would be likely to win. Given this, player B might be willing to hand over a larger share of the period-2 prize if player A abstained from fighting in period 1. However, such promises or contracts are not time consistent in a world without external enforcement. Player B may easily make such promises. Once player A has abstained from action in period 1, player B will not stick to the promise. The time-consistent outcome is the sharing rule determined by the relative strength of A and B in period 2. The only way for player A to make use of the superiority in period 1 and to attain a larger share in the prize that is allocated in period 2 might therefore

[10] See also Fearon (1995) for a discussion of the argument and further examples.

be to try and defeat player B in period 1, or to use own fighting capacity in period 1 to weaken player B's fighting ability in the second period.

The second example draws on a formal analysis carried out by Slantchev (2003). His argument is also based on a failure to commit, and can also be described verbally, using the two-stage framework just outlined. Suppose that two players A and B have to divide a prize of a given size in stage 2 between them. Let us assume the size of the prize is normalized again to unity. For reasons that are beyond consideration here, this division problem may have two possible coordination equilibria, I and II: in equilibrium I player A receives 80 percent of the prize (=0.8) and player B receives 20 percent (=0.2). In equilibrium II the distribution is just the reverse: player B receives 80 percent of the prize and player A receives 20 percent. Clearly, player A prefers coordination on equilibrium I and player B prefers the coordination equilibrium II. Players may succeed in coordinating on one of the equilibria, in particular if any other outcome has a lower payoff for both. But which of the two coordination equilibria is chosen in stage 2 may simply be random, or it may well depend on anything that happens in stage 1. For instance, suppose that player B may attack player A in stage 1 with no particular purpose, but coordination on equilibrium II may occur if and only if B attacks A in this stage, whereas coordination on equilibrium I occurs if B does not attack. Even if attacking is just resource wasteful for B (and presumably also for A) and has no further fundamental consequences apart from this waste, it may be advantageous for player B to initiate such an attack in period 1, provided that this wasteful attack has a cost for player B that is lower than the difference in his payoffs (0.8) – (0.2) in the two coordination equilibria in stage 2. The choice of whether to incur a wasteful conflict in stage 1 may simply be caused by players who try to influence the selection among the coordination equilibria in stage 2.

Optimal timing

Having found reasons to explain why expending resource-wasteful effort in a contest may be inevitable, and why options to negotiate and to reach a Coasian bargaining outcome may fail, the second question in a dynamic framework emerges: when is the optimal timing for entering into a stage of fighting in which the contestants expend resource-wasteful effort? During the times of the Cold War, the two major powers expended considerable amounts of resources to build up weapons or to prepare for a military showdown, but compared to the welfare cost of an actual showdown, these costs were small, and fortunately the actual showdown never took place. Similarly, adversaries inside a firm, a political party or an organization more generally may watch each other for a whole series of periods. In each period, each player must decide whether to open the battle or not.

What determinants are important for the decision to strike now, or to be willing to delay the showdown? As each side in a conflict can initiate the showdown, observed delay requires that both parties prefer a delay. In particular, if two rivals both wait for the optimal moment to open the battle, if a given period is inconvenient for one side, it should be even more convenient for the other side. This suggests an early resolution of an enduring conflict. However, as the examples mentioned show, in many cases both adversaries in a dynamic contest are willing to delay the showdown.

At least two reasons can be identified. One reason traces back to Clausewitz (1832/1976). He claimed that a showdown is not symmetric: one side attacks, the other side defends, and the side that initiates the showdown is usually the attacker. Clausewitz explains that the side that competes on the defense has several advantages compared to the side that attacks. Bester and Konrad (2004) analyzed this in a simple two-period framework in which relative and absolute strength of the adversaries may change over time. It turns out that what may cause a player to attack is the expectation that his relative strength deteriorates strongly over time, such that, even having the advantage of the defense in a future period does not compensate for the deterioration of his relative strength. They show that absolute fighting capacity (and the cost it involves) also matters.

An important aspect of a dynamic framework is uncertainty about own and competitors' strength in future periods. This aspect is developed more formally in Bester and Konrad (2005) and Polborn (2006). Both papers analyze a conflict between two contestants that possibly lasts for an infinite number of periods. Players may consider fighting in any given period or waiting for the optimal period to initiate fighting in the future. If at least one player initiates a showdown in a given period, this 'showdown' terminates the conflict and settles the property rights conflict between the two rivals for all times. Some characteristics of the players that are important for their fighting ability or their willingness to fight are developing stochastically over time, and the key question becomes when the situation is sufficiently advantageous for a player to initiate the showdown. In this problem, if only one player can initiate the showdown, as in Polborn (2006), this player sacrifices the option of initiating the showdown at a later date, when the situation might even be superior for him. Accordingly, for it to be attractive to attack in a given period, the expected benefit from attacking must be sufficiently large to overcompensate for the lost option value of attacking later. In Bester and Konrad (2005), both players have the option to attack and change an initially symmetric situation, gaining everything by winning the showdown, or losing everything otherwise. Here the decision problem is more complex, because a player has to wage the expected benefit from attacking now against a more blurred picture regarding future options: if the showdown does not take place today, the situation may be even better for him tomorrow, or it may become so much worse that his adversary becomes tempted to initiate the showdown.

To illustrate the option value of waiting, consider a simple parametric variant of the problem that is studied in Polborn (2006). Two players, A and B, compete in a dynamic framework with periods $t = 0, 1, 2, \ldots$, that is depicted in Figure 8.5. Each player owns some assets at $t = 0$ that generate an amount of income in each period of size $w_A(t)$ and $w_B(t)$. For simplicity, let $w_A(t) \equiv 1$ for all t, and let the $w_B(t)$ be independent draws from the uniform distribution $G_B(w)$ with expected value $Ew = 1/2$ and support $[0, 1]$. At period 0, each player observes his own income and the income of his competitor. In line with Polborn, let only player A decide whether to initiate a resource-wasteful conflict in any given period: the showdown. If A does not initiate the showdown, both consume their respective period income in this period and time moves to the next period, $t = 1$. In the

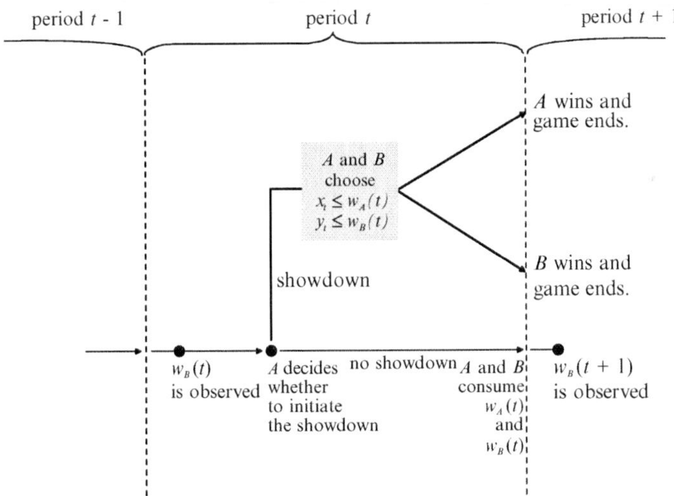

Figure 8.5 Timing in a period prior to which no showdown had been triggered: the income of player B is revealed. Then A decides whether to trigger the showdown. If peace prevails, A and B consume their incomes. Otherwise the showdown takes place. The showdown is an all-pay auction in which each player chooses fighting effort and this choice is constrained by the own income in the respective period.

next period, income materializes and the decision problem repeats. This continues up to the period in which A initiates the showdown. Suppose the showdown is triggered in period t. Then a fight takes place in this period. The fight can be described by an all-pay auction. Both players choose simultaneously the amounts of contest efforts $x_t \in [0, 1]$ and $y_t \in [0, w_B(t)]$. The contest success function (2.1) maps these efforts into a contest outcome, by which the player who expended the higher effort wins. If player A wins, A takes over the property rights in the income-generating assets of player B for all future periods and receives the future income generated by these resources for all future periods. Analogously, if B wins, B receives the property rights in A's resources and the income they generate for all future periods. The player who loses the fight loses all future income and is left with the period income in the period of fighting, net of his own fighting effort. If a fight takes place in a particular period, the outcome of the fight essentially eliminates one of the two players from the picture and shifts ownership of the property of the defeated player to the winning player.

Consider players' local strategies. If a showdown took place prior to period t, no decisions are made in all future periods as the showdown settled the conflict. Consider a period t for which no showdown had taken place prior to t. Player A has to choose whether or not to initiate the showdown. If A initiates the showdown, players choose $x_t \in [0, 1]$ and $y_t \in [0, w_B(t)]$ respectively. As A can mobilize more resources than B, player A can initiate the showdown and expend sufficient resources to make winning an outcome that has probability 1. Let us constrain the set of strategies of players to stationary Markov strategies: A's choice of whether to initiate a showdown at t is only a function of $w_B(t)$, but not of the history of previous incomes, and the choice of $x_t \in [0, 1]$ and $y_t \in [0, w_B(t)]$ in the showdown is only a function of the observed respective period incomes $(1, w_B(t))$ in the period of the showdown. Finally, the payoffs of players are given by the sum of their discounted period incomes, net of fighting efforts, with $\delta \in (0, 1)$ the discount factor that applies.

It is easy to confirm that the one-stage deviation principle applies to this problem. It is also intuitive that a Markov perpect equilibrium has a simple property: there is a cut-off value w^* such that player A will initiate the showdown if the observed value of B's income $w_B(t)$ is not larger than this cut-off value, and will wait if it is not. To identify this cut-off value, we consider the condition of indifference, assuming that such a cut-off value exists and that the attack occurs if the actual $w_B(t)$ in period t is smaller than the cut-off value.

In any period, player A can initiate the showdown and choose $x_t = w_B(t)$ and win. Using the logic applied in Chapter 2 on the all-pay auction without noise and budget constraints, this yields an expected present value of payoff of

$$(1 - w_B(t)) + \frac{\delta}{1-\delta}(1 + 0.5). \tag{8.11}$$

Note that, in equilibrium, A does not choose $x_t = w_B(t)$ with probability 1, but randomizes, with $w_B(t)$ being in support of his equilibrium strategy. However, one can use any of the efforts that are in the equilibrium support for player A in calculating the equilibrium payoff. Alternatively A may wait and attack at a later time when the value of $w_B(t)$ drops for the first time below the critical level w^*. The expected payoff that emerges from this behavior is equal to

$$1 + \delta\left[w^*\left[\left(1 - \frac{w^*}{2}\right) + \frac{\delta}{1-\delta}(1.5)\right] + (1 - w^*)\right]\sum_{k=0}^{\infty}\delta^k(1 - w^*)^k. \tag{8.12}$$

This makes use of $E(w_B(t)\,|w_B(t) < w^*) = w^*/2$. Further, (8.12) can be written equivalently as

$$1 + \delta\left[w^*\left[\left(1 - \frac{w^*}{2}\right) + \frac{\delta}{1-\delta}(1.5)\right] + (1 - w^*)\right]\frac{1}{1 - (\delta(1 - w^*))}. \tag{8.13}$$

For the critical level of $w_B(t) = w^*$, player A needs to be just indifferent between initiating the showdown or continuing to wait. Accordingly, w^* is obtained from replacing $w_B(t)$ in (8.11) by w^*, equating the resulting expression to (8.13) and solving for w^*. This yields

$$w^* = \frac{1}{2\delta}\left(2\delta - 2 + 2\sqrt{2\delta^2 - 2\delta + 1}\right). \tag{8.14}$$

This function is depicted in Figure 8.6.

Note that, for $\delta \to 0$, we have $w^* \to 0$; that is, if only the present period matters, then the player A would not like to initiate the showdown in this period, as this has fighting cost in the current period and yields benefits only in future periods, which are heavily discounted. However, if the future income is valued more highly, then the player A is willing to initiate the showdown, even though it costs contest effort today. The threshold up to which player A is willing to fight is increasing in the discount factor. This is one of the key results in the analysis by Polborn (2006).

A limitation of the approach by Polborn is that only one player can attack at a time. There are applications like the incumbent-entrant situations analyzed by Stephan and Ursprung (1998) that were outlined in

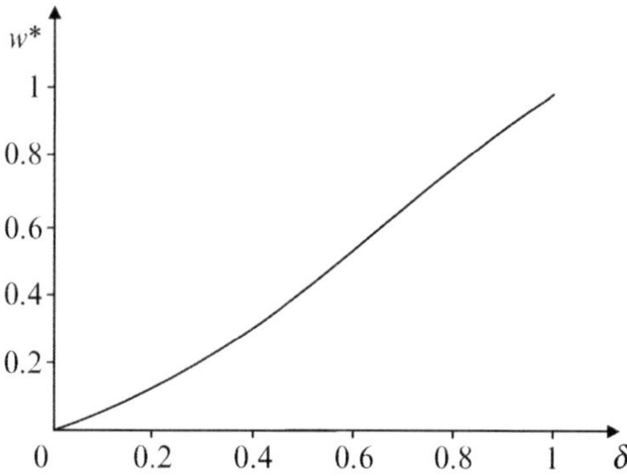

Figure 8.6 The threshold value w^* as a function of the discount factor δ if the period income $w_B(t)$ from player B's initial resources is independently and uniformly distributed on the interval $[0, 1]$.

section 8.4, in which this is a plausible assumption. However, in many contexts the option to attack is mutual for the whole group of players. Thinking, for instance, of the Cold War period, both the USA and the Soviet Union were able to initiate the final showdown, but still both sides decided to delay the conflict for decades. This simultaneity of the option to initiate the fighting characterizes many dynamic problems in which the initial status of two or more contestants is similar. The framework considered by Bester and Konrad (2005) allows for both adversaries to initiate the showdown, and assumes that they are symmetric from an ex ante point of view. Each player can unilaterally initiate the showdown. However, if both players decide to delay the showdown, this has two upsides and one downside for each player. The first upside is that the player does not need to expend any effort on fighting in the respective period. A second upside is that the strategic position of the player may improve in the next period; he may have higher income, or his adversary may have lower income than in the previous period. In this case, the player's success from initiating the showdown in the next period becomes more likely and less costly for this player. On the downside, the realization of incomes in the next period may improve the strategic position of the adversary, turning the player into an easier target for his adversary. Bester and Konrad characterize conditions for a Markov perfect equilibrium to exist for which both players delay the showdown until one of them becomes a sufficiently easy target that is, until one player has a sufficiently low income, and hence, a sufficiently low fighting ability in that particular period and can be defeated by the other player with little effort in expectation. Hence, both players wait to see whether a situation emerges in which the rival player is weak, such that it is inexpensive to defeat this player. The player who first reaches such a situation of weakness essentially loses. Empirically this outcome maps the type of enduring rivalries observed in politics or between rival companies or persons in organizations and makes a prediction: players wait until their adversaries are weak or vulnerable, and then hit.

8.6. Summary: the discouragement effect

Contests with multiple rounds of the types illustrated here have a common feature which will essentially provide an intuition for their equilibrium properties which could be termed the 'discouragement effect'. This effect can be illustrated for an elimination tournament as in Figure 8.5 with only four players and two rounds. Suppose, for simplicity, that the players' abilities and valuations of winning are common knowledge, and let players be perfectly symmetric for simplicity. Players 1 and 2 anticipate that a victory in the semi-final will not give them a prize, but that it allows the victorious player w_1 to enter the final, where he expects to meet player w_2. Symmetry implies that each of the two winners of the semi-finals will receive a payoff

$$\pi_F = p(x^*, x^*) - x^* \tag{8.15}$$

if x^* is the symmetric equilibrium effort in the final and if the final prize is normalized to 1. This payoff is only a fraction of the prize, and, depending on the nature of the battle that constitutes the final, this fraction can be very small. Recall that, in the lottery contest with symmetric players, this fraction is 1/4, and if the contest success function in the final is that of the all-pay auction with complete information as in (2.1), the fraction is even zero. Accordingly, when competing in the semi-final, players 1 and 2 compete for a possibly very small prize. The fact that most of the final prize is dissipated in contest effort in the final discourages the contestants in the semi-final from expending much effort.

Discouragement effects occur in many dynamic contests and have been discussed for several types in this chapter. In the race, a disadvantaged player could try and win some component battles, returning to a state in which the situation between the players is again more symmetric. However, the incentive to do this is small, given that the players will expend considerable effort having once returned to a state of symmetry. In the tug-of-war, the discouragement effect caused two very different types of equilibrium. In one case, all fighting takes place in a small set of interior states in which players are fairly symmetric. Once the process leaves this set, one of the players essentially gives up. Returning to states in which the contestants are more symmetric is feasible, but not much is gained for the disadvantaged player by returning to these states, as the component contests in these symmetric states dissipate much of what can be gained in the tug-of-war. In the other case, the discouragement effect caused players to avoid approaching states next to the terminal states, and to stay effortlessly in the set of interior states of the tug-of-war. A discouragement effect was also important for the dynamics of sequences of incumbent-challenger fights. If any winner of a championship knows that new challengers will come up and contest for the championship, the winner of a current incumbent-challenger fight wins less than the present value of all future benefits of being champion. The prize of winning is essentially the period prize, plus the benefit of entering into future conflict from an incumbent's position.

The discouragement effect suggests that players do not expend much effort in early rounds of an elimination tournament, or in asymmetric states in a race or in a tug-of-war, and this prediction may partially hold in the data when considering such games. But overall, we do not observe tennis players leaving the court before the game is over, and we observe intense competition in early rounds of soccer world championships and in many other grand contests. There could be several reasons for this. The first reason is incomplete information. However, as was already observed by Rosen (1986), a formal treatment of incomplete information in grand contests is difficult, due to the possible signalling value of players' choices or observed outcomes in early stages.[11] Second, grand contests with several rounds typically have a complex prize structure with prizes for the best, second best, third best, etc. There could also be intermediate prizes from winning single battles in a grand contest. Konrad and Kovenock (2008c) have analyzed the race, and have shown that such intermediate prizes prevent the race from becoming trivial and boring once one of the players has accumulated some advantage. Such intermediate prizes can make the race 'pervasive' in the sense that, from a given state, all further feasible trajectories have a positive probability of being reached, and players who are lagging far behind may catch up, take over the lead, and finally win. A third reason is variability of ability of players over time. As is shown in

[11] See, e.g., Meyer (1991), Moldovanu and Sela (2006), and Münster (2006a) for further considerations on repeated contests with incomplete information.

Konrad and Kovenock (2008a) and discussed in section 3.2, if contestants' ability or their unit cost of expending effort are not time invariant but instead are random draws for each of the states of a grand contest, this will also counterbalance the discouragement effect. Moreover, players whose ability is more variable benefit more from participating in a contest and, in expectation, they are more successful at reaching later stages of grand contests. This asymmetry in benefits has implications for the self-selection of individuals: in a population in which players differ in terms of the variability of their ability, and in which individuals have to choose whether to enter into a contest or do something else, the individuals whose variability is high should be more likely to decide to enter the contest, because their expected gain from entering is higher. Moreover, as these individuals are, in expectation, more successful in the course of a grand contest, one should observe that the ability of the set of participants in the later stages of grand contests is even more variable.

9

Conclusions

Contest competition shares properties with other types of competition which are more prevalent and have been more carefully studied in economic theory, but it also has some important differences. Some insights that have been developed are seemingly robust and these are collected also in the summary sections at the ends of the chapters. The fundamental role of heterogeneity of contestants and the discouragement effect in dynamic contests figure prominently in the theory of contests.

Contest competition is an important and widespread principle for solving allocation problems. This has been illustrated in the examples in Chapter 1. Contests sometimes emerge naturally, or their rules are designed by forces that are outside human control. War technology develops and shapes the rules of military combat. The physiology of animals and much of their social behavior develop along the laws of evolution. Contests play an essential role in evolutionary selection processes, but are also outcomes of the evolutionary process. In some other areas contests are conscientiously and carefully designed, examples being sports tournaments, political competition, tournaments in labor markets and in organizations, or state lotteries.

The analysis of contests in this book has been mostly positive. Contests differ in the likelihood of allocating the prize to the player(s) who value(s) it more highly. If contestants differ in the values they attribute to winning the prize, efficiency requires that the contestant with the highest valuation wins. This is not always the case for contests. The properties of the different types of contests with respect to the efficiency of the allocation of the prize can be studied considering the equilibrium analysis that was carried out for the different types of contests.

Players expend effort in contests. Some of this effort is simply wasteful from a social point of view. This is seemingly most evident for armies which aim at destroying each other in order to determine the victorious country. There are also contests in which the welfare conclusions are less obvious. Campaign effort or litigation effort may be useful if it helps overcome information problems, but may be less useful for other channels by which they may affect decision-making. Tullock (1980) considered rent-seeking as a contest and determined equilibrium rent-seeking effort as a share of the rent that is contested for. Implicitly suggesting that rent-seeking effort is wasteful, he called this rate the dissipation rate. As has been discussed in Chapter 2, if the rent-seeking contest is seen as a process that produces and reveals information about the quality of policy proposals, the picture becomes less clear. Also, there are contexts in which contest effort is basically a good thing. Examples could be the labor market if contests are used as incentive payment mechanisms, sports contests, if spectators enjoy the good performance of athletes, or R&D contests in which contest effort yields new valuable knowledge. Even in these cases, however, the welfare analysis is not straightforward. R&D contests produce new information and allow innovations that generate profits and consumer rents. However, they involve the potential of duplicating research effort. For this and other reasons, welfare analysis on R&D is a rather difficult problem and this explains why the analysis did not focus on welfare considerations.

The theory of contests is a very active field of research, and I will abstain from trying to predict its future directions. I tried to look at contests as structures governing the allocation of valuable resources from a particular perspective, focusing on aspects of commitment and design issues, and on the interaction between component contests in a dynamic contest environment. The idea was to abstract from particular institutional contexts and to detect more general patterns. This may complement other analyzes that are more focused on a particular institutional context or policy area.

References

Aidt, Toke S., and Arye L. Hillman, 2008, 'Enduring rents', *European Journal of Political Economy* (forthcoming).

Alexander, Herbert E., 1996, 'Financing presidential election campaigns', *Issues of Democracy*, USIA Electronic Journals, 1(13) (<http://usinfo.state.gov/journals/itdhr/0996/ijde/alex.htm> 12.10.2006).

Amaldoss, Wilfred, and Amnon Rapoport, 2008, 'Excessive expenditures in two-stage contests: theory and experimental evidence', in: Ingrid N. Haugen and Anna S. Nielsen (eds.), *Game Theory: Strategies, Equilibria and Theorems*, Nova Publishers, New York (forthcoming).

Amann, Erwin, and Wolfgang Leininger, 1996, 'Asymmetric all-pay auctions with incomplete information: the two-player case', *Games and Economic Behavior*, 14(1), 1–18.

Amegashie, J. Atsu, 1999, 'The design of rent-seeking competitions: committees, preliminary and final contests', *Public Choice*, 99(1–2), 63–76.

——— 2000, 'Some results on rent-seeking contests with shortlisting', *Public Choice*, 105(3–4), 245–53.

——— and Marco Runkel, 2007, 'Sabotaging potential rivals', *Social Choice and Welfare*, 28(1), 143–62.

——— and Ximing Wu, 2004, 'Self selection in competing all-pay auctions', mimeo, University of Guelph.

Anbarci, Nejat, Stergios Skaperdas, and Constantinos Syropoulos, 2002, 'Comparing bargaining solutions in the shadow of conflict: how norms against threats can have real effects', *Journal of Economic Theory*, 106(1), 1–16.

Anderson, Lisa R., and Sarah L. Stafford, 2003, 'An experimental analysis of rent seeking under varying competitive conditions', *Public Choice*, 115(1–2), 199–216.

Anderson, Simon P., Jacob K. Goeree, and Charles A. Holt, 1998, 'Rent seeking with bounded rationality: an analysis of the all-pay auction', *Journal of Political Economy*, 106(4), 828–53.

Appelbaum, Elie, and Eliakim Katz, 1986a, 'Transfer seeking and avoidance: on the full social cost of rent-seeking', *Public Choice*, 48, 175–81.

——— 1986b, 'Rent seeking and entry', *Economics Letters*, 20(3), 207–12.

Arrow, Kenneth J., 1973, 'Higher education as a filter', *Journal of Public Economics*, 2(3), 193–216.

Austen-Smith, David, 1995, 'Campaign contributions and access', *American Political Science Review*, 89(3), 566–81.

—— 1998, 'Allocating access for information and contributions', *Journal of Law, Economics and Organization*, 14(2), 277–303.

Baik, Kyung Hwan, 1993, 'Effort levels in contests: the public-good prize case', *Economics Letters*, 41(4), 363–7.

—— 1998, 'Difference-form contest success functions and effort levels in contests', *European Journal of Political Economy*, 14(4), 685–701.

—— 2007, 'Equilibrium contingent compensation in contests with delegation', *Southern Economic Journal*, 73(4), 986–1002.

—— and In-Gyu Kim, 1997, 'Delegation in contests', *European Journal of Political Economy*, 13(2), 281–98.

—— and Sanghack Lee, 1998, 'Group rent seeking with sharing', in: Michael R. Baye (ed.), *Advances in Applied Microeconomics*, Vol. 7, JAI Press, Stamford, Conn., 75–85.

—— and Jason F. Shogren, 1992, 'Strategic behavior in contests—comment', *American Economic Review*, 82(1), 359–62.

—— and Sunghyun Na, 2001, 'Bidding for a group-specific public-good prize', *Journal of Public Economics*, 82(3), 415–29.

Banks, Jeffrey S., 2000, 'Buying supermajorities in finite legislatures', *American Political Science Review*, 94(3), 677–81.

Barros, Pedro P., and Lars Sørgard, 2000, 'Merger in an advertising-intensive industry', mimeo, University of Bergen.

Barut, Yasar, and Dan Kovenock, 1998, 'The symmetric multiple prize all-pay auction with complete information', *European Journal of Political Economy*, 14(4), 627–44.

—— —— and Charles Noussair, 2002, 'A comparison of multiple-unit all-pay and winner-pay auctions under incomplete information', *International Economic Review*, 43(3), 675–708.

Batina, Raimond G., and Toshihiro Ihori, 2005, *Public Goods: Theories and Evidence*, Springer, Heidelberg.

Baye, Michael R., and Heidrun C. Hoppe, 2003, 'The strategic equivalence of rent-seeking, innovation, and patent-race games', *Games and Economic Behavior*, 44(2), 217–26.

—— Dan Kovenock, and Casper G. de Vries, 1993, 'Rigging the lobbying process: an application of the all-pay auction', *American Economic Review*, 83(1), 289–94.

—— —— —— 1994, 'The solution to the Tullock rent-seeking game when R > 2: mixed-strategy equilibria and mean dissipation rates', *Public Choice*, 81(3–4), 363–80.

—— —— —— 1996, 'The all-pay auction with complete information', *Economic Theory*, 8(2), 291–305.

—— —— —— 1998, 'A general linear model of contests', mimeo, Kelley School of Business, Indiana University, Bloomington, Ind.

——— ——— 1999, 'The incidence of overdissipation in rent-seeking contests', *Public Choice*, 99(3–4), 439–54.

——— ——— 2005, 'Comparative analysis of litigation systems: an auction-theoretic approach', *Economic Journal*, 115(505), 583–601.

——— ——— 2008, 'Contests with rank-order spillovers', unpublished manuscript, Indiana University, Bloomington, Ind.

Bell, David E., Ralph L. Keeney, and John D. C. Little, 1975, 'A market share theorem', *Journal of Marketing Research*, 12(2), 136–41.

Bergstrom, Ted, Larry Blume, and Hal R. Varian, 1986, 'On the private provision of public goods', *Journal of Public Economics*, 29(1), 25–49.

Bester, Helmut, and Werner Güth, 1998, 'Is altruism evolutionarily stable?', *Journal of Economic Behavior and Organization*, 34(2), 193–209.

——— and Kai A. Konrad, 2004, 'Delay in contests', *European Economic Review*, 48(5), 1169–78.

——— ——— 2005, 'Easy targets and the timing of conflict', *Journal of Theoretical Politics*, 17(2), 199–215.

——— and Karl Wärneryd, 2006, 'Conflict and the social contract', *Scandinavian Journal of Economics*, 108(2), 231–49.

Blackett, Donald W., 1954, 'Some Blotto games', *Naval Research Logistics Quarterly*, 1(1), 55–60.

——— 1958, 'Pure strategy solutions to Blotto games', *Naval Research Logistics Quarterly*, 5(2), 107–9.

Bloch, Francis, Santiago Sánchez-Pagés and Raphaël Soubeyran, 2006, 'When does universal peace prevail? Secession and group formation in conflict', *Economics of Governance*, 7(1), 3–29.

Borel, Émile, 1938, *Traité du Calcul des Probabilités et de ses applications: Applications aux Jeux de Hazard*, Gauthier-Villars, Paris.

Börgers, Tilman, and Christian Dustmann, 2003, 'Awarding telecom licenses: the recent European experience', *Economic Policy*, 36, 215–68.

Brandauer, Stefan, and Florian Englmaier, 2005, 'A model of delegation in contests', mimeo, Harvard Business School.

Brander, James A., and Barbara J. Spencer, 1985, 'Export subsidies and international market share rivalry', *Journal of International Economics*, 18(1–2), 83–100.

Broom, Mark, Chris Cannings, and Glenn T. Vickers, 2000, 'Evolution in knockout conflicts: the fixed strategy case', *Bulletin of Mathematical Biology*, 62(3), 451–66.

——— ——— 2001, 'Evolution in knockout conflicts: the variable strategy case', *Selection*, 1, 5–21.

Buchanan, James, Robert Tollison, and Gordon Tullock, 1980, *Toward a Theory of the Rent-seeking Society*, Texas A&M University Press, College Station.

Carmichael, H. Lorne, 1983, 'The agent-agents problem—payment by relative output', *Journal of Labor Economics*, 1(1), 50–65.

Chan, William, 1996, 'External recruitment versus internal promotion', *Journal of Labor Economics*, 14(4), 555–70.

Che, Yeon-Koo, and Ian Gale, 1997, 'Rent dissipation when rent seekers are budget constrained', *Public Choice*, 92(1–2), 109–26.

—— —— 1998, 'Caps on political lobbying', *American Economic Review*, 88(3), 643–51.

—— —— 2000, 'Difference-form contests and the robustness of all-pay auctions', *Games and Economic Behavior*, 30(1), 22–43.

Chen, Kong-Pin, 2003, 'Sabotage in promotion tournaments', *Journal of Law, Economics, and Organization*, 19(1), 119–40.

Chung, Tai-Yeon, 1996, 'Rent-seeking contest when the prize increases with aggregate efforts', *Public Choice*, 87(1–2), 55–66.

Clark, Derek J., and Kai A. Konrad, 2007, 'Asymmetric conflict: weakest link against best shot', *Journal of Conflict Resolution*, 51(3), 457–69.

—— —— 2008, 'Fragmented property rights and incentives for R&D', *Management Science*, 54(5), 969–81.

—— and Christian Riis, 1996, 'A multi-winner nested rent-seeking contest', *Public Choice*, 87(1–2), 177–84.

—— —— 1998a, 'Contest success functions: an extension', *Economic Theory*, 11(1), 201–4.

—— —— 1998b, 'Competition over more than one prize', *American Economic Review*, 88(1), 276–89.

—— —— 2000, 'Allocation efficiency in a competitive bribery game', *Journal of Economic Behavior and Organization*, 42(1), 109–24.

Clausewitz, Carl von, 1832/1976, *On War*, Princeton University Press, Princeton.

Cole, Harold L., George J. Mailath, and Andrew Postlewaite, 1992, 'Social norms, savings behavior and growth', *Journal of Political Economy*, 100(6), 1092–125.

—— —— —— 1998, 'Class systems and enforcement of social norms', *Journal of Public Economics*, 70(1), 5–35.

Congleton, Roger D., 1984, 'Committees and rent-seeking effort', *Journal of Public Economics*, 25(1–2), 197–209.

—— 1986, 'Rent-seeking aspects of political advertising', *Public Choice*, 49(3), 249–63.

—— 1989, 'Efficient status seeking: externalities, and the evolution of status games', *Journal of Economic Behavior and Organization*, 11(2), 175–90.

—— Arye L. Hillman and Kai A. Konrad, 2008, *40 Years of Research on Rent Seeking* Vols. 1 and 2, Springer, Heidelberg.

Corchón, Luis C., 2007, 'The theory of contests: a survey', *Review of Economic Design*, 11(2), 69–100.

—— and Matthias Dahm, 2007, 'Foundations for contest success functions', Universidad Carlos III, Working Paper 07-04 Economic Series 01.

Cornes, Richard, and Roger Hartley, 2002, 'Dissipation in rent-seeking contests with entry costs', *Keele Economics Research Papers*, KERP 2002/11.

—— —— 2003, 'Risk aversion, heterogeneity and contests', *Public Choice*, 117(1–2), 1–25.

——— 2005, 'Asymmetric contests with general technologies', *Economic Theory*, 26(4), 923–46.

——— 2007, 'Aggregative public good games', *Journal of Public Economic Theory*, 9(2), 201–19.

—— and Todd Sandler, 1986, *The Theory of Externalities, Public Goods and Club Goods*, Cambridge University Press, Cambridge.

Coughlin, Peter J., 1992, 'Pure strategy equilibria in a class of systems defense games', *International Journal of Game Theory*, 20(3), 195–210.

Davis, Douglas D., and Robert J. Reilly, 1998, 'Do too many cooks always spoil the stew? An experimental analysis of rent-seeking and the role of a strategic buyer', *Public Choice*, 95(1–2), 89–115.

——— 1999, 'Rent-seeking with non-identical sharing rules: an equilibrium rescued', *Public Choice*, 100(1–2), 31–8.

Dechenaux, Emmanuel, Dan Kovenock, and Volodymyr Lugovskyy, 2003, 'A comment on "David vs. Goliath: an analysis of asymmetric mixed-strategy games and experimental evidence", Krannert Working Paper Series, Working Paper No. 1162, Purdue University.

———— 2006, 'Caps on bidding in all-pay auctions: comments on the experiments of A. Rapoport and W. Amaldoss', *Journal of Economic Behavior and Organization*, 61(2), 276–83.

Democratic National Convention, 2000, 'The 2000 Democratic National Platform: Prosperity, Progress, and Peace', Democratic National Convention Committee, Inc., Washington, DC.

Deneckere, Raymond J., and Dan Kovenock, 1992, 'Price leadership', *Review of Economic Studies*, 59(1), 143–62.

——— and Robert Lee, 1992, 'A model of price leadership based on consumer loyalty', *Journal of Industrial Economics*, 40(2), 147–56.

Dixit, Avinash K., 1987, 'Strategic behavior in contests', *American Economic Review*, 77(5), 891–98.

Drook-Gal, Bat-Sheva, Gil S. Epstein, and Shmuel Nitzan, 2004, 'Contestable privatization', *Journal of Economic Behavior and Organization*, 54(3), 377–87.

Dupuy, Trevor N., 1977, 'Analyzing trends in ground combat', *History, Numbers and War*, 1(2), 77–83.

Eaton, Curtis B., and Mukesh Eswaran, 2003, 'The evolution of preferences and competition: a rationalization of Veblen's theory of invidious comparisons', *Canadian Journal of Economics*, 36(4), 832–59.

Eggert, Wolfgang, Jun-ichi Itaya, and Kazuo Mino, 2006, 'A dynamic model of conflict and cooperation', mimeo, University of Paderborn.

Ellingsen, Tore, 1991, 'Strategic buyers and the social cost of monopoly', *American Economic Review*, 81(3), 648–57.

Epstein, Gil S., and Carsten Hefeker, 2003, 'Lobbying contests with alternative instruments', *Economics of Governance*, 4(1), 81–9.

Epstein, Gil S., and Shmuel Nitzan, 2003a, 'The social cost of rent seeking when consumer opposition influences monopoly behavior', *European Journal of Political Economy*, 19(1), 61–9.

———2003b, 'Political culture and monopoly price determination', *Social Choice and Welfare*, 21(1), 1–19.

——2004, 'Strategic restraint in contests', *European Economic Review*, 48(1), 201–10.

——2006, 'The politics of randomness', *Social Choice of Welfare*, 27(2), 423–33.

——2007, *Endogenous Public Policy and Contests*, Springer, Berlin.

Esteban, Joan M., and Debraj Ray, 1999, 'Conflict and distribution', *Journal of Economic Theory*, 87(2), 379–415.

——2001, 'Collective action and the group size paradox', *American Political Science Review*, 95(3), 663–72.

—and József Sákovics, 2003, 'Olson vs. Coase: coalitional worth in conflict', *Theory and Decision*, 55(4), 339–57.

Fabella, Raul V., 1995, 'The social cost of rent-seeking under countervailing opposition to distortionary transfers', *Journal of Public Economics*, 57(2), 235–47.

Farmer, Amy, and Paul Pecorino, 1999, 'Legal expenditure as a rent-seeking game', *Public Choice*, 100(3–4), 271–88.

Fearon, James D., 1995, 'Rationalist explanations for war', *International Organization*, 49(3), 379–414.

Feess, Eberhard, Gerd Muehlheusser, and Markus Walzl, 2002, 'When bidding more is not enough: all-pay auctions with handicaps', Bonn Econ Discussion Papers, No. 14/2002, Bonn.

Fernández, Raquel, and Jordi Galí, 1999, 'To each according to ...? Markets, tournaments, and the matching problem with borrowing constraints', *Review of Economic Studies*, 66(4), 799–824.

—and Dani Rodrik, 1991, 'Resistance to reform: status quo bias in the presence of individual-specific uncertainty', *American Economic Review*, 81(5), 1146–55.

Ferrall, Christopher, and Anthony A. Smith Jr., 1999, 'A sequential game model of sports championship series: theory and estimation', *Review of Economics and Statistics*, 81(4), 704–19.

Frank, Robert H., 1984a, 'Are workers paid their marginal products?', *American Economic Review*, 74(4), 549–71.

—1984b, 'Interdependent preferences and the competitive wage structure', *Rand Journal of Economics*, 15(4), 510–20.

—1985a, 'The demand for unobservable and other nonpositional goods', *American Economic Review*, 75(1), 101–16.

—1985b, *Choosing the Right Pond, Human Behavior and the Quest for Status*, Oxford University Press, New York.

—1987, 'If homo economicus could choose his own utility function, would he want one with a conscience?' *American Economic Review*, 77(4), 593–604.

Frank, Robert H., 1988, *Passions Within Reason: The Strategic Role of the Emotions*, W.W. Norton, New York.

—— 1989, 'If homo economicus could choose his own utility function, would he want one with a conscience? Reply', *American Economic Review*, 79(3), 594–6.

Friedman, Lawrence, 1958, 'Game-theory models in the allocation of advertising expenditures', *Operations Research*, 6(5), 699–709.

Fu, Qiang, 2006, 'A theory of affirmative action in college admissions', *Economic Inquiry*, 44(3), 420–8.

—— and Jingfeng Lu, 2007, 'The optimal multiple-stage contest', *NAJ Economics*, 14(2).

Fullerton, Richard L., and R. Preston McAfee, 1999, 'Auctioning entry into tournaments', *Journal of Political Economy*, 107(3), 573–605.

Garfinkel, Michelle R., 2004, 'On the stability of group formation: managing the conflict within', *Conflict Management and Peace Science*, 21(1), 43–68.

—— and Stergios Skaperdas, 2000, 'Conflict without misperceptions or incomplete information: how the future matters', *Journal of Conflict Resolution*, 44(6), 793–807.

—— —— 2007, 'Economics of conflict: an overview', in: Todd Sandler and Keith Hartley (eds.), *Handbook of Defense Economics*, Vol. 2, North-Holland, Amsterdam, 649–710.

Gasmi, Farid, Jean-Jacques Laffont, and Quang Vuong, 1992, 'Econometric analysis of collusive behavior in a soft-drink market', *Journal of Economics and Management Strategy*, 1(2), 277–311.

Gavious, Arieh, Benny Moldovanu, and Aner Sela, 2002, 'Bid costs and endogenous bid caps', *RAND Journal of Economics*, 33(4), 709–22.

Gibbons, Robert, and Michael Waldman, 1999, 'Careers in organizations: theory and evidence', in: Orley Ashenfelter and David Card (eds.), *Handbook of Labor Economics*, North-Holland, Amsterdam, 2373–437.

Glazer, Amihai, and Mark Gradstein, 2005, 'Elections with contribution-maximizing candidates', *Public Choice*, 122(3–4), 467–82.

—— and Refael Hassin, 1988, 'Optimal contests', *Economic Inquiry*, 26(1), 133–43.

—— —— 2000, 'Sequential rent seeking', *Public Choice*, 102(3–4), 219–28.

—— and Kai A. Konrad, 1999, 'Taxation of rent-seeking activities', *Journal of Public Economics*, 72(1), 61–72.

Gneezy, Uri, and Ran Smorodinsky, 2006, 'All-pay auctions—an experimental study', *Journal of Economic Behavior and Organization*, 61(2), 255–75.

Goeree, Jacob K., and Charles A. Holt, 1999, 'Classroom games—rent-seeking and the inefficiency of non-market allocations', *Journal of Economic Perspectives*, 13(3), 217–26.

—— Emiel Maasland, Sander Onderstal, and John L. Turner, 2005, 'How (not) to raise money', *Journal of Political Economy*, 113(4), 897–918.

Gonzalez, Francisco M., 2007, 'Effective property rights, conflict and growth', *Journal of Economic Theory*, 137(1), 127–39.

——and Hugh M. Neary, 2004, 'Optimal growth policy under privately enforced property rights', Discussion Paper No. 04-15, University of British Columbia.

Gradstein, Mark, 1993, 'Rent seeking and the provision of public goods', *Economic Journal*, 103(420), 1236–43.

Gradstein, Mark, 1995, 'Intensity of competition, entry and entry deterrence in rent seeking contests', *Economics and Politics*, 7(1), 79–91.

——2004, 'Governance and growth', *Journal of Development Economics*, 73(2), 505–18.

——and Kai A. Konrad, 1999, 'Orchestrating rent seeking contests', *Economic Journal*, 109(458), 536–45.

——and Shmuel Nitzan, 1989, 'Advantageous multiple rent seeking', *Mathematical and Computer Modelling*, 12(4–5), 511–18.

Groh, Christian, Benny Moldovanu, Aner Sela, and Uwe Sunde, 2003, 'Optimal seedings in elimination tournaments', SFB/TR 15 Discussion Paper, No. 140.

Groseclose, Tim, and James M. Snyder, Jr., 1996, 'Buying supermajorities', *American Political Science Review*, 90(2), 303–15.

Güth, Werner, and Menahem E. Yaari, 1992, 'An evolutionary approach to explain reciprocal behavior in a simple strategic game', in: Ulrich Witt (ed.), *Explaining Process and Change—Approaches to Evolutionary Economics*, The University of Michigan Press, Ann Arbor, 23–34.

Hamilton, Jonathan H., and Steven M. Slutsky, 1990, 'Endogenous timing in duopoly games: Stackelberg or Cournot equilibria', *Games and Economic Behavior*, 2(1), 29–46.

Harbaugh, Rick, and Tilman Klumpp, 2005, 'Early round upsets and championship blowouts', *Economic Inquiry*, 43(2), 316–29.

Harbring, Christine, and Bernd Irlenbusch, 2008, 'How many winners are good to have? On tournaments with sabotage', *Journal of Economic Behavior & Organization*, 65(3–4), 682–702.

————Matthias Kräkel, and Reinhard Selten, 2004, 'Sabotage in asymmetric contests, an experimental analysis', *Bonn Econ Discussion Papers*, No. 12/2004, Bonn.

Harris, Christopher, and John Vickers, 1985, 'Perfect equilibrium in a model of a race', *Review of Economic Studies*, 52(2), 193–209.

————1987, 'Racing with uncertainty', *Review of Economic Studies*, 54(1), 1–21.

Harsanyi, John C., 1977, *Rational Behavior and Bargaining Equilibrium in Games and Social Situations*, University Press Cambridge, Cambridge.

Hazlett, Thomas W., and Robert J. Michaels, 1993, 'The cost of rent-seeking: evidence from cellular telephone license lotteries', *Southern Economic Journal*, 59(3), 425–35.

Hehenkamp, Burkhard, Wolfgang Leininger, and Alex Possajennikov, 2001, 'Evolutionary rent-seeking', CESifo Working Paper No. 620, Munich.

Heller, Michael A., and Rebecca S. Eisenberg, 1998, 'Can patents deter innovation? The anticommons in biomedical research', *Science*, 280(5364), 698–701.

Hess, Gregory D., and Athanasios Orphanides, 1995, 'War politics, an economic, rational-voter framework', *American Economic Review*, 85(4), 828–46.

Hillman, Arye L., 1989, *The Political Economy of Protection*, Harwood Academic Publishers, Chur.

——and Eliakim Katz, 1984, 'Risk-averse rent seekers and the social cost of monopoly power', *Economic Journal*, 94(373), 104–10.

————1987, 'Hierarchical structure and the social costs of bribes and transfers', *Journal of Public Economics*, 34(2), 129–42.

——and John G. Riley, 1989, 'Politically contestable rents and transfers', *Economics and Politics*, 1(1), 17–39.

——and Dov Samet, 1987, 'Dissipation of contestable rents by small numbers of contenders', *Public Choice*, 54(1), 63–82.

——and Heinrich W. Ursprung, 1988, 'Domestic politics, foreign interests, and international trade policy', *American Economic Review*, 78(4), 729–45.

Hirsch, Fred, 1976, *Social Limits to Growth*, Harvard University Press, Cambridge, Mass.

Hirshleifer, Jack, 1983, 'From weakest-link to best-shot: the voluntary provision of public goods', *Public Choice*, 41(3), 371–86.

——1989, 'Conflict and rent-seeking success functions: ratio vs. difference models of relative success', *Public Choice*, 63(2), 101–12.

——1991, 'The paradox of power', *Economics and Politics*, 3, 177–200.

——and John G. Riley, 1992, *The Analytics of Uncertainty and Information*, Cambridge University Press, Cambridge.

Hoehn, Thomas, and Stefan Szymanski, 1999, 'The Americanization of European football', *Economic Policy*, 14(28), 203–40.

Huck, Steffen, Kai A. Konrad, and Wieland Müller, 2002, 'Merger and collusion in contests', *Journal of Institutional and Theoretical Economics*, 158(4), 563–75.

——and Jörg Oechssler, 1999, 'The indirect evolutionary approach to explaining fair allocations', *Games and Economic Behavior*, 28(1), 13–24.

Hurley, Terrence M., and Jason F. Shogren, 1998, 'Effort levels in a Cournot Nash contest with asymmetric information', *Journal of Public Economics*, 69(2), 195–210.

Inderst, Roman, Holger M. Müller, and Karl Wärneryd, 2005, 'Influence costs and hierarchy', *Economics of Governance*, 6(2), 177–97.

Jehiel, Philippe, Benny Moldovanu, and Ennio Stacchetti, 1996, 'How (not) to sell nuclear weapons', *American Economic Review*, 86(4), 814–29.

Jost, Peter J., and Matthias Kräkel, 2000, 'Preemptive behavior in sequential tournaments', IZA Discussion Paper, No. 159.

Kalra, Ajay, and Mengze Shi, 2001, 'Designing optimal sales contests: a theoretical perspective', *Marketing Science*, 20(2), 170–93.

Kaplan, Todd R., Israel Luski, and David Wettstein, 2003, 'Innovative activity and sunk cost', *International Journal of Industrial Organization*, 21(8), 1111–33.

Katz, Eliakim, Shmuel Nitzan, and Jacob Rosenberg, 1990, 'Rent-seeking for pure public goods', *Public Choice*, 65(1), 49–60.

——and Julia Tokatlidu, 1996, 'Group competition for rents', *European Journal of Political Economy*, 12(4), 599–607.

Keem, Jung Hoon, 2001, 'The social cost of monopoly when consumers resist', *European Journal of Political Economy*, 17(3), 633–9.

Klumpp, Tilman, and Mattias K. Polborn, 2006, 'Primaries and the New Hampshire effect', *Journal of Public Economics*, 90(6–7), 1073–114.

Kolmar, Martin, and Dana Sisak, 2007, 'Multi-prize contests as incentive mechanisms for the provision of public goods with heterogenous agents', unpublished manuscript.

——and Andreas Wagener, 2007, 'Contests and the private provision of public goods', unpublished manuscript.

Konrad, Kai A., 1990, 'Statuspräferenzen: Soziobiologische Ursachen, Statuswettrüsten und seine Besteuerung' (With English summary), *Kyklos*, 43(2), 249–72.

——1992, 'Wealth seeking reconsidered', *Journal of Economic Behavior and Organization*, 18(2), 215–27.

——1993, 'Selbstbindung und die Logik kollektiven Handelns, *Habilschrift*, 70–72.

——2000a, 'Sabotage in rent-seeking contests', *Journal of Law, Economics and Organization*, 16(1), 155–65.

——2000b, 'Trade contests', *Journal of International Economics*, 51(2), 317–34.

——2002, 'Investment in the absence of property rights: the role of incumbency advantages', *European Economic Review*, 46(8), 1521–37.

——2004a, 'Altruism and envy in contests: an evolutionary stable symbiosis', *Social Choice and Welfare*, 22(3), 479–90.

——2004b, 'Bidding in hierarchies', *European Economic Review*, 48(6), 1301–08.

——2004c, 'Inverse campaigning', *Economic Journal*, 114(492), 69–82.

——2004d, 'Mobilität in mehrstufigen Ausbildungsturnieren', in: Wolfgang Franz, Hans Jürgen Ramser, and Manfred Stadler (eds.), Bildung, Mohr Siebeck, Tübingen.

——2006, 'Silent interests and all pay auctions', *International Journal of Industrial Organization*, 24, 701–13.

——2007, 'Strategy in Contests: An Introduction', Discussion Paper SPII 2007–09, Social Science Research Center, Berlin.

——and Dan Kovenock, 2005, 'Equilibrium and efficiency in the tug-of-war', CEPR Discussion Paper No. 5205.

————2007b, 'Self-enforcing norms and the efficient non-cooperative organization of clans', CEPR Discussion Paper No. 6333.

————2008a, 'Contests with stochastic abilities', *Economic Inquiry* (forthcoming).

————2008b, 'The alliance formation puzzle and capacity constraints', CEPR Discussion Paper No. 6741.

——— 2008c, 'Multi-battle contests', *Games and Economic Behavior* (forthcoming).

——— and Wolfgang Leininger, 2007a, 'The generalized Stackelberg equilibrium of the all-pay auction with complete information', *Review of Economic Design*, 11(2), 165–74.

——— Wolfgang Peters, and Karl Wärneryd, 2004, 'Delegation in first-price all-pay auctions', *Managerial and Decision Economics*, 25(5), 283–90.

——— and Harris Schlesinger, 1997, 'Risk aversion in rent-seeking and rent-augmenting games', *Economic Journal*, 107(445), 1671–83.

Kooreman, Peter, and Lambert Schoonbeek, 1997, 'The specification of the probability functions in Tullock's rent-seeking contest', *Economics Letters*, 56(1), 59–61.

Korte, Karl-Rudolf, 2006, Wahlkampfkosten, Bundeszentrale für Politische Bildung (<http://www.bpb.de/themen/V1BR0N,0,0,Wahlkampfkosten.html> 12.10.2006).

Kotler, Philip, and Friedhelm Bliemel, 2001, *Marketing-Management*, Schäffer-Poeschel, Stuttgart.

Kovenock, Dan, and Brian Roberson, 2006, 'Terrorism and the optimal defense of networks of targets', mimeo, Purdue University.

——— 2008, 'Coalitional Colonel Blotto games with application to the economics of alliances', Discussion Paper SP II 2008–02, Social Science Research Center, Berlin.

Kräkel, Matthias, 1998, 'Zur Ambivalenz einer unternehmensinternen Verwendung von Wettbewerbsmechanismen—eine personalpolitische Diskussion am Beispiel relativer Leistungsturniere', *Zeitschrift für Wirtschafts- und Sozialwissenschaften*, 118, 61–85.

——— 2006, 'Splitting Leagues', *Journal of Economics*, 88(1), 21–48.

——— and Dirk Sliwka, 2006, 'Strategic delegation and mergers in oligopolistic contests', *Journal of Economics and Business*, 58(2), 119–36.

Krishna, Vijay, and John Morgan, 1997, 'An analysis of the war of attrition and the all-pay action', *Journal of Economic Theory*, 72(2), 343–62.

Krüger, Anne O., 1974, 'The political economy of the rent-seeking society', *American Economic Review*, 64, 291–303.

Kura, Takuya, 1999, 'Dilemma of the equality: an all-pay contest with individual differences in resource holding potential', *Journal of Theoretical Biology*, 198(3), 395–404.

Lagerlöf, Johan, 1997, 'Lobbying, information and private and social welfare', *European Journal of Political Economy*, 13(3), 615–37.

——— 2007, 'A theory of rent seeking with informational foundations', *Economics of Governance*, 8(3), 197–218.

Lange, Andreas, John A. List, and Michael K. Price, 2007, 'Using lotteries to finance public goods: theory and experimental evidence', *International Economic Review*, 48(3), 901–27.

Lazear, Edward P., 1989, 'Pay equality and industrial politics', *Journal of Political Economy*, 97(3), 561–80.

——1995, *Personnel Economics*, MIT Press, Cambridge, Mass.

——and Sherwin Rosen, 1981, 'Rank-order tournaments as optimum labor contracts', *Journal of Political Economy*, 89(5), 841–64.

Leach, Andrew, 2004, 'Subgame, set and match. Identifying incentive response in a tournament', Cahier de recherche no. IEA-04-02, HEC Montréal.

Lee, Sanghack, 1995, 'Endogenous sharing rules in collective-group rent-seeking', *Public Choice*, 85(1–2), 31–44.

Leidy, Michael P., 1994, 'Rent dissipation through self-regulation: the social cost of monopoly under threat of reform', *Public Choice*, 80(1–2), 105–28.

Leininger, Wolfgang, 1991, 'Patent competition, rent dissipation, and the persistence of monopoly: the role of research budgets', *Journal of Economic Theory*, 53, 146–72.

——1993, 'More efficient rent-seeking—a Münchhausen solution, *Public Choice*, 75(1), 43–62.

——2003, 'On evolutionarily stable behavior in contests', *Economics of Governance*, 4, 177–86.

——and Chun-Lei Yang, 1994, 'Dynamic rent-seeking games', *Games and Economic Behavior*, 7(3), 406–27.

Levin, Jonathan, 2002, 'Multilateral contracting and the employment relationship', *Quarterly Journal of Economics*, 117(3), 1075–03.

Lewis, Michael, 2006, *Liar's Poker*, Coronet Books, Philadelphia.

Linster, Bruce G., 1993a, 'Stackelberg rent-seeking', *Public Choice*, 77(2), 307–21.

——1993b, 'A generalized model of rent-seeking behavior', *Public Choice*, 77(2), 421–35.

Lizzeri, Alessandro, and Nicola Persico, 2000, 'Uniqueness and existence of equilibrium in auctions with a reserve price', *Games and Economic Behavior*, 30(1), 83–114.

Lockard, Alan, and Gordon Tullock, 2001, *Efficient Rent Seeking: Chronicle of an Intellectual Quagmire*, Kluwer Academic Publishers, Boston.

Long, Ngo van, and Neil Vousden, 1987, 'Risk-averse rent seeking with shared rents', *Economic Journal*, 97, 971–85.

Loury, Glenn C., 1979, 'Market structure and innovation', *Quarterly Journal of Economics*, 93(3), 395–410.

Lugovskyy, Volodymyr, Daniela Puzzello, and Steven Tucker, 2006, 'Experimental investigation of overbidding in the all-pay auction', mimeo, University of Canterbury.

Mailath, George J., 1993, 'Endogenous sequencing of firm decisions', *Journal of Economic Theory*, 59(1), 169–82.

Malcomson, James M., 1984, 'Work incentives, hierarchy, and internal labor markets', *Journal of Political Economy*, 92(3), 486–507.

Malueg, David A., and Andrew J. Yates, 2004, 'Rent seeking with private values', *Public Choice*, 119(1–2), 161–78.

———2006, 'Best-of-three contests between equally skilled players', mimeo, Tulane University.

Matros, Alexander, 2006, 'Stochastic K-player Blotto games', Discussion Paper, No. 206, University of Pittsburgh.

Matsumura, Toshihiro, 1999, 'Quantity-setting oligopoly with endogenous sequencing', *International Journal of Industrial Organization*, 17(2), 289–96.

Maynard Smith, John, 1982, *Evolution and the Theory of Games*, Cambridge University Press, Cambridge.

——and George R. Price, 1973, 'The logic of animal conflict', *Nature*, 246, 15–18.

McBride, Michael, and Stergios Skaperdas, 2006, 'Explaining conflict in low-income countries: incomplete contracting in the shadow of the future', Working Paper, No. 050606, University of California at Irvine.

McAfee, R. Preston, 2000, 'Continuing wars of attrition', unpublished manuscript.

Mehlum, Halvor, and Karl O. Moene, 2004, 'So much fighting, so little success', mimeo, University of Oslo.

Meland, Frode, and Odd Rune Straume, 2007, 'Outsourcing in contests', *Public Choice*, 131(3–4), 315–31.

Meyer, Margaret A., 1991, 'Learning from coarse information: biased contests and career profiles', *Review of Economic Studies*, 58(1), 15–41.

Michaels, R., 1988, 'The design of rent seeking competitions', *Public Choice*, 56(1), 17–29.

Milgrom, Paul, 1988, 'Employment contracts, influence activities and efficient organization design', *Journal of Political Economy*, 96, 42–60.

——and John Roberts, 1988, 'An economic approach to influence activities in organizations', *American Journal of Sociology*, 94(1), 154–79.

Millner, Edward L., and Michael D. Pratt, 1989, 'An experimental investigation of rent seeking', *Public Choice*, 62, 139–51.

——and Michael D. Pratt, 1991, 'Risk aversion and rent-seeking, an extension and some experimental evidence', *Public Choice*, 69(1), 81–92.

Mills, Harland D., 1961, 'A study in promotional competition', in: Frank M. Bass et al. (eds.), *Mathematical Models and Methods in Marketing*, R. D. Irwin, Homewood, 245–301. Reprinted from: Research Paper No. 101–103, December 1959, Mathematica, Princeton.

Moldovanu, Benny, and Aner Sela, 2001, 'The optimal allocation of prizes in contests', *American Economic Review*, 91(3), 542–58.

———2006, 'Contest architecture', *Journal of Economic Theory*, 126(1), 70–96.

———and Xianwen Shi, 2007, 'Contests for status', *Journal of Political Economy*, 115(2), 338–63.

Morgan, John, 2000, 'Financing public goods by means of lotteries', *Review of Economic Studies*, 67(4), 761–84.

——2003, 'Sequential contests', *Public Choice*, 116(1–2), 1–18.

——and Martin Sefton, 2000, 'Funding public goods with lotteries: experimental evidence', *Review of Economic Studies*, 67(4), 785–810.

Müller, Holger M., and Karl Wärneryd, 2001, 'Inside versus outside ownership: a political theory of the firm', *RAND Journal of Economics*, 32(3), 527–41.

Münster, Johannes, 2006a, 'Repeated contests with asymmetric information', mimeo, Social Science Research Center, Berlin.

——2006b, 'Contests with an unknown number of contestants', *Public Choice*, 129(3–4), 353–68.

——2006c, 'Lobbying contests with endogenous policy proposals', *Economics and Politics*, 18(3), 389–97.

——2007a, 'Selection tournaments, sabotage, and participation', *Journal of Economics & Management Strategy*, 16(4), 943–70.

——2007b, 'Simultaneous inter- and intragroup conflict', *Economic Theory*, 32(2), 333–52.

Myerson, Roger B., and Karl Wärneryd, 2006, 'Population uncertainty in contests', *Economic Theory*, 27(2), 469–74.

Nalebuff, Barry, and Joseph E. Stiglitz, 1983, 'Prizes and incentives: towards a general theory of compensation and competition', *Bell Journal of Economics*, 14(1), 21–43.

Nitzan, Shmuel, 1991a, 'Collective rent dissipation', *Economic Journal*, 101(409), 1522–34.

——1991b, 'Rent-seeking with nonidentical sharing rules', *Public Choice*, 71(1–2), 43–50.

——1994, 'Modelling rent-seeking contests', *European Journal of Political Economy*, 10(1), 41–60.

——and Kaoru Ueda, 2008, 'Collective contests for commons and club goods', mimeo, Bar-Ilan University.

Noh, Suk Jae, 2002, 'Resource distribution and stable alliances with endogenous sharing rules', *European Journal of Political Economy*, 18(1), 129–51.

Nti, Kofi O., 1997, 'Comparative statics of contests and rent-seeking games', *International Economic Review*, 38(1), 43–59.

——1998, 'Effort and performance in group contests', *European Journal of Political Economy*, 14, 769–81.

——1999, 'Rent-seeking with asymmetric valuations', *Public Choice*, 98(3), 415–30.

OECD, 2005, *Education at a Glance 2005*, OECD, Paris.

O'Keefe, Mary, W. Kip Viscusi, and Richard J. Zeckhauser, 1984, 'Economic contests: comparative reward schemes', *Journal of Labor Economics*, 2(1), 27–56.

Öncüler, Ayse, and Rachel Croson, 2005, 'Rent-seeking for a risky rent—a model and experimental investigation', *Journal of Theoretical Politics*, 17(4), 403–29.

Parco, James E., Amnon Rapoport, and Wilfred Amaldoss, 2005, 'Two-stage contests with budget constraints: an experimental study', *Journal of Mathematical Psychology*, 49(4), 320–38.

Pérez-Castrillo, J. David, and Thierry Verdier, 1992, 'A general analysis of rent-seeking games', *Public Choice*, 73(3), 335–50.

Piga, Claudio A.G., 1998, 'A dynamic model of advertising and product differentiation', *Review of Industrial Organization*, 13(5), 509–22.

Polborn, Mattias K., 2006, 'Investment under uncertainty in dynamic conflicts', *Review of Economic Studies*, 73(2), 505–29.

Posner, Richard A., 1975, 'The social costs of monopoly and regulation', *Journal of Political Economy*, 83(4), 807–27.

Potters, Jan, Casper G. de Vries and Frans van Winden, 1998, 'An experimental examination of rational rent-seeking', *European Journal of Political Economy*, 14(4), 783–800.

Priks, Mikael, 2002, 'Egalitarian wage schedules in small firms and in co-operatives—rent seeking at work', mimeo, University of Munich.

——2005, 'Delegation in legal disputes, the role of competition and different litigation systems', mimeo, University of Munich.

Quintero, Jose E., 2004, 'Moral hazard in teams with limited punishments and multiple outputs', mimeo, Universidad Carlos III de Madrid.

Rapoport, Amnon, and Wilfred Amaldoss, 2004, 'Mixed-strategy play in single-stage first-price all-pay auctions with symmetric players', *Journal of Economic Behavior & Organization*, 54(4), 585–607.

Rees, Ray, and Ekkehard Kessner, 1999, 'Regulation and efficiency in European insurance markets', *Economic Policy*, 29, 365–99.

Reiter, Michael, 2000, 'Relative preferences and public goods', *European Economic Review*, 44(3), 565–85.

Rekkas, Marie, 2007, 'The impact of campaign spending on votes in multiparty elections', *Review of Economics and Statistics*, 89(3), 573–85.

Riaz, Khalid, Jason F. Shogren, and Stanley R. Johnson, 1995, 'A general model of rent seeking for public goods', *Public Choice*, 82(3–4), 243–59.

Roberson, Brian, 2006, 'The Colonel Blotto game', *Economic Theory*, 29(1), 1–24.

Robson, Alexander R.W., 2005, 'Multi-item contests', Series in Economics and Econometrics, No. 446, Australian National University.

——and Stergios Skaperdas, 2008, 'Costly enforcement of property rights and the Coase theorem', *Economic Theory*, 36(1), 109–28.

Romano, Richard, and Huseyin Yildirim, 2005, 'On the endogeneity of Cournot-Nash and Stackelberg equilibria: games of accumulation', *Journal of Economic Theory*, 120(1), 73–107.

Rosen, Sherwin, 1986, 'Prizes and incentives in elimination tournaments', *American Economic Review*, 76(4), 701–15.

——1988, 'Promotions, elections and other contests', *Journal of Institutional and Theoretical Economics*, 144(1), 73–90.

Rothschild, Michael, and Joseph E. Stiglitz, 1970, 'Increasing risk: I. A definition', *Journal of Economic Theory*, 2, 225–43.

Salant, Stephen W., Sheldon Switzer, and Robert J. Reynolds, 1983, 'Losses from horizontal mergers: the effects of an exogenous change in industry structure on Cournot-Nash equilibirum', *Quarterly Journal of Economics*, 98(2), 185–99.

Sahlins, Marshall D., 1963, 'Poor man, rich man, big-man, chief: political types of Melanesia and Polynesia', *Comparative Studies in Society and History*, 5(3), 285–303.

Samuelson, Larry, 1997, *Evolutionary Games and Equilibrium Selection*, MIT Press, Cambridge, Mass.

Sánchez-Pages, Santiago, 2007, 'Endogenous coalition formation in contests', ESE Discussion Papers, No. 158, University of Edinburgh.

Schaffer, Mark E., 1988, 'Evolutionarily stable strategies for a finite population and a variable contest size', *Journal of Theoretical Biology*, 132(4), 469–78.

Schelling, Thomas C., 1960, *The Strategy of Conflict*, Oxford University Press, New York.

Schmalensee, Richard, 1976, 'Model of promotional competition in oligopoly', *Review of Economic Studies*, 43(3), 493–507.

Schmitt, Pamela, Robert Shupp, Kurtis Swope, and John Cadigan, 2004, 'Multi-period rent-seeking contests with carryover: theory and experimental evidence', *Economics of Governance*, 5(3), 187–211.

Schoonbeek, Lambert, 2004, 'Delegation in a group-contest', *European Journal of Political Economy*, 20(1), 263–72.

—— 2007, 'Delegation with multiple instruments in a rent-seeking contest', *Public Choice*, 131(3–4), 453–64.

Shavell, Steven, 1982, 'Suit, settlement and trial: a theoretical analysis under alternative methods for the allocation of legal costs', *Journal of Legal Studies*, 11, 55–82.

Shogren, Jason F., and Kyung Hwan Baik, 1991, 'Reexamining efficient rent-seeking in the laboratory markets', *Public Choice*, 69(1), 69–79.

Shubik, Martin, 1954, 'Does the fittest necessarily survive?' in: Martin Shubik (ed.), *Readings in Game Theory and Related Behavior*, Doubleday, New York, 43–6.

—— 1971, 'The dollar auction game: a paradox in noncooperative behavior and escalation', *Journal of Conflict Resolution*, 15(1), 109–11.

—— and Robert Weber, 1981, 'Systems defense games: Colonel Blotto, command and control', *Naval Research Logistics Quarterly*, 28(2), 281–87.

Singh, Nirvikar, and Donald Wittman, 1998, 'Contest design and the objective of the contest designer: sales promotions, sporting events, and patent races', in: Michael R. Baye (ed.), *Advances in Applied Microeconomics*, vol. 7, JAI Press, Stanford, Calif, 139–67.

—— —— 2001, 'Contests where there is variation in the marginal productivity of effort', *Economic Theory*, 18(3), 711–44.

Skaperdas, Stergios, 1992, 'Cooperation, conflict, and power in the absence of property rights', *American Economic Review*, 82(4), 720–39.

—— 1996, 'Contest success functions', *Economic Theory* 7(2), 283–90.

——1998, 'On the formation of alliances in conflict and contests', *Public Choice*, 96(1–2), 25–42.

——2002, 'Warlord competition', *Journal of Peace Research*, 39(4), 435–46.

——2003, 'Restraining the genuine homo economicus: why the economy cannot be divorced from its governance', *Economics and Politics*, 15, 135–62.

——and Li Gan, 1995, 'Risk-aversion in contests', *Economic Journal*, 105(431), 951–62.

——and Bernard Grofman, 1995, 'Modeling negative campaigning', *American Political Science Review*, 89(1), 49–61.

——and Constantinos Syropoulos, 2001, 'Guns, butter, and openness: on the relationship between security and trade', *American Economic Review*, 91(2), 353–57.

Slantchev, Branislav L., 2003, 'The power to hurt: costly conflict with completely informed states', *American Political Science Review*, 97(1), 123–33.

Spier, Kathryn E., 2007, 'Litigation', in: A. Mitchell Polinsky and Steven Shavell (eds.), *The Handbook of Law and Economics*, Vol. 1, North-Holland, Amsterdam, 259–334.

Stackelberg, Heinrich von, 1934, *Marktform und Gleichgewicht*, Verlag von Julius Springer, Vienna and Berlin.

Stein, William E., 2002, 'Asymmetric rent-seeking with more than two contestants', *Public Choice*, 113(3–4), 325–36.

Stephan, Joerg, and Heinrich Ursprung, 1998, 'The social cost of rent seeking when victories are potentially transient and losses final', in: Karl-Josef Koch and Klaus Jaeger (eds.), *Trade, Growth, and Economic Policy in Open Economies: Essays in Honour of Hans-Jürgen Vosgerau*, Springer, Berlin, 369–80.

Stewart, Mark F., and C. L. Wu, 1997, 'The right to host the Olympic games should be auctioned to the highest bidder', *Economic Papers—Economic Society of Australia*, 16(1), 40–5.

Stratmann, Thomas, 2005, 'Some talk: money in politics. A (partial) review of the literature', *Public Choice*, 124(1–2), 135–56.

Szidarovszky, Ferenc, and Koji Okuguchi, 1997, 'On the existence and uniqueness of pure Nash equilibrium in rent-seeking', *Games and Economic Behavior*, 18(1), 135–40.

Szymanski, Stefan, 2003, 'The economic design of sporting contests', *Journal of Economic Literature*, 41(4), 1137–87.

——and Tommaso M. Valletti, 2005, 'Incentive effects of second prizes', *European Journal of Political Economy*, 21(2), 467–81.

Tan, Guofu, and Ruqu Wang, 1997, 'Endogenous coalition formation in rivalry', QED Working Paper No. 956, 09-1997, Queen's University, Kingston, Ont.

Tsoulouhas, Theofanis, 1999, 'Do tournaments solve the two-sided moral hazard problem?', *Journal of Economic Behavior and Organization*, 40(3), 275–94.

——Charles R. Knoeber, and Anup Agrawal, 2007, 'Contests to become CEO: incentives, selection and handicaps', *Economic Theory*, 30(2), 195–221.

Tullock, Gordon, 1967, 'The welfare cost of tariffs, monopolies, and theft', *Western Economic Journal*, 5, 224–32.

——1980, 'Efficient rent seeking', in: James Buchanan, Roger Tollison, and Gordon Tullock (eds.), *Towards a Theory of the Rent-Seeking Society*, Texas A&M University Press, College Station, Tex., 97–112.

Ueda, Kaoru, 2002, 'Oligopolization in collective rent-seeking', *Social Choice and Welfare*, 19(3), 613–26.

Ursprung, Heinrich W., 1990, 'Public goods, rent dissipation, and candidate competition', *Economics and Politics*, 2, 115–32.

Wärneryd, Karl, 1998, 'Distributional conflict and jurisdictional organization', *Journal of Public Economics*, 69(3), 435–50.

——2000, 'In defense of lawyers: moral hazard as an aid to cooperation', *Games and Economic Behavior*, 33(1), 145–58.

——2001, 'Replicating contests', *Economics Letters*, 71(3), 323–27.

——2003, 'Information in conflicts', *Journal of Economic Theory*, 110(1), 121–36.

Weiss, Yoram, and Chaim Fershtman, 1998, 'Social status and economic performance: a survey', *European Economic Review*, 42(3–5), 801–20.

Welch, John F. Jr., 2001, *Jack, Straight From the Gut*, Warner Books, New York.

Windham, Patrick H., 1999, 'Appendix A, A taxonomy of technology prizes and contests', excerpted from: 'Background Paper: Workshop on the Potential for Promoting Technological Advance through Federally Sponsored Contests and Prizes', mimeo, National Academy of Engineering, Washington, DC.

Xu, Lin, and Ferenc Szidarovszky, 1999, 'The stability of dynamic rent-seeking games, *International Game Theory Review*, 1(1), 87–102.

Young, Hobart Peyton, 1978, 'A tactical lobbying game', in: Peter C. Ordeshook (ed.), *Game Theory and Political Science*, NYU Press, New York, 391–404.

Index